# EXECUTIVE REORGANIZATION AND REFORM IN THE NEW DEAL

## THE GENESIS OF ADMINISTRATIVE MANAGEMENT, 1900–1939

*Barry Dean Karl*

CAMBRIDGE, MASSACHUSETTS

HARVARD UNIVERSITY PRESS

1963

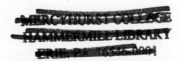

Distributed in Great Britain by Oxford University Press, London

Publication of this book has been aided by a
grant from the Ford Foundation

---

Library of Congress Catalog Card Number: 63-13813
Printed in the United States of America

FOR

*Alice Woodard Karl*

IN 1939, through a series of plans submitted to the Congress, Franklin Roosevelt reorganized the presidency of the United States. The action caused scarcely a ripple in the still apprehension of a world awaiting a war. Less than a year earlier proposals for executive reorganization had become involved in the furor over executive dictation, court packing, and a multitude of similarly fearful accusations. Clothed now in compromise and mantled in the mutual adjustments long characteristic of the Roosevelt revolution, executive reorganization helped effect the transition from the government of the New Deal to that of the Second World War.

What did this mean in fact? There was still one President, elected to a four-year term. He had become neither Prime Minister, nor King, nor Dictator, nor Consul, nor indeed any other of the historical definitions of leadership raised as threat or salvation by those who criticized FDR and his habits of governing. He was still subject to the same constitutional restraints and responsibilities. Reorganization had not re-established his relation to the courts or the Congress. What had it done, then?

From a purely practical point of view it had set up the Executive Office of the President and a White House staff which now included the Bureau of the Budget and the National Resources Planning Board. It had enabled the President to appoint administrative assistants. It had given the President the authority to shift certain of the existing offices of government and to reorganize them by reorganization plans, submitted to Congress to become law if not vetoed by that body. It had affected the President's method of working by affecting the tools with which he worked; but had it changed the presidency?

In fact the presidency had been neither seriously altered nor, in any profound sense, revised. It had been reorganized by men whose intense respect for the traditions of the office and whose fundamental faith in its efficacy led them to seek revision in methods rather than in scope, in the tools of power rather than in power itself. In doing this they had not only the support of the President but of the traditions to which they belonged.

To a public already bored with the alphabet of bureaucracy, reorganization meant little more than another move in the accumulation of government characteristic not only of the New Deal but of what had come to be the heart of twentieth-century American government—the executive branch. The New Deal had dramatized the complexity of modern government but it had not invented it. Roosevelt had brought to national prominence a variety of social instrumentalities new to the federal government; but he had found the techniques and the men who espoused them in the fabric of American government, not in its federal form but in its dispersed collectivity—the assemblage of cities and states long accustomed to experimentation often more daring than even the New Deal could propose. The White House and the Capitol may have been new to many of the young men the Roosevelt administration brought to Washington; but the city halls and the state-houses throughout the land were not. The same was often true of their ideas.

To the professional students of government, many of whom had contributed much time and interest to the study of the presidency, the reorganization of 1939 may have seemed more dependent upon political maneuver than upon the social sciences as objective analyses of social facts. Never agreed on what they wanted government to be, the social scientists could measure the quality of their common dissatisfaction by the degree to which this reorganization deviated from their individual dreams.

The reality satisfied no one completely, although each of them was more or less responsible for what the various partisanships had in fact produced.

The partisanships of those who concerned themselves with reorganization were more than a matter of politics, although politics played an inevitably important role as the ultimate refuge of all partisanships. From the President and other men whose practical careers had been in government to the academicians and specialists whose systematic analyses had long sought understanding of the structure of government, one could plot a virtual continuum of degrees and gradations of interest in the efficient or the economical or the honest operation of offices held in public trust. Indeed, the three terms, honesty, efficiency, and economy, had formed the hooks on which reformers had, from the early days of the republic, hung not only the various strands of criticism and complaint but also the increasingly vast web of solutions spun out of traditional senses of public responsibility, or experience, or the various areas of specialized knowledge. Between the professional practitioners and the academic theorists stood men who saw government as one of their many responsible interests as citizens and those whose particular technical training was of use to government without being necessarily governmental.

The partisanships in point of view concerning the operations of government tended to fall into four categories. The career politician was forced of necessity to divide his attention between running for office and executing the offices he won, with the two professional functions exerting an obvious influence upon one another. Secondly, the politically interested citizen often held views generated by his activities in citizen associations for the improvement of government or his experience in appointed positions in government, although as a distinct group such men rarely sought or achieved elective office. If the first group comprised politicians ranging in style and background from Al Smith to Franklin Roosevelt, the second included members of the Adams family after their effective disenfranchisement early in the ninteenth century and privately public servants of the order of Henry L. Stimson and R. Fulton Cutting. Thirdly, one could see the professionals in such careers as banking and finance, engineering, or the various forms of industrial manufacture, who moved periodically in and out of government in their professional capacity, sometimes as adviser, sometimes as director of some governmental operation; but it was the specialized knowledge which such men held more often than administrative skills or political interest which gave direction and purpose to their governmental careers. While current uses of scientific advisers point to obviously striking examples, it has certainly been the case since 1900 that government has sought advice on the building of bridges and railroads, the formulation of fiscal policy, and the elaboration of needs and methods of social improvement from experts borrowed from their specific fields. Finally, the developing academic professions in the social sciences produced individuals whose interest in government came from the study of it and its special functions, as political scientists, economists, sociologists, and others concerned with the relation between social knowledge and social policy sought to impress their views upon the operations of society. Franklin Roosevelt's Brain Trust was by no means the first attempt to organize extragovernmental academic information for governmental use.

That the above four groups scarcely deserve close distinction from one another is illustrated by the efforts continually underway to break down boundaries created by professional or personal commitment and to invade the one sure repository of power: public office achieved by popular election. The attempt to separate politics from administration during the first third of the twentieth century only served to point out more sharply the presence of difference and the desire to surmount it. For example, the City Manager as an appointed official, a professional engineer at first, brought his specialized knowledge within the realm of politics, but often with a distinct commitment to being anti or at least nonpolitical. Academicians, businessmen, and public-spirited citizens alike lamented their virtual proscription from elective office by entrenched political machinery. Wealthy men stopped buying legislatures and began buying universities, partly out of guilt, perhaps, but possibly out of a recognition of the new and complex ways in which society could be remade in the image they deemed honorable and just. The intermingling did not blend the groups, but it did reveal the values they held in common.

Through the nineteenth century and into the twentieth, differences in point of view sharpened as an increasingly more complex society sought solutions to social and political problems. New investigation brought new alternatives and new alternatives reinforced the expansion of professionalisms and the possibility of greater disagreement. Professional points of view became political interests. Unlike traditional interests which followed patterns of class or community, professional interests followed the logic of increasingly more educated debate, often technically complex. Systematic beliefs came to be embodied in professional standards and the training which could presumably produce them. The more "scientific" the study of society became, both in method and in principle, the less "political" it could be, the less subject to compromise and the tradition of the "deal." Scientific truth, if it were indeed scientific, could not be made more or less true by agreement, or by majority decision, or, above all, by personal preference. To bring the sciences of society into the realm of democratic politics would not be easy. It would require a new deal, indeed.

Practical alternatives came to be expressed in partisanships both beyond and within traditional party structure. Franklin Roosevelt, in effect, embodied in his methods of judgment among alternatives one of the more important phenomenon of his age. He imposed an old-fashioned notion of relative interests pragmatically defined on self-consciously rigorous types of systematic thought in economics, sociology, and government which had for almost a century been growing more and more committed to the necessary logic of the scientific approach to life. The atmosphere of social knowledge available in 1932 from the country as a whole constituted a chaos of professional interests formulated institutionally in a variety of associations— vestiges of old reform groups, philanthropic foundations, professional academic and technical associations, research institutes for the study of government—with the professional politician maintaining his control over the organization of the traditional two parties through which all effective interests would have to be expressed.

Within the activity of government itself, however, partisanships were to be compromised, much as they had always been. New ideas and new methods, however rigorous the arguments from which they sprang, had to be subjected not only to the traditions of constitutional structure but also to the rough-and-tumble of American politics. Disputes had to be squeezed into the rhythmic pattern set by fixed terms of office.

The reorganization of the presidency in 1939 was a compromise. But what were the positions in dispute? How old were they, and how new? Despite the fact that, from the point of view of a single event—the reorganization of the presidency— one can see the convergence of many ideas, the nature of American government—its dispersion, its federalism, indeed, its chaos—gives an air of the overstructured to any structure one tries to describe. The values one can claim as common to American society as a whole constitute a handful of generalities which, by virtue of the mass of beliefs they must encompass, make difficult the outlining of any systematic analysis of any single circumstance. Yet if the fact of convergence can be shown to exist, such a convergence must have a history.

The method chosen for this study borders tentatively on biography without pretending to be that in any rigorous sense. This may be a fault, but it is hoped that other purposes which seemed more important will override the severe limitations deliberately imposed upon the relation of the backgrounds of the three men whom Franklin Roosevelt appointed to his Committee on Administrative Management in 1936, Louis Brownlow, Charles E. Merriam, and Luther H. Gulick. I have followed the technique of "imbedding" the more general relation of their earlier backgrounds in particular aspects of their careers which seemed to me to be central to their response to the problem of analyzing the presidency. Such particulars chosen for detailed emphasis—city management, social science planning, municipal research and budgeting, and similar interests to which they gave much attention—are not necessarily the major concerns of their careers except insofar as those interests influenced, in my opinion, their work on the President's Committee. In presenting the material in this form I realize that, biographically speaking, I am distorting the relative importance of these factors. But these were versatile men whose interests touched numerous aspects of American society during the years I shall seek to describe. My intention has been to create a balanced distortion, if I may use the phrase, which has as its purpose the illumination of a single event from the vantage point of the society and the men who produced it.

The event is the preparation and issuance of the Report of the President's Committee on Administrative Management, the legislation which that report suggested, the response of Congress to the proposals, and the subsequent reorganization. As a single event the report would be comparatively unimportant but for its relation to the history which preceded it and to the course of history since. It is for that reason that I have used its authors as a means of documenting that history by relating aspects of their particular lives and interests to the trends which culminated—as they have continued to culminate—in the question of the relation between executive leadership and the liberal base of a democratic society. For ultimately the problem of an individualist, democratic ethic, egalitarian in its fundamental philosophy, existing and continuing to exist in a society growing more and more dependent upon specialized skills and technical elites is the problem which twentieth-century history has posed to those of world society whose route to modern industrialism took them through the utopian dreams of the eighteenth century. If today it often appears that those societies which were deprived of that amiable journey are better attuned to the music of the machine than we, it is even more important to look back, if only nostalgically, on the men of this study. They sought neither the negation nor the destruction of the dreams, but rather their transformation. It might be well to recapture the spirit of their endeavor.

I owe much to the many people who have helped me along the way, not least of all the colleagues and students who have listened patiently to my monologues and opinions. That I have not always taken as much of their advice as I should have may be as obvious to them as it now seems to me. I want to express my gratitude without implicating them in my errors.

My greatest debt for such knowledge as I have been able to gain of the material of this study is to Louis Brownlow who has willingly bartered the wisdom of his years for the energies of my youth, leaving me immeasurably more enriched than I deserve. He introduced me to the subject of Public Administration exactly as I fancy others had introduced it to him: as an exciting potpourri of genuinely responsible public services strung together by anecdotes and techniques bound by the common desire to make effective government as useful as the needs of democratic society and the limitations of human nature would allow. Profoundly aware of vaster knowledge than he could ever hope to possess he set about making the minds of others useful to society without bowing meekly either to wisdom or to training and, above all, without confusing the two.

I doubt that I should ever have had the courage to make this use of that friendship had it not been for the willing support of Frank Freidel, who originally suggested that I make a study such as this and who then proceeded to guide it step by step. I am deeply grateful to him for his advice and for the generosity and kindness with which he has given it.

The family of Charles E. Merriam and particularly his son, Robert E. Merriam, kindly made the Merriam papers available to me. Herman Pritchett of the University of Chicago and his assistant, Doreen Herlihy, were most helpful in having the papers shipped to me.

# PREFACE

Luther Gulick was generous in his contribution of a wonderful day of reminiscences and helpful in his criticism of my text.

Mrs. Lucile Keck was immensely helpful, not only in her capacity as librarian of the Joint Reference Library at "1313" but as friend of many of those who participated in the work this study describes—and not least as an important participant herself.

The diaries of Herbert Emmerich are an invaluable source of a sense of the day-to-day activities of a Washington official during the New Deal. I am grateful to him for lending them to me.

Don K. Price read the manuscript in its original form and gave me much valuable criticism and advice. John Gaus and William Y. Elliott were very generous both with their own recollections of their work on the Committee on Administrative Management and with relevant manuscripts from their personal papers. A grant from the Sloan Fund of the School of Industrial Management at MIT financed a trip to New York for initial conversations with Richard S. Childs, Pendleton Herring, and officers of the Society for the Advancement of Management. My earliest plans for a study of this subject benefited much from the criticism of Elting E. Morison of MIT.

Helpful encouragement, criticism and advice during the final stages of my work came from V. O. Key Jr., Luella Gettys Key, William N. Chambers, and Rowland Berthoff.

Kenneth B. Murdock read and commented upon large parts of the original manuscript, providing throughout a patient and sustaining friendship for which I shall always be deeply grateful.

My wife, Alice Woodard Karl, has read every word of every conceivable form this study has taken. It bears the impress of her criticism and advice, as well as her own intimate knowledge of the field. It should be added that she has also made life not only possible but worth while.

St. Louis, Missouri

1963

# CONTENTS

# 6

# EXECUTIVE
# REORGANIZATION
# AND REFORM
# IN THE NEW DEAL

# REFORMERS OLD AND NEW
## The Meeting Ground

I

IN OCTOBER of 1931 as the Great Depression moved toward its seemingly bottomless trough, the *Survey Graphic* presented to its public a cover from which smiled a sun moving out of an eclipse. In the center of the sun stood a towered and columned building, composite of countless American courthouses and city halls, the symbol of local government. Beneath it ran the slogan, "A New Deal at City Hall." This special issue on city government included articles by Lincoln Steffens, Harold W. Dodds, Luther H. Gulick, Leonard D. White, and Louis Brownlow. Brownlow's essay gave the issue its title. While the phrase "a new deal" would, in other contexts and in other hands, become famous in less than a year, in October of 1931 one could certainly question the degree of warmth it cast on those who found the reforms in city government over the previous twenty-five years too small a ray of hope in the darkness of a national catastrophe.[1]

Even in darkness and concern there resided a sense of hopefulness born of an assurance soon to be tested by responsibility. The professorial Wilson, elevated to the presidency, had given the growing group of professionals in the social sciences reason to believe that their usefulness to American society could come through the practice of government as well as through the study of it. The utilization of professional opinion by men as disparate in their beliefs as Theodore Roosevelt and Herbert Hoover had given greater encouragement to those who were bent upon seeing the twentieth century as the new, technological age of knowledge and skill. But everyone did not look upon the immediate past with equal enthusiasm.

Lincoln Steffens' *The Shame of the Cities* had appeared some twenty-seven years earlier. He was now being asked, he said, to take up his rusty rake and return to the muck; but he refused: "I balked because all the propositions made to me expected a repetition of the old muckraking. And one should not repeat. It is precisely the repetitions of history, whether in large experiences like war, or in such small adventures as political reforms, that should be avoided."

Steffens was not too optimistic about new reforms. They should, he thought, begin "somewhere near where the old muckrakers left off. That may be asking too much. But certainly the new muckrakers—the editors, reporters and reformers—might set out upon their quest with some of the general conclusions in their minds that we old muckrakers drew from our decade of exposure." [2]

In a way it was asking too much indeed, and in a way not much at all. When Steffens looked forward into history, he saw himself, improved by repetition and enlightened by experience. The new reform, he thought would come from "editors, reporters, and reformers." Had he looked around at his company in *Survey Graphic* he might have wondered. Brownlow was a director of the newly formed Public Administration Clearing House, Dodds a professor of politics at Princeton, Gulick a professor of municipal government at Columbia. "Editors, reporters, and reformers" were of Steffens' generation. The new generation were of another stamp; and if they looked back on Steffens with respect, they also took his advice—but for reasons of their own.

Speaking of the "new deal at City Hall," Brownlow wrote, "Did the reformers get it? I fear not. The very word 'reformer' has become an epithet of opprobrium. No one applies it to himself. Nor to anyone he loves. It is less popular than 'racketeer,' and in many minds means the same thing." [3]

# REFORMERS OLD AND NEW

Reform meant many things by 1931, too many perhaps. It meant a stirring up, fuss, noise, and the clash of rakes among the reformers themselves, each eager to uncover an abuse, destroy an evil. The limited public response to the exposure of scandal in the Harding administration had already given hints of an appetite jaded by excesses of shocked concern. It was immoral to question the morality of the President of the United States and in any case it was probably useless. It was better to look at the morality of the reformers, the disturbers of the peace of "normalcy."

Steffens' article was introduced with a cartoon by F. Opper, reproduced from *Puck* of 1894. A guillotine, its blade labeled "reform movement" was being constructed for a group of public malefactors who stood, each tagged with his respective "ism" and shivering with fear, in a roughly constructed prison. Interestingly enough, and apparently by an artistic inadvertence, the construction of the guillotine itself communicates much that made such reform a confusion. The blade hangs expectantly from its hook. One reformer, his hand resting carelessly beneath the blade, drives a nail into the frame. A second, his leg resting across the neck groove, hammers another nail. A third stands eagerly with his eye on his victims and hand on the release rope. In some senses, reform and reformers were never too far from destroying one another.

The many reform movements which enlivened the broad, brisk scene of nineteenth-century American life were often brightly colored reflections of specific, individually conceived aims which derived their design not always from what they were in themselves but from the relations they bore to one another in the constantly changing framework of history. In America the frameworks were constructed by the possibilities of a new world, by the Constitution of 1787, by the dream of an infinitely perfectible man. But the very size of the frame and the local and regional views which could be taken of it made the details at times seem the more grotesque for their specificity. Abolitionism, the most terrifying of all of the reforms because of the war it helped foment, could be hope to one man and horror to another without ever achieving the reality which some had fought for and others had feared.

The specificity of the ends of reform and the isolation of particular means could scarcely avoid being both self-liquidating and disillusioningly self-destructive. If slavery were *the* major social evil in America, then the abolition of slavery must abolish not only evil but the abolitionist societies as well. And while it had in any case done the latter, the fact that it could not do the former could very effectively turn zeal into disillusion.

This specificity, particularly with respect to methods of reform, meant that the achievement of new legislation, new constitutional amendments, or new elected officials, would be expected to achieve social ends. The movements which produced them could die. Those who had contributed to such movements could sit back in satisfaction and live bravely in their new world. The difficulty, of course, lay in the fact that the new world was indeed new, as well as disillusioningly old. The successes of reform could not compete with the development of new problems or the persistence of old ones. The excesses of reform could not be justified in the light of the failures. They could seem shabby, embarrassing, and best forgotten.

One of the difficulties involved in any attempt to give a social or political characterization of American reform movements arises, at least in part, from the peculiarities of the federal system. Unlike the tradition of British government where centralization has tended of necessity to channel reform issues into a course of national debate, the American tradition of local control has operated as an irregular and sometimes irrational filtering system. Issues such as labor legislation, suffrage restrictions, and devices for improving social welfare, for example, succeeded ultimately in various state governments but suffered from a series of rebuffs by the federal legislature and federal courts until much local experimentation had led to more general ideas of practices which could be debated nationally. Where a more centralized system might have had a tendency to turn all reform issues into national political issues and all reformers into politicians, decentralization could localize not only the issues but also the men who espoused them. Thomas Hart Benton's antibank crusade of the Jackson era and William Jennings Bryan's silver crusade both share the rampant moralism of earlier religious reform as well as that of some of the more localized and relatively nonpolitical reforms of their own era—prohibition, for example—but both men sought political ends through political office in the national government. By contrast the work of Emerson, Channing, or even Garrison and Phillips, like some of the later magazine and newspaper muckraking exposés, approached reform as a problem of appeal to individual conscience and intelligence. The reform arguments, like the occupations of their authors, were nonpolitical and often antipolitical.

Those who emphasized political ends recognized that no reform could be lasting unless it were institutionalized in laws which could enforce obedience. Those who emphasized nonpolitical ends and methods recognized that without a reform of mental and moral attitude, law was unenforceable and hence useless. Politics with its compromises was an offence to the moralist's faith in immutable truths. Rigid moralisms had indeed the power to inflame individual understanding, but without a willingness to accede to the age-old demands of political compromise they could only consume those they had inflamed. Reform, if it sought its ends in politics, ran the risk of making a joke of its morality. Bryan standing under a beach umbrella hawking Florida land or fighting science in the heat of a Tennessee summer became the ultimate symbol of the joke. Reform, if it sought its ends in a rejuvenation of the minds of men, faced defeat through the intransigency of its material. Public attention proved again and again too short and too unreliable. Steffens' disillusion was a recognition of this fact.

[ 5 ]

# REORGANIZATION AND REFORM

In general, reform movements in nineteenth-century America followed lines of argument suggestive of the distinction between political and nonpolitical approaches. That they often blended and borrowed aspects of one another's procedures, aims, and intentions makes strict categorization useless. Yet, those which chose to operate through politics and the legal process differed in methods, problems, and personnel from those which took some form of re-education of opinion and attitude through the presumably uninterpreted presentation of the facts as their method of public education. Any given crusade could contain aspects of current and previous reform drives; but practices tended to divide them into two camps held together, if at all, by the presumption of common purpose. The various stages and aspects of the prohibition movement, for example, were often divided between those who sought enforceable laws as the answer to the evil and those who viewed the problem in terms of public, moral education. The chicken-or-egg aspect of the argument—whether laws produced moral education or moral education the laws—disappeared once the conflict could be drawn between those who wished to prohibit drinking, sale, and manufacture of alcohol and those who sought temperance which would retain for the individual his right to decide what or how much he chose to imbibe.

Where law was primary, reform took the shape of the redevelopment of political institutions and practices or in supposed reversions to institutions which had degenerated from their pure, original form. Where the minds of men were primary, reform took the shape of moral exhortation which could direct citizens and politicians alike toward the paths of honesty and virtue. Post-Civil War agrarian reformers took an expansion of the institutional, regulative practices of government as the end of their crusade, just as the Jacksonian reformers had sought their ends in a presumed return to a pure rendering of the Constitution. Although the two groups could have differed violently on the question of the just and proper function of government protection, both looked to government for satisfaction of their grievances, both took "interests" and "privilege" as their enemies.

If one took the view, however, that institutions could not be primary, either because laws could not and should not control the mind of the individual or because politics was in any case a source of chronic evil, then reform tended to confine itself to the enlightened arousal of the community. This point of view, ideally speaking, could direct itself against evil men, who could be replaced by honest ones, or against government itself, from whom unauthorized authority could be wrested.

In either institutional or individualist reform, however, certain of the classic problems of democratic society tended to interfere. Institutional reform was slow, full of compromise, fraught with complexities which were apt to go far beyond the general knowledge and information of the voter. If a responsible electorate was needed to effect such reform in a democratic society, its interest would have to be maintained calmly and steadily over long periods of time, through innumerable defeats and quiet compromises. The audience could be kept in its seats with exciting specifics—silver, tariff reform, out-and-out thievery, and the like. But failure or compromise was apt to produce either cynicism and boredom or a dangerous mob excitement which went beyond the political realities of most situations. It was the latter danger which tended even more to dog the footsteps of the individualist reformers who, in their efforts to arouse understanding, too often were destroyed by the less rational responses they also aroused. The lessons of the hateful days which preceded the Civil War had been painfully learned.

By the 1880's and nineties the phenomenal growth of cities and concentrations of industrial wealth had not only created new reform concerns but had, in varieties of ways, combined elements of past reform and reformers in useful fashion. Cities provided, if nothing else, multitudes of specifics. Here for the environmentalist devotees of the perfectible individual was the ultimate environment, a Sodom which offered sins beyond biblical imagination in quantity if not in quality. Here was wealth malevolently employed, government corrupted and disdained. The new reformers—newspapermen and a sprinkling of academics—could direct their attention to individuals, to institutions of government, and to the various relationships they saw between them. They could attack both politics *and* politicians, business *and* businessmen, dividing politics and business right down the middle, praising what they believed to be basic structures and concepts, attacking what evil men had done to them.

Confusions between the morality demanded of institutions and the morality demanded of individuals plagued efforts of the public and the government alike to define the newer evils. The construction of commissions, presumably independent of politics, to judge the actions of individuals and corporate groups, the agitation for more effective public voice through initiative, referendum, and recall, the arguments for more responsive leadership through modification of government in the direction of the British cabinet system, all of these sought more responsible government through some form of institutional reconstruction. But the relation among the methods was bound to remain obscure, given their vastly differing origins and the different audiences to which they appealed. Civil Service reform measures had begun to make some small dents in the incidence of abuse of federal office, but in city and state government abuses were a method of operation substitutes for which were difficult to find. The supposed rascality of John D. Rockefeller or of Cornelius Vanderbilt seemed to call for public control. But the rascality of Tammany leaders posed other problems. As long as the institutional structures of city government remained the same, changes in leadership, even under the aegis and enthusiasm of public-spirited citizens, had a tendency to reproduce the evils they had been instituted to correct. The new tensions and strains of city life had pressed well beyond the capacity of older governmental forms. Corruption was often the only available method for solving problems which went beyond the capabilities of traditional methods. New brooms could not sweep away new problems. The injustices of corruption could be preferable to the injustices of total neglect.

The reform movements of the eighties and nineties were, like those of previous periods, a chaos of specifics. But the development of the railroad, itself an object of reform zeal, and the increasing spread of national public media of communication had aided the consolidation of reform in lines which would become familiar to the nation as a whole. The assassination of President Garfield in 1881 by a disappointed office-seeker called dramatic attention to movements for Civil Service reform. C. W. Curtis, a leader in the movement, combined the role of publicist (as editor of *Harper's*) with that of administrator (as a member of the Civil Service Commission). Agrarian reform amassed specific concerns ranging from free silver to initiative and referendum; but it was carried to national prominence, in part at least, on the rhetoric of William Jennings Bryan. Muckrakers exposed misuses of wealth and local governmental corruption in carefully, soberly documented articles in widely circulated *McClure's*. The strains of older moral forces continued to press for prohibition and woman suffrage, but through organizations which developed national membership, working locally while hoping ultimately for federal action.

While these movements, each of which captured public imagination in its own way, continued to capture headlines as well, other groups, less spectacular for the moment, were seeking answers of another sort to the difficulties which seemed to them to face American society.

The universities of Germany, their science and their scholarship, had, ever since the close of the Civil War, exerted increasing influence on young Americans. In their search for higher education men like Albion Small and Herbert Baxter

Adams turned to Europe, and particularly Germany, for graduate studies in the old and, more importantly, the new sciences of society. The founding of The Johns Hopkins as an institution of advanced study, and the development of schools of graduate study at Columbia and the new University of Chicago were conceived and directed by men whose studies in Germany had convinced them of the effectiveness of German methods and aims in education.[4] But there was more. The efficiencies of German government produced cities whose order and cleanliness were in marked contrast to the sprawling chaos of the American city. In addition, the role of the German professor vis-à-vis his government could undoubtedly be attacked on those occasions when criticism hobbled academic freedom; but the relationship existed, and the possibilities had much appeal, particularly with respect to the potential influence of university research on government. For men like Dean Burgess at Columbia, Albion Small at Chicago, and H. B. Adams at The Johns Hopkins, the model was clear: combine the free traditions of American democracy, presumably Anglo-Saxon in origin anyway, with the standards of science and efficiency of Germany. By 1909 Herbert Croly in *The Promise of American Life* could formulate the possibilities with a clarity which left no doubt of his admiration of Germany but which took as base in the American tradition the relationship between Alexander Hamilton and Thomas Jefferson. Combine the order and efficiency of the one with the democratic humanity of the other. The American tradition could be preserved; the German could be utilized; reform—if one can extend his argument to this—could be given an intellectual and scientific reality which it had so often seemed to lack.[5]

The party platforms of the presidential campaign of 1912 managed both to compromise and consolidate nationally the varied reforms of the previous twenty years and to attach, wherever they could be attached, the trailing strands which could not logically be fitted in to party argument. Theodore Roosevelt rejoiced in his new discovery of the virtues of Jane

Addams[6] who, in 1908, he had called "foolish," and "a striking example of the mischievous effect produced by the teachings of a man like Tolstoi upon a mind without the strength, training and natural ability to withstand [them]." [7] In his "Confession of Faith" Roosevelt, who had not hidden his annoyance with the presumed radicalism of reformers in general, felt himself forced to acknowledge President Van Hise of the University of Wisconsin as "one of those thoroughgoing but sane and intelligent radicals from whom much of leadership is to be expected. . . ." [8]

Roosevelt placed much emphasis upon the ascendance of Germany in the world of commerce, attributing it to the happy relationship established there between business and government. Senator Albert Beveridge's keynote address at the Progressive Party Convention had spoken to the point in even more glowing terms.[9] A pamphlet in support of the image of Woodrow Wilson as a gentleman of culture worthy of public attention noted that he employed a German governess for the education of his daughters.[10] Elsewhere German cities were compared with their American counterparts and conclusions drawn highly unfavorable to the latter, with the suggestion that American municipal government might model itself on the intelligent order so clearly present in cities of the thriving empire.[11] Roosevelt's references to Van Hise and the University of Wisconsin's helpful influences on Wisconsin government helped make the connection between the German sciences, the universities of America, and modern American politics.

Theodore Roosevelt's espousal of the Progressive program in 1912 was an acceptance perhaps more of its moral zeal than of the specifics which were of necessity attached. That the specifics were, by standards of his prior statements as President, to be associated more often than not with "radicalism" was not necessarily a denial of the fact that they could be utilized for the kind of public political purposes which he set himself to serve. The Progressive program had been built out of varied and independent crusades. Roosevelt was a tough crusader. But he was also, in his own terms, a "Bull Moose." It is possible that his followers were not so wholly committed to the breed. They had directed their efforts toward institutional reform, concentrating their attack upon legislative bodies and their methods. Strong executive leadership and executive independence had not always been an important part of their battles. But if Roosevelt was using the progressive party movement to fight for ends with which progressives had not been identified, the progressives were also using him to give them something which alone they would not have had: an entrée to the only strictly unified objective offered by American national politics—the presidency.

In some respects Theodore Roosevelt's most immediate opponent, President Taft, more effectively fulfilled at least one of the images of the presidency one can build from progressive argument. Taft's interest in government was institutional, judicial, and, above all, administrative. He had concerned himself, in part at least, with problems relating to the efficient and economic operation of his office, eschewing the popular public leadership which so appealed to Roosevelt. The battle between Roosevelt and Taft was to some extent over opposing images of the presidency. Yet to gain the nominations in 1912 each was forced to use methods and alliances which would have been more consistent in the hands of the other. Taft became a political maneuverer. Roosevelt became a man of rigorous, legal principle.

Woodrow Wilson was, in 1912, a newcomer, innocent of sin because, perhaps, of his limited exposure to temptation. He had been in politics for two years. As Governor of New Jersey he had been able to exercise the kind of intelligent political morality which came to characterize him ultimately to friends and critics alike. The accidents of his career gave him the best of the worlds open to him in his day. He was intimately associated with the academic profession, but he had early disavowed German methodology. In 1887 he had begun discussion of problems of administration in an article in the

*Political Science Quarterly*, in which he suggested to his colleagues that they had best stop struggling with constitutions of government and get down to the actual operations of government.[12] But his study, *Congressional Government*, had seemed to disassociate him from the idea of the President as the strong executive in American government. His behavior both as President of Princeton and as Governor of New Jersey had focused attention on him as an individual willing to fight for principles of democratic society. He was, politically speaking, a systematic reformer but a Democrat, an academician but a traditionalist American of Virginia identification, an executive with a strong faith in the legislative process, and above all a man who projected the image of a firm, logical, moral individual. The battle between Roosevelt and Taft may have put him in the White House; but the fact that he combined so many aspects of the sides of that battle put him in position to take advantage of the dispute. He had inherited the by then tattered mantle of Bryan, but he added to it his own concerns with the structure of government and its applicability to the practice of administration. The relationship among the three contestants in 1912 might best be described by the fact that Croly, who had idolized Roosevelt, but who might have found Taft a more explicit exponent of some of his own best arguments, turned ultimately to the support of Wilson.

Yet, in the three candidates, plus the still powerful shadow of Bryan, one could find the strands of reform which had moved public interest for almost a century. Bryan, who most exemplified the moral and theological base of earlier reforms, lost out at the beginning; but his concerns lived on in Roosevelt and Wilson. Roosevelt's battles with the intractable and imperfectible in man continued to place on the process of election the responsibility for the choice of new leaders who would utilize traditional methods for the achievement of new ends.

Of the four, Taft and Wilson seemed most to represent

the new methods, with Taft the exponent of current concerns with economy and efficiency, while Wilson's emphasis lay in the expansion of services and protection against "interests." Both men seriously questioned the primacy of leadership as the sole determining factor in democratic government and sought their solutions in laws which could subject the immoral in man to the morality of great institutions of government.

In any case, the cries of moral reform seemed less a part of the debate than the effort to organize moral ends in structures of law and government. The specificity of older arguments had, by reaching the level of national debate for the presidency, been generalized to the point where public concern could be less directed to individuals and particular abuses and more to methods and law. From the point of view of government and those most directly involved in it, the change could only signify improvement. But from the point of view of the public whose emotional involvement with problems of reform had been a motivating force in public debate, the exhaustion of its enthusiasm was perhaps imminent.

With respect to that enthusiasm, World War I served a unique and awful purpose. Any gaps left by the decline of interest in individual moral reform were filled by the new crusade which provided the opportunity for a massive direction of zeal into world-wide channels. The failure of the moral crusade in Europe brought to a dramatic if enervating conclusion fourscore years of moral reform. Prohibition, one of the last vestiges of the old battles, succeeded in enshrining itself in the constitution only to pave the way for one of the more chaotic displays of national lawlessness and disorder in American history.

World War I was a violent experience in the demise of moral reform, but it was neither the end of reform nor the sole or principle cause of the changes which took place. Like the Civil War it provided a passionate outlet for attitudes which had grown too violent to control and too varied to compromise. Such an expansion of attitudes was in some respects an indication of the fact that they had in reality outlived their usefulness. For those who, after World War I, sought a continuance of the reforms of previous decades, it was this, the dangers of public response, which seemed at times an overriding concern. Torn between an awareness of the rapid need for change in modern society and their traditional faith in popular democracy, they attempted, some of them, to salvage bits and pieces of the past, to understand them more fully, and to put them together again in ways which would be less susceptible to failure. They were joined by others, who, educated in traditions more conscious of new values, launched out in directions dictated by new sciences and new attitudes toward the organization of society.

## II

The frontispiece of *Survey Graphic*'s special issue on city government presented the new problems in their most romantic, traditional terms. A color print engraving from 1856 showed a dignified looking gentleman standing on a platform built of rough logs situated under the shading branches of a gnarled and ancient tree. He is a politician, and the print, which the editors entitled "To the Voters," shows him in an attitude of wise and intelligent appeal to a group of country folk. Most of the audience is seated on the ground. One or two, more richly but still simply attired, are on tree stumps. Children are playing at the feet of the speaker; dogs are frolicking in one corner, and a barn in the distance is limned against the afternoon sky. The paragraph beneath the print comments:

This color print of an eager electorate all attention for the details of government might, we venture to suggest, have been an idyllic interpretation even in the less distracting days of 1856 when it was engraved. Even then government was not so simple as President Jackson had described it a generation earlier. In our era of radio and headlines the people are torn with divers distractions. Meanwhile government grows more and more complicated. Do we come to an impasse or is a solution developing?[13]

The idyll of representative government required an interested participation by the electorate. For men like Walter Lippmann who, as one of the young men at Versailles, agonized through the tragic treaty negotiations and later watched the failure of the League in its appeal for American public approval, the problem lay not only in "divers distractions" but in the capacity to be distracted, the conscious and unconscious desires of a public called upon to control the actions of a complex state. Solutions for Lippmann lay in education, specialization, and rational systematizations of the methods of democratic government. In his book, *Public Opinion*, he asked questions similar to those which the editors of *Survey Graphic* had asked; similar, too, to those which Croly had asked.[14]

Reforms had revealed the extent to which an aroused public could go, stimulated by an awareness of immediate ends and hampered by large-scale lacks of information. Lippmann saw the answers in a frank recognition of the chaos, conscious and unconscious, which attended public discussion. Government would have to lead the public by being patient with and aware of its potential irrationality, and by making decisions in ways which would guard against that damaging influence. Lippmann's systematic appraisal of the problem was echoed, angrily and chaotically, by H. L. Mencken who, with godless Nietzsche as his god, attacked the reforming habits of public and government alike, demolishing forms and institutions of society as the dangerous tools of a dangerous herd. For those, however, who chose not to see the problem at that stage as a threat to democratic institutions, the answer lay in another area.

In the campaign of 1912 four of the parties had gone to the public with planks urging economy and efficiency in government.[15] Arguments for economy in the federal government were old in American history, having been one of the original sources of contention between the Federalists, who sought higher salaries for public officials as a means of recruiting a professional group, and the Jeffersonians, who saw government as a sacrificial civic duty not to be disturbed by temptations of personal gain. The proliferation of government services occasioned by the Civil War and its aftermath had turned the attention of Congress to questions of economy, not necessarily in the Congress itself, but in the executive branch whose expenditures Congress jealously controlled. Congressional efforts to inquire into executive operations were inevitably failures, and not until Theodore Roosevelt's appointment of the Keep Commission, under the direction of the Assistant Secretary of the Treasury whose name it bore, did the executive branch of the government undertake inquiry into its own workings. The difference in point of view—executive rather than legislative—tended to effect the relationship between economy and efficiency. The executive position gave efficiency a status equal to economy, if not prior to it, placing the method of expenditure on a level with the amount expended.

Arguments with respect to efficiency as separate from or prior to those with respect to economy were to some extent a newer concern and, for the public at large, a less clearly definable one. In its simplest form, efficiency tended to be defined by relation to economy, although it was developing a newer definition, partly as a result of its alliance with the growth of industry in the nineteenth century. From the point of view of capital investment, efficiency meant cheaper production and hence the economy which could produce greater profit. It was difficult to fit such an image directly into the existing images of government, if only by virtue of the fact that the end of productive efficiency and economy was more production, while from many points of view the end of government efficiency and economy was definitely not more government.

For industrial utopians like Edward Bellamy and Frederick W. Taylor, efficiency led to cheaper production, lower prices, wider distribution, and, finally, to a more uniformly happy society. This last sense did not ally efficiency with economy on the basis of frugality but of social improvement in a scientific age. When Taylor was called upon to defend his system before a committee of Congress against the charge that it threatened the position of the laboring man both with loss of his independent identity and with technological unemployment, he took a firm stand midway between management and labor, calling for a change in mental attitude, a new morality which would bring a reign of peace—efficiently and scientifically organized—to the industrial world.[16]

The uses to which Taylor and other efficiency theorists were put by the industrial community were at times a far cry from the aims of scientific management. The real conflict was best illustrated by what happened to notions of efficiency when they reached the level of governmental administration. For here the greatest selling point of efficiency arguments lay in lowering the cost of government and hence lowering taxes. This could most effectively be accomplished by cutting down on government services as well as their cost. The same methods and the same ideals were to be used to increase production and to narrow government.

The problem of the cost of government was intimately connected with problems in attitudes toward political morality. For, after the muckraking of the nineties it seemed clear enough that the cost of government was directly proportional to the dishonesty of politicians. Services were more expensive, it could be argued, because their accomplishment was padded with graft and corruption. Hence, "honesty and efficiency" could lead directly to economy; an honest and economic government was obviously an efficient one; and if you could combine efficiency and economy, you could reduce all temptations to, as well as opportunities for, dishonesty. The confusions among these three terms—honesty, efficiency, and economy—and the differing motivations which led to emphases on one rather than the others had, by the end of World War I, a common object of abhorrence which could account for what-

and the processes employed, but having also, and
, a practical knowledge of how to observe, record,
, and compare essential facts in relation to wages,
s, expense accounts, and all else that enters into or
the economy of production and the cost of the
t.[17]

pecialist's awareness of greater need for the practical
of his knowledge continued to be debated in the
ssemblies of professional societies, the public aware-
e problem would ultimately follow. On the national
years 1920 to 1930 provided dramatic evidence of
reness. Woodrow Wilson, supposed idealist and aca-
as replaced in the White House by Warren G. Hard-
se presumed practical honesty and dignity fairly shone
face. At his death thrift entered the White House in
of Calvin Coolidge, who, in word and deed, exempli-
stringent economies of the New England household.
the booming machinery of the economy seemed to
at the throttle a hand which would exercise only
guidance. Herbert Hoover, respected as an engineer,
food administrator of World War I, beloved symbol
hold efficiency and management, became the public
f the new-era man. But the fortunes which had made
a household word turned that name to satiric uses
pression moved households into makeshift slums and
rk benches. The era of the businessman-scientist-
had turned upon itself in one painful revolution.
oming of the New Deal and the depression which
its urgency vastly overshadowed questions of manage-
hether for purposes of honesty or efficiency. Economy
y element on both sides of the campaign of 1932, but
y in the sense of frugality, living within one's means,
ng taxes for new investments which in any case never
to come. For those who held onto older moral notions
lity the bank failures had been a serious blow. The

ever imbalance one found. The common object was "politics."
Politics made government inefficient, expensive, or dishonest,
depending upon how one chose to set up the argument. But
the fact that politics also by tradition made the country democratic served as a serious concern for whatever line of argument one took.

By the 1920's one could outline three strands of argument
which tended to reflect combinations of the above terms.
Those who concerned themselves with honesty and efficiency
presumed that economy would naturally follow or that economy was not an end with which government needed necessarily to be concerned. Economy was, in their terms, a natural
by-product rather than an end. The only reason government
was uneconomical was that it was dishonest or inefficient.
Such men had made the Progressive and the Populist platforms. They had fought for civil service reform as well as for
expanded governmental regulation and control of public
services. They had attempted to reform corrupt governments
by the introduction of honest men and had, by 1920, begun
to acknowledge their failure.

Those who chose to combine efficiency and economy tended
to presume that honesty would, of its own accord, follow
such an alliance, since it would automatically exclude opportunities for dishonesty. Of such were the schools of scientific
management and administration, made up of former followers
of Taylor, Henry George, and Bellamy, as well as a sprinkling
of socialists and near-socialists, and, above all, the newest breed
of executive reformer, the city manager. Their successes were
counted in the number of local civic groups which were clean-
ing up governments by changing city charters, appointing
managers, and dealing with the city as a business for experts.
Their difficulties—and in some instances their failures—lay in
the inability or unwillingness of the public to continue to center
its attention on the operations of the city. Politics continued
to be more exciting and, at times, even unintentionally destructive to the ends of the new management.

Part of the difficulty of both of the above groups resulted

from a third combination of the terms, a combination which often seemed more fruitless and destructive than useful and which contributed to the downfall of many of the management reforms. Traditional, fundamentalist, political attitudes tended to look upon honesty and economy as the major terms of governmental virtue. High standards of morality and thrift were bound to produce efficiency. Any man could run a city, be a governor, or execute the office of President. The requirement of special knowledge or status was in violation of the fundamental tenets of American democracy. If efficiency was not directly the result of individual morality and thrift, efficiency was a threat to representative institutions and the equal dignity of men.

Lincoln Steffens had recognized the fact that corruption in government was related more to the problems which modern industrial society posed for traditional forms of government than to the honesty of the men who governed. But, perhaps in his disillusion, he turned to new ideologies, specifically communism, as his answer. His companions in the October *Survey Graphic* agreed only with his emphasis upon forms of government. Their choice of alternatives lay, however, in areas far from his new political ideology.

One of the heroes of the new concept of efficiency was the city manager, the first of whom were engineers who understood street construction, railways, and bridges—the old plums of the grafters. In 1908 Charles E. Ashburner, a railway engineer educated in England, France, and Germany, became general manager of Staunton, Virginia. The action which was supposed to have brought this about—he revealed to the city fathers the extent to which local contractors were fleecing them—became the St. George legend of the city manager movement. Technical knowledge could save money and provide service. The new profession could command high salaries and, as each manager proudly sought to prove, save the city not only the cost of the salary but impressive additional sums in the first year of his service. John N. Edy, who became

manager of Berkeley, California,
Texas, successively, graduated w
ing from the University of Mis
railroad construction. He becal
after having been chief enginee
the Montana State Highway L
continued his studies at the Univ
in political science. Henry M. V
at the Massachusetts Institute of
a national reputation as an engin
of city management.

Engineers had built the iron ro
nent and had given imagination a
developing industry in the revo
country since the Civil War. Sta
to educate them and the only oth
ing country gave the status of tl
For the nineteenth-century Amer
man of the laboratory but the ma
brought development to the land.
were recognizing that the engine
solely to the specifics and techni
have to be more than a craftsman
his craft. While Woodrow Wilso
expansion of the knowledge and
political scientist in his article on
R. Towne, a member of the Ame
Engineers and a friend and suppor
was exhorting his colleagues to an
In a speech, later an article, ent
Economist," he wrote:

To ensure the best results, the
labor must be directed and cont
only good executive ability, a
familiarity of a mechanic or en

duced
equall
analyz
suppli
effects
produ

If the
expansior
private a
ness of t
scene th
that awa
demic, w
ing, who
from his
the form
fied the
By 1928
demand
efficient
famed as
of house
model o
his nam
as the d
onto pa
enginee

The
dictated
ment, w
was a k
econom
and savi
seemed
of frug

end of the gold standard was perhaps an additional attack on the hard security of the saving public. Honesty seemed less relevant than the system under which dishonesty existed. Incidents of bank failures could be blamed, of course, on individual malefactions; but much of the debate centered on the question of the efficacy of systems. Dissident groups professing various remedies seemed more inclined to attack institutions of government and their forms rather than to seek substitutes in individual leadership. Despite the personal public appeal which men like Huey Long, Father Coughlin, and Francis Townsend possessed, their basic arguments lay in revisions of system and rebuilding or obliteration of what seemed useless institutions. Their appeals were based on the presumed efficacy and efficiency of the institutional changes they proposed, not necessarily, if at all, on their economy. Efficiency had to be defined in terms of the immediate alleviation of urgent conditions. To this extent the New Deal could at first be judged publicly by the speed with which it could act on any given problem, not by the rationality of the structures through which it chose to act or the money it consumed. The ultimate pragmatic test of the New Deal was the fact that it had effects; it took action; it moved. When the honesty and economy attacks began, they leaned heavily for their data on the obvious inefficiencies of the quick solution.

In a sense the public arguments against New Deal chaos drew their material from the New Deal rather than from prior arguments readily associated with Hoover and Republicanism. The sources of such criticism in the past tended to be obscured by the revolutionary air of the New Deal and the powerful personality of its leader. Even the most reactionary of critics could not easily look back without frightening both himself and the public. For those who idealized the New Deal and for those who criticized it, it was the future. They debated their respective attitudes toward that future, whether it was socialistic, communistic, or, that new, important word, fascistic. That all of them were working with and within a past seemed obscured at times by a fear of the past, by a dream of a future, and, for those who found time to observe current events in Europe, by a terrifying reappraisal of democratic government being enacted in the present. Whatever the New Deal was, it was difficult for even its most enthusiastic adherents to find the ways in which it was, in the traditional sense of American government, democratic. The search for a definition of the New Deal which would relate it to the past took the form most traditional in American history: the struggle among the members of Congress, the President, and the Supreme Court over the location and limits of power. The defeat of the President's so-called "court packing" bill was followed quickly by the defeat of the "dictator bill," the plan to make more efficient the executive branch of the federal government.

The battle brought to the fore old quarrels which could now be seen in the light of changes wrought by the New Deal and the years which had preceded it. Efficiency and economy, watchwords inseparable to a generation which included the members of the Court, much of the Congress, and indeed the President himself, were being separated by events taking place in a world over which no one seemed capable of exercising control. Measured by standards of industrial production rapidly developed to monumental proportions in the previous century, democracy, in a society economically depressed, seemed notoriously inefficient. And the paths toward efficiency in the world outside of America led away from democracy. In some of the nations of Europe, democratic government could be singled out by those appealing to mass sentiment as the cause of depressing inefficiency. Efficiency became the threat to democratic government because it was, in the face of newer and greater demands being made upon such governments, the most obviously weak link. The equation of efficient government with nondemocratic government seemed to be the ultimate product of industrialism, of science, and even of knowledge itself. To meet the challenges, government would have to become efficient. But could it continue to offer the freedom which democracy had traditionally prized?

The Supreme Court could only point to the danger. Yet, in attacking the legislation of the New Deal, it could provide no alternatives which would not prove the case against the form of government it was trying to preserve. If American government was not constitutionally empowered to deal with crises, then it would have to be destroyed by them. From the Congressional point of view the problem was even more complex. At first Congress joined with the President in sanctioning and contributing to the broad range of experimentation which the crisis seemed to require. But the gradual awareness of the apparently limitless expenditure required by the New Deal moved conservative Democrats like Harry Byrd to return to older efficiency-economy questions. And liberal Democrats watching the increasing concentration of power in the hands of the executive could scarcely avoid a questioning of the efficiency which this entailed. If the preservation of democracy depended upon the weakening of democratic institutions, then all might be lost in any case.

The man least concerned with the problem seemed to be the President himself. But he was aware of it. In his inaugural address in 1933 he had issued a clear warning that "broad executive power" to meet the emergency might be beyond even the most advanced of traditional methods for dealing with national troubles. By the beginning of his second term, despite the overwhelming electoral victory, it was clear that, should he need such powers, neither Congress nor the courts would willingly concede them. Roosevelt's plans for coping with an obstructive court and the equally obstructive processes of executive management were defeated resoundingly, not only by Congress but by public opinion as well.

Reorganization of the executive office for purposes of greater efficiency in the exercise of its powers was a concern almost as old as the office itself. Few Presidents had failed to complain of the problems inherent in an amorphous administrative structure of which much was demanded and to which little was given, whether from jealousy or ignorance, or useful combinations of the two. Congressional efforts to bring about solutions to the many problems of executive administration were generally oriented toward a desire for economy to which was often added the intention of circumscribing expanded executive power. While it remained easy to identify efficient management with the saving of money, by 1935 it was no longer possible to define efficiency in terms of a reduction of executive authority—quite the contrary. The early years of the depression had demonstrated that Congress could not cope with an emergency without the leadership of executive authority. While such an idea had always been accepted of necessity in wartime, its espousal in peacetime seemed tantamount to a surrender of Congressional authority and the acceptance of an all-powerful executive. Roosevelt had, with consummate rhetorical skill, identified the emergency as "war" for all practical purposes. But wars were specific occurrences to which specific causes could be assigned and for which temporal limits could be expected. It was becoming difficult to view the depression and the measures taken to combat it as temporary. Emergency actions were beginning to appear permanent.

While it would be difficult to find the point at which Roosevelt might have realized that the New Deal was effecting permanent changes in the structure of American government, or even that such changes were required, those whom he chose as advisers on the subject of executive organization had long been aware of the problem. Moreover, they had long been persuaded, in varying degrees and for varying reasons, that changes which would have to be reflected in modern American government were taking place in the world. This awareness had not, however, been produced by either the depression or the New Deal. It had developed in the years which followed the Civil War and had grown to professional maturity through training in the cities, the universities, and the industries of pre-World War I America. Its practical expression had been and continued to be reform.

On March 22, 1936, the White House released to the press letters sent by the President to the Senate and House announcing his intention of appointing a committee to make "a careful study of the organization of the Executive branch of the Government . . . with the primary purpose of considering the problem of administrative management." In the course of presenting the background of the idea, the President said "many new agencies have been created during the emergency, some of which will, with the recovery, be dropped or greatly curtailed, while others, in order to meet the newly realized needs of the Nation, will have to be fitted into the permanent organization of the Executive branch." [18] The letters had been drafted by Louis Brownlow, whom the President was to appoint as chairman of his Committee on Administrative Management. Charles E. Merriam and Luther H. Gulick were to be appointed to serve with him. It was recommended that the House and Senate appoint committees to work conjointly on the same problem to prevent duplication of research efforts. The letters had been discussed with and approved by both the Vice-President and the Speaker of the House prior to their being made public.

It is interesting that no emphasis is placed here either on economy or efficiency, although subsequent events would show that the Congress made much of both terms in their investigations. From the beginning the major intention of the President and his committee was to give the President the "authority" to carry out "his responsibilities under the constitution." That this touched upon major constitutional questions was clear to the President. He told Gulick, according to a memorandum prepared by the latter following a meeting of Brownlow, Gulick, and the President on November 14, 1936, "that since the election he had received a great many suggestions that he move for a constitutional convention for the United States and observed that there was no way of keeping such an affair from getting out of hand what with Coughlin and other crackpots about. 'But,' he said, 'there is more than one way of killing a cat, just as in this job I assigned you.'" [19]

In the course of the discussion potential difficulties with

respect to conservative Congressional concern with economy were raised. The President, according again to Gulick, expressed himself clearly on this point: "We have got to get over the notion that the purpose of reorganization is economy. I had that out with Al Smith in New York. I pleaded with him not to go before the people with the pledge of economy. But he did, and his first budget after reorganization was way up over the previous budget, though there was some saving in administrative salaries. The reason for reorganization is good management." [20]

These statements are particularly important in view of two points: first, as Governor of New York, Roosevelt had based his public arguments for reorganization in local government on the economies and resultant savings in taxation which could be effected, and secondly, that, as President, when he presented his reorganization plans to members of the House and Senate at an informal meeting in the White House, he used economy arguments persuasively and persistently. The battle between efficiency as frugality and efficiency as administrative authority would not break out into the open, however, until the congressional debates over reorganization reached their peak. The problems of the terms usable for public presentation would here, as in the court fight, bedevil efforts to explain and to understand.

III

The chaos of the thirties in many parts of the western world seemed to force a hasty and sometimes hysterical reach backward into the bag of history for whatever structures would prove useful for present demands and seem reasonable for future possibilities. Out of Teutonic legends and national pride Nazism built a butchery based on forms of mass persuasion unknown to the past but useful as a model for the future operation of any government dependent upon mass acceptance. Italy resurrected Rome only to have it crumble into new ruins; but the early Mussolini attracted world-wide attention and much general approval for demonstrating that central control of an industrial society could promote efficiency and general welfare, as well as relieve a depressed economy without seeming to threaten productive ownership. The world was being rebuilt on old philosophies to which were conjoined, as method, new sciences which denigrated the hopeless uncertainties of past moralities. This was as true of America as it was of Germany, Italy, or the new Soviet Union. But for America the new sciences were often being learned and used by men steeped in the idealism of an old morality, whereas in Europe many of the exponents of the new sciences had long been disillusioned by conflicting varieties of moral dogma. Max Weber could be the messiah of European social science because he questioned the utility of messianic morality, finding the ends of government in government and the objectification of reason in the working machinery of government.

Louis Brownlow, Charles Merriam, Luther Gulick, and the President himself, reflected aspects of a generation which had set for itself the continuing reformation of American society; but the reformation was based upon the unquestioned assumption that the morality with which they had been raised would continue to be the morality of the institutions they reformed. World War I and the depression had not destroyed their aim, but it had modified their methods. Woodrow Wilson might conceivably have called a constitutional convention to decide the issues of the thirties, or centered the problems in the debate of a national election. Franklin Roosevelt could not.

The President's Committee on Administrative Management and the men who guided it were representative of the changes which had been taking place in America since the Civil War. Each of the three brought to the task of fitting the presidency to cope with contemporary society a different but an extensive experience in the problems of modern administration and modern social science. Two of them, Merriam and Gulick, were academics by training; but Merriam had spent his career attempting to reconcile theories of politics with the practical operations of politics, while Gulick had concentrated upon a science of administration which would separate it from the vagaries of either the theory or the practice of politics. In some senses, the systematic differences between them were compromised by Brownlow. His observations of politics as a newspaper reporter from the 1890's until his appointment as Commissioner of the District of Columbia in 1915 had left him with a deep and abiding love of the political in American life; but his subsequent career as a city administrator and as Director of the Public Administration Clearing House had given him a knowledge of and respect for the problems involved in executing the ends which politics determined.

Each of the three brought to the study of the presidency a background and experience which was unique but for the common concern with the improvement in the processes of democratic government. This concern had, in each of the three men, been centered originally on problems in local government. Like an ever-widening pattern of concentric waves, the concern had broadened to meet more general, federal problems as it sought more efficiently to cope with the needs of American society as a whole. Its focus on the presidency in 1936 was in some senses the pinnacle of an endeavor which had begun well before the turn of the century.

To use the presidency as the center of a discussion of administrative reform in America invites at the outset problems as interesting in their origins as the central one of the presidency itself, and in many respects more difficult to discuss. For it is only in the twentieth century that the President of the United States has become a genuinely national figure of daily concern to the politically interested public throughout the country. Even Lincoln, the most heroic of nineteenth-century Presidents, achieved his status in the holocaust of a Civil War and the assassination which crowned his participation in it. American Presidents are the subjects of controversy and the objects of heated political temper. The presidency itself has often been treated as some drastic cure for serious but temporary discomforts, necessary when required but better shelved during periods of national good health. It is this attitude, perhaps, which accounts for the fact that American Presidents are rarely and only briefly symbols of national leadership, that they do not constitute a tradition of heroes—or villains—and that generations are required to build about them even the most rudimentary legendary background. The country is effectively "de-presidentized" after each administration.

Yet Presidents sometimes share in the mythology of their times through the contemporary literature which is used to describe them. Contemporary accounts of Woodrow Wilson often bear striking resemblance to the Confederate heroes of post-Civil War fiction. The whole episode at Versailles has entered historical literature as a tragedy wrought by the personal defects of a stern, unsmiling, firmly Presbyterian moralist. Again, the public descriptions of Theodore Roosevelt share much in common with the heroes of Dreiser and Norris, so much so that one can only with some difficulty grope one's way through them toward a genuinely political analysis of the man as President. Characteristically enough, perhaps, one of the few novels to deal even obliquely with the presidency, Henry Adams' *Democracy*, pictures the President as the least heroic figure of the book. Still, one can reasonably say that American Presidents, at least at the beginning of their elected careers, fulfill in some measure currently accepted ideals of the public hero. Their campaign propaganda describes them as such, and their success in the campaign must in some measure depend upon the degree to which they project to the public a satisfying sense of heroic reality.

The executive is the hero of the twentieth century, but his image rests on criteria which, in America at least, prevent anything approximating accurate focus. He entered the scene in the nineteenth century, in the first rich surge of America's industrialization; but his most obvious representation, the Horatio Alger hero, effectively documents the confusion. For there are two heroes to each adventure: the virtuous innocent who succeeds through the light of his promise and the purity of his endeavor, and the giver of success, the man who recognizes the virtue and rewards it. The career of the first is the plot of the novel, but the career of the second is built on the unstated assumptions. The first is the preindustrial hero whose success is compounded of virtue and luck; the second is the new hero, a product of knowledge and skill and cunning. He may or may not practice the virtues he recognizes. Like all of the strange adaptations in America of the Darwinian idea, his fitness may be measured by his awareness of moral quality, but his survival depends upon his selective application of it.

That such a duality affects the presidency becomes obvious when one compares the growing technical complexity of the scope of presidential responsibility with the nature and method of selection of the executive. Presidents are not chosen because they are skilled, trained administrators, but because they have evidenced certain publicly required virtues, attitudes, and responses to whatever the public conceives as current challenges. This is a subtler difference, certainly, than that which marks the division in the Alger hero, but it has been formed according to a similar cultural design. For, as this study will attempt to show, the report of the President's Committee on Administrative Management sought to create a presidency which would contain within it the efficiency and technological skills which a modern industrial society required, at the same time that the American public would be left free to choose its President as it willed and in accordance with criteria firmly and properly rooted in its national traditions. The preservation of this tradition—the Jeffersonian-Jacksonian base of the democratic process—was one of the chief aims of the committee and one of the central sources of the criticism which could be leveled at it. Interestingly enough, when such criticism came, it would come from both sides, from those who found the committee's strengthening of the office a threat to democratic traditions as well as from those who found its support of the traditionally individual and technically irrational aspect of the office a threat to the needs of a complex industrial society. Nonetheless, the committee embodied the duality of past virtues and present problems in the President and the presidency—a phrase which Brownlow later took as the title of his lectures on the subject. They were to be dealt with not as oppositions but as inherently necessary coordinates in the continuity of American society.

To open this study with a detailed analysis of the problems of the presidency would in some respects be a serious misstatement of the case, although the fact that the office will be the eventual goal of the argument makes an initial explanation necessary. Ever since the summer of 1787 when the Constitutional Convention in almost mysterious fashion produced the outlines of the presidency as the end process of a debate which somehow failed to get completely on the record, the presidency has been the conclusion of experiment and dispute more often than the originator. It has absorbed change. It has responded to experiment which has been begun in other sectors of national life more often than it has initiated it. Whether one deals with the standard public response to leadership in America as a traditional and troublesome apathy or as considered reluctance to be led where inner motives have not yet directed, the President of the United States faces a problem in his personal capacity to lead which, quite frequently, he alone seems to understand. Experts press programs and advisers compound advice which he either dawdles with or ignores as he listens to some inner counsel—his own sense of public opinion based not on polls but on his awareness of his responsibilities. The New Deal presidency, despite its pragmatic aura and the image of bold experimentation which surrounded it, was experimenting with innovations most of which had been tested in local government over the previous three decades. The great contribution which those decades of progressivism in its many forms made to the New Deal were precisely the multitude of successes and failures in governmental experimentation. These experiments provided examples in the form of case studies of attempts in local governments across the nation to solve problems which could not yet be considered by the federal government, let alone by the Chief Executive. For with the exception of foreign affairs, problems of government reach the federal level only after a series of attempts locally to cope with them. Even so recent an effort as the proposal to set up a department of urban affairs reveals the sustained reluctance of many to bring the Executive Branch any closer than it already is to one of the chief facts of this century. When such change does come it will be another in the long series of examples of the slow and painful process of adapting the American executive to the demands of social and political necessity.

The demand for a new concept of executive responsibility began within the decade which followed the Civil War; but the voices which carried it were the quietly conservative ones—like those of the Adams family—fighting unsuccessfully a trend which was becoming dominant in business enterprise as well as in government. Charles Francis Adams Jr. in "A Chapter of Erie" sought to bring the businessman back to his presumably traditional responsibilities, while Henry Adams in his two articles, "The Session," and his angry discussion of the Legal Tender Act called for a more effective federal executive to cope with the emergent economic and political problems of the new age. Brooks Adams ultimately systematized the problem in philosophical orders in "The Law of Civilization and Decay"; but none of the voices seemed to break through the direction which history was taking. Henry Adams' pleas to President Grant certainly went unheard, particularly by the President himself who was clear and explicit in his belief that the President was the servant of the will of Congress.

The scandals of the Grant administrations and their reflections in local government called for reform; and while the voice of morality continued to describe both causes and cures, administrative solutions in the form of Civil Service reform and more businesslike methods (a curiously recurrent term given the known role which business played in corruption) of operating government were being suggested and experimented with locally. Systematic bookkeeping was revolutionizing control over industrial production, pointing out the direction not only of efficiency and greater profit but honesty as well. Translations to government were clearly on the way.

Cleveland's assertion of executive power through the veto came at a time when young intellectuals like Professor Woodrow Wilson had already begun to despair of the possibility of a firm executive in the White House and had begun to look for him in the House of Representatives. But a quietly shrewd McKinley marked a trail which would be more publicly blazed by Theodore Roosevelt, making it possible for Woodrow Wilson to become the kind of President he had once thought necessary but unlikely. The war through which he led the country revealed finally the immense power contained within the industrial community and its vast potential. But it was still difficult to see the connections which could usefully relate that community to the responsibilities of government, as the period following the war so amply demonstrated.

The New Deal sought to cope with problems which had been in a process of development for half a century at least. The real question where the Executive Branch itself was concerned was one of method. Were there really available in the traditions of American government the means of solving problems which confronted the country in 1933? No one could answer, least of all the President himself, except with a faith that what had always been would always be; that from within the very chaos of national energy and ambition which had produced the dilemma would come the solution. This was the faith with which the President's Committee on Administrative Management worked in its effort to consolidate the gains of the New Deal and to enable it to profit by its failures.

This study will examine the background and experience of the men who formed the President's Committee on Administrative Management. Subsequent chapters will then seek to place them and their report into the context of the history of executive reorganization. The problems posed by the editors of the *Survey Graphic* might then be seen in a broader perspective.

A nostalgic look back to the Jacksonian idyll did not easily reveal the elements of that era which could be salvaged to provide value and purpose for a democratic society in a technologically complex world. And a disillusioned glance at the reformers of the immediate past did not disclose methods clearly transferable. The old reform had failed—or had simply been outlived, it was hard to say. Steffens' rake had rusted, but whether from misuse or disuse would be a matter of some argument. In any case, there were now new tools.

---

## CHARLES EDWARD MERRIAM
### Politics, Planning, and the Academy

I

IN DECEMBER of 1929 President Hoover appointed a research committee to study social trends. The public press, gradually devoting more and more of its attention to the worsening economic crisis, greeted the announcement with little enthusiasm or interest. White House appointments of study groups, committees of investigation, and advisory units of one sort or another had become a fairly common occurrence in the ten years since the end of the war. Fluctuations in the situations under study often moved faster than the studies themselves. The reports issued rarely seemed to evoke much in the way of clear-cut action and the problems with which they dealt sometimes disappeared before—or in spite of—the issuance of the report. On occasion comment could become bitter and bemused. "Making a study" of a problem seemed an alternative to facing it. In any case, no one could say much about a study of "social trends." No one was sure what it meant; and by 1932 when the study was completed, public preoccupation with problems of the depression made the question seem even more academic than the personnel of the committee which was asking it.

The President's Research Committee on Social Trends[1] was headed by Wesley C. Mitchell, director of the Social Science Research Council and professor of economics. Its vice-chairman was Charles E. Merriam, founder of the Council and professor of political science. William F. Ogburn, sociologist, was named director of research. The completed report of the committee, a three-volume work, was announced by the President in October of 1932 and published early in 1933. Some fifteen individual monographs were planned as supplements to the basic report. The long list of participants, stellar in academic terms, was virtually unknown to the public.[2] These were not the prominent citizens at large, the traditional "public men" of American politics. Their associations were not with reform but with research, the term which they had been proud to place in the official title of their committee.

While the committee was pleased with what it considered its unprecedented position as social science adviser to the President, Mr. Hoover was quick to remind them that, in his opinion, the true breaking of ground had been the work of the Committee on Waste in Industry, of which he had been chairman. The question of precedent was relevant, despite the President's injunction. The committee felt itself at a turning point in American intellectual history. The academic community and the effective system of professional associations into which academics had been organizing themselves for almost half a century were now being asked to comment directly on problems facing the national government. It was the culmination of a complex dream, a triumph of past efforts even to have been called into existence as a group of scientists for the purpose, as the President put it in his introduction, of helping "all of us to see where social stresses are occurring and where major efforts should be undertaken to deal with them constructively." [3]

Charles Merriam in particular exemplified the academic in this new role. It was an image which he had done much to create over the previous decade. As President of the American Political Science Association he had led in the founding of the Social Science Research Council, in the modernizing of philanthropy through the formation of the Spelman Fund, in the effort to create a new association of public administration and political science at the University of Chicago. Entrepreneurial and political, an activist in the achieving of any new relationship which could promise to break through the restrictions of academic tradition, Merriam saw the social sciences as constellations of a new universe coming to be. The key concept in that universe was "research." The idea for the President's committee had originated in the Social Science Research Council. Success in persuading Mr. Hoover that such a committee could be useful seemed to indicate a new relation between the federal government and the dispersed knowledge of the American academic world.

Merriam's chapter in the committee report provided that document with its peroration. Entitled "Government and Society," it concluded with a series of questions, typical of which was the following: "How shall we blend the skills of government, industrial and financial management, agriculture, labor and science in a new synthesis of authority, uniting power and responsibility, with a vivid appeal to the vital interest of the day, able to deal effectively with the revolutionary developments of our social, economic and scientific life, yet without stifling liberty, justice and progress?" [4]

Such were the questions to which Merriam and his generation addressed themselves, and to which they felt they were beginning to find answers. *Recent Social Trends,* the title which the committee finally chose for its published report, was a beginning in that it demonstrated the possibility of bringing the organized research of the academic community to the service of the federal government. But this was the product of movements which had been going on in American society for the previous fifty years.

The President's Research Committee on Social Trends was supported by the Social Science Research Council, a recently founded "super" society of academic societies in the various areas of the social studies: economics, politics, psychology, sociology, statistics, anthropology, and history. Money supplied to the Social Trends group by the Social Science Research Council came from the Rockefeller Foundation. The interrelation and interdependence of the three groups—organized academic research, the academic society, and the philanthropic foundation—form a history of the development into a community of the dispersed and independent segments of American academic interest.

The academic and scientific society, so important to the development of science and learning in England and on the continent of Europe, was a particular and peculiar necessity in the United States. American intellectual associations, in common with their old-world counterparts, served the function of facilitating interchange of ideas through meetings and various forms of publication. But such societies in England and Europe rested on hierarchical systems of education which provided a common social and intellectual experience for those who, later in their careers, would constitute the membership of either the academy or other portions of the society. Such men had been social contemporaries in school, at the university, and in government positions as well as in the libraries or laboratories in which their professional labors were carried on. At the center of the educational system one found a university or a limited group of universities which served the national function of providing personnel for intellectual activities wherever they occurred in national life. Americans had discussed the possibility of a national university ever since Washington's day, but there had never been even the beginnings of agreement concerning the utility of such an institution, let alone its form. Americans had continued to found colleges and universities for every conceivable reason and, given the traditional adherence to the sanctity of local control in education, in every conceivable form. By the end of the nineteenth century the chaos of American higher education could be documented impressively by the number of colleges which dotted every segment of American landscape without regard to kind or quality, and without regard, certainly, to the question of intercommunication.

Thus the major function of the American academic society, almost from its beginnings, lay in compensating for the lack of common base. The result was that such groups were, of necessity, professional groups in the sense of being more concerned with the establishment of identity and the definition of personnel and standards than with the interchange of ideas as such. Although ideas were by no means ignored—as the journals founded will testify—the introduction of men to one another was as important as the exchange of their ideas. The common educational background which united scholars of the old world did not even begin to exist in the new. While those who formed the American academic societies were not seeking to duplicate that common background in society as a whole, they were using the academic society as a means of creating a common intellectual experience within the disciplines themselves. The problem of relating this experience to government, equally difficult in American society, would occupy the generation which, having satisfied in part its need for identification, now sought to impress that identity on the affairs of government.

In America the development of academic societies was in some ways a substitute for a national university or educational system in that it could attempt to provide a common ground of communication not only among members of a given discipline but among the disciplines themselves and ultimately between academic disciplines and the government. The first stage was accomplished by the founding of the associations within the separate fields; the second could be found in the creation of the American Council of Learned Societies and the Social Science Research Council; but it was the difference between those two bodies which indicated the emergence of the third stage, the relation between academic disciplines and the government. For the common bond among members of the ACLS was quite clearly their status as learned societies. There could be no further ideological unity among groups so widely dispersed in interest. The emphasis was on personnel and professionalism rather than ideas. Inherent in the founding of the Social Science Research Council, however, was the idea of social science as a general intellectual discipline with distinctive methods and purposes as well as principles. Among the purposes was, unmistakably, the desire to have a useful relationship with and effect upon the governing of American society. The appointment by President Hoover of the Committee on Social Trends was, in formal, public terms, the first major achievement of that end.

Much of the above development had depended upon the problem of gaining financial support. Universities and colleges had done little for the growth of professional societies beyond employing their members—that in itself, of course, a massive contribution. But the growth of such groups had important effects on the operations of universities and colleges, particularly with the emergence of "super" organizations with little or no necessary affiliation with particular institutions.

Through the nineteenth century the various institutions of higher learning had developed their own special relationships to the individuals and social or religious groups who acted as philanthropic sources of revenue. The academic societies, however, not only crossed lines among institutional centers but held a new appeal for donors, particularly donors whose industrial interests had given them respect for the great concept, efficiency. Donors who had either satisfied or tired of the desire to be memorialized in institutional masonry were impressed by the power of the professional groups to provide projects in which they could invest. For those who already had a building with their name above the door it was interesting to find specific endeavors in which they could see the active effects of their contribution, either in objects moved from the tombs of Egypt to the museums of New York and Chicago or in systematic attempts to improve social conditions in slums. The institutionalization of the intellectual community paralleled the institutionalization of philanthropy; and as academic societies sought to improve the nature and conditions of learned investigation, philanthropy reformed itself in foundations dedicated to a similar appreciation of new forms of efficiency.

Thus not only was academic research brought to the service

of the federal government through Hoover's use of the Social Science Research Council, but the Rockefeller fortune as well.[5] As founder of the Social Science Research Council, vice-chairman of the Committee on Social Trends, and director of the Spelman Fund of the Rockefeller Foundation, Charles Merriam was a central instrument in these transactions. His major ambition rested on his belief that American government was as seriously in need of the knowledge possessed by the academic community as that community was in need of the responsibility and experience of serving its government. The conviction that there would have to be a relationship established between government responsibly conducted and information reliably obtained came to constitute the basic definition of the term "planning" for Merriam and many of his contemporaries. But it was a particular conception of the idea of planning and, in the minds of his critics, a debatable one. It had, nonetheless, evolved out of the circumstances of his career in the academic and political life of America.

Gaining support for extra-university associations was not an easy matter in 1900 when Merriam first moved from Columbia to the University of Chicago. William Rainey Harper was not unique among university presidents in his firm, personal control over university policy as well as over sources of financial supply. Although he had been active in the development of systems of adult education, his belief in the relation between the university and the community was oriented toward an academic view of society. Merriam's desire to enter Chicago politics as a participant in public office did not meet with open approval from Harper who drew lines between the responsibilities of the teacher and those of the citizen. Merriam's earliest proposals that the university create a center for training in government and citizenship were likewise shunted aside by Harper who either questioned their utility or saw them as a rival for available funds, but in any case politely failed to back them. Like other university administrators, Harper viewed government as a historical study in the university, not as the training and research enterprise which Merriam understood it to be.[6]

For twenty years Merriam sought university support for one institutional scheme after another. The rebuffs from successive university presidents ranged from cool ignorance to the statement that the university could scarcely be expected to provide funds for the writing of every faculty member's books—the only interpretation which historically oriented academics could give to Merriam's constant pleadings for what he called "research in politics."[7] Success, finally, came not from a university administration but from the academic society which, in 1921, named Merriam as its president—The American Political Science Association. Merriam was responsible there for the development of a committee on research. The committee was formed along lines suggested by Merriam's presidential address to the Association in 1921. His plan, however, went beyond research confined solely to political science. He sought as well what he considered the supporting research being done in psychology, sociology, economics, statistics, history, and any other discipline which chose to call itself a science of society. It was clear, not only to Merriam but to political science colleagues like A. B. Hall and Robert T. Crane, that the plan was rapidly—and happily—exceeding the boundaries of the Political Science Association alone. By 1923 Merriam was engaged in correspondence with other associations and academic groups. The topic for discussion was an entity tentatively titled the "Social Research Council."

The title itself is interesting. It was copied, and rather directly, from the National Research Council, a group founded in 1916 for the purpose of supporting and interrelating work in the natural sciences. One of its guiding lights was John C. Merriam, brother of Charles Merriam, and a prominent paleontologist and geologist. The breadth of John Merriam's interests and concerns had aided in the broadening of the active interest of the Council which, by the beginning of the twenties, was considering projects larger in scope than its original boundaries of "natural" science. One such was a study of "human migration," a project also to be partly financed by the Russell Sage Foundation. Wesley C. Mitchell had been named director of the study, which had as its purpose an investigation of the effects and influences of population movement on American society. This, too, had been broadened to include the effects of "mechanization" on American industry. Beneath this, to be sure, lay the outlines of Veblen's emphasis upon scientific inquiry into the effects of industrialism and its consequent new utilizations of men and machines. Viewed in relation to the heated concern with immigration during this period, on the one hand, and, on the other, the necessity-for-self-study-to-see where-we-are-going technique which motivated not only progressivism but the Committee on Recent Social Trends, the migration study reflected broader aims than those originally envisioned by those who had proposed it.

Mitchell was impressed with Merriam's plans for a research council for social studies, and by 1924, through efforts sustained and furthered by Merriam, such a council was formed and incorporated in the state of Illinois. It borrowed part of the Mitchell migration study from the National Research Council and the Russell Sage Foundation. With funds from the Laura Spelman Rockefeller Memorial it set about its new business.[8]

The organization of the Social Science Research Council, the name finally settled upon, was not a matter, however, of undiluted happiness on the part of all concerned. Initially, only the Political Science Association and the Sociological Society were unqualified in their approval. The economists, who had been interested from the beginning, nonetheless took several months to come to agreement, perhaps as a result of the internecine turmoil in which that group had often found itself. The historians, who had continued to meet with the other three during the period of discussion, were for a time the major holdouts, a disagreement which, because it indicates some of the deeper and more continuing problems in American social science, is worth describing.

The American Historical Association, through Charles H. Haskins of Harvard, had from the beginning voiced objections to the development of such a council, although the historians expressed agreement in full with the aims Merriam had proposed. The difficulty centered around the American Council of Learned Societies, a group which, as Haskins wrote Merriam, "plans to do for the humanities and social sciences somewhat the same kind of work which the National Research Council is doing for the natural sciences, and which similar organizations, like the British Academy, have accomplished for these fields of study in other countries." [9] J. Franklin Jameson, director of the Carnegie Institution's department of historical research, voiced the same concern, although he, too, conceded that among the many problems which separated some members of the ACLS from others, one of the more important was a lack of funds. But the differences were more significant than this. As Jameson pointed out, it was unlikely that the American Philological Association could find much in common with the American Political Science Association. But he felt that the historians stood midway between both groups. Moreover, he continued, "I think we may all well feel, that there are common interests of all humanistic studies much in danger of being neglected in the United States, and which will be better cared for if the entire group of students of the humanities hold together, with a united effort; and out of these common interests there arise certain common problems and enterprises that may well be looked out for by an organ representing the whole group of the humanistic sciences." [10]

Herein lay the crux of the matter. "Humanistic sciences" from Merriam's point of view was a contradiction in terms. Undoubtedly he had responded rather pointedly to his reading of Haskins' contention that the creation of a new research council would not only split off the fields under discussion from the ACLS, but, more important, apparently, create "at least two separate bodies in the non-scientific fields as over against the single body in the field of the natural sciences [the National Research Council]." [11] To call "non-scientific" the very areas of study whose scientific nature Merriam and his colleagues were working to establish was to decide the question at the outset—and in favor of views which Merriam had for twenty years been opposing. He had already been told that there was no such thing as research in politics. He did not need to be told it again.

While Haskins and Jameson were apparently unaware of the meaning of this dispute, they were aware of the strange rumblings of new ideas coming out of the Midwest. Haskins coyly ("informally" was the word he used) suggested that the ACLS might benefit from more membership from the "Middle West," and promised to do something to see that this was brought about.[12] True, there had always been a relatively fierce competition between the growing schools of the west and the older ones of the east, and this certainly influenced the tendency of the western scholars to go their own way. But in this case the problem was overshadowed by newer concerns. More telling was the question of "common problems and enterprises." Whatever Merriam and his colleagues may have thought of the teachers of English literature and the scholars of ancient oriental studies, these were not part of the community of scholarship and research they were trying to create. He did not consider himself in opposition to the National Research Council. He wished to emulate, not oppose their endeavors. For Merriam and for those who joined with him in the founding of the Social Science Research Council, the model for research was built on the methods of experimental science. Merriam was willing to defer questions of humanizing influence, partly because he doubted that such a concern was really valid, partly because he felt that he and those who shared his beliefs could provide all the humanizing necessary.[13]

The establishment of the SSRC fulfilled needs not only for

the social scientists but for the philanthropies which were beginning to support them. The choice between the ACLS and the National Research Council was made not only by Merriam but by those whose willingness to support "useful" public endeavors led them to social problems rather than to cultural ones. Support by wealthy patrons of humanistic pursuits had always been, and continued to be, a private affair. But toward the later decades of the nineteenth century private philanthropy more and more had sought outlet in social reform. Bestowers of fortunes created by industrial empires becoming geared to efficiency and proper management could scarcely fail to see the inefficiency of piecemeal efforts to dispense largesse gracefully rather than usefully. For those newly engaged in foundation and fund management the problems of where to give and how to give posed problems which charity had not raised. Charity had looked to palliatives, nickeling and diming the poor to keep them alive. The new philanthropy tended to search out causes—of disease, of poverty, of war—and these, unlike the poor, were harder to recognize at first glance.

Professional educators had, in the first decades of the century, sought out and guided the rich to America's universities, that they might endow old ones, found new ones. Like the art and music impresarios of the previous decades, they attempted to exercise rigid control over the judgments of their benefactors, building institutions which accorded with tastes more exclusively their own. Specific interests in social research, however, combined with the vanity of salvation when men like John D. Rockefeller took up the hookworm as a disease to be conquered and the perpetuation of all that was good in the Baptist faith through the University of Chicago and the Laura Spelman Rockefeller Memorial, later the Spelman Fund.[14]

Among the professional advisers who directed the wealthy to the support of art, music, and education were those who directed them also to the support of society itself, not through cures of disease but cures of basic social evils, the causes of which could also, presumably, be discovered through research. The latter group, however, faced difficulties which the former had not had to contend with, if "difficulties" is the proper term. Those who chose to put their new riches into the purchase of paintings or symphony orchestras often needed detailed guidance and were willing at times to admit their need. The minds of those who turned to the support of welfare work were, on the contrary, full of ideas, methods, evils, cures, and directives, both of a specific and general nature. Difficult as it was to guide men who often did not feel the need to be led, those who accomplished this task, like Beardsley Ruml of the Spelman Fund and Edward Pierce, secretary to E. A. Filene, served as the link between philanthropies, the universities, and government, both local and federal. Ruml's interest in and respect for Merriam and Merriam's high regard for Ruml provided Ruml with a social project for the Spelman Fund and Merriam with the SSRC. While it was through the SSRC, the Spelman Fund, and the Rockefeller Foundation that much of the support was obtained for the financing of the studies which comprised the report of the President's Research Committee on Social Trends, this was the same combination which would, for the next two decades, provide new ideas and new personnel for American government.

For those who were studying the previous three decades of American society the point at which they stood—1932—was not necessarily a disadvantage. The way ahead looked difficult, but the challenge had an excitement bred out of assurances that the evils besetting society could be conquered, not by faith alone nor by the chaos of individual works, but by organized knowledge supported by foundations, universities, and, if need be, by the government itself. The public sanction which President Hoover gave to the work of his committee seemed a promise of the ultimate in cooperation—the government of the United States and the knowledge which could give it life and endurance. A President was being advised—directly aided in his responsibility of planning the future of America—by members of the academic community, not as friends or former classmates and colleagues, but as professionals in the study of society.

II

The transition from reform to research was not the product of design, although a retrospective view reveals much pattern to the years which saw individuals trained in the Social Gospel movement turning to Progressivism and local reform groups in major cities giving their attention to what were now being called Bureaus of Municipal Research. Merriam's efforts to found an Institute for Government at the University of Chicago, like his desire to create a group for the furtherance of research in the social sciences, grew out of an era which found not only in the progressive movement but in the whole technological revolution the belief that specialized knowledge systematically applied was necessary for the preservation of democratic government. Merriam's approach centered upon two basic points: first, to encourage the development of technical research in politics in an academic community nurtured on the belief that politics was a historical study; and secondly, to bring the results of that research, the newly acquired knowledge, to the immediate use of government itself at its highest levels. If his approach to the first problem attacked traditions within the university, his approach to the second touched springs of dissent deep in the society of America as a whole; for the faith in self-evident truths as the basis of liberal, democratic self-government could not help but come into conflict with the doctrine that specialized knowledge and training were somehow to be considered requirements of governmental operation. Merriam's concerns, however, were not new.

The bringing of privately acquired knowledge to bear upon public problems had been the aim of that branch of liberal thought which distinguished between "public" and "private" in a fashion later described by John Dewey in *The Public and its Problems,* a work which became a handbook for theorists of public administration.[15] Dewey's analysis had been precast, however, by the development through the nineteenth-century's closing years of groups of private citizens in major cities of America who devoted themselves to the investigation of public problems and the endowment of private institutions for studying them. Shock over the ravages of "sin" and "corruption" helped bring private funds to the founding of bureaus of research, committees of vigilance, and various institutes for civic education.[16]

The early years of the twentieth century saw a transition taking place—from the older emphasis upon sin and corruption to be investigated by vigilantes armed with public virtue to a new emphasis, now upon "efficiency and economy," to be investigated by experts armed with technical training and science, a phrase applied often to describe systematic bookkeeping, then strangely new to city halls and courthouses. For a period of time the objects of investigation and those leading the investigations remained the same—interested citizens looked into crime, prostitution, slums, and the corrupt leadership which, presumably, condoned such abuses. Calling the purpose of the investigation a wiping out of sin or the instituting of efficiency and economy often did not reflect any differences in the problems being argued.

Even before World War I, however, one could begin to distinguish groups of men who professionalized the activity of reform, who brought to it particulars of training which classified problems and methods and encouraged the development of specialization. The word "reform" was dropped. It had developed associations with the suppression not only of corruption but of the liberty to be corrupt in areas where one traditionally had been able to choose for one's self. For the middle-class German who had come to live in Chicago the liberty to visit the saloon of one's choice after a hard day's work did not necessarily imply the liberty to engage in white slavery, but for others the connection was obvious. When

Charles Merriam ran for mayor of Chicago in 1911 he was defeated, in part at least, by the argument that he was a reformer who would close the saloons. A college professor, his opponent argued, would be bad enough, but the election of a professor who was also a reformer would mean the end of individual liberty in Chicago. For many years after, Merriam felt that his reputation as a moral man had led to his defeat, although he reflected upon this less with cynicism than with an appreciation of the discovery of technique in politics of the period. Merriam had used his own sense of morality with equal political skill when, as a member of the aldermanic council of Chicago, he had introduced a motion during an economy and efficiency inquiry he was conducting that the words, "Thou Shalt Not Steal," be placed on the wall in the Council chamber. He was persuaded to withdraw the motion by fellow aldermen who recognized that a vote for the motion would be an admission of the charges Merriam was leveling at the council—that wholesale stealing was going on—while a vote against it would obviously place them in the camp of Satan himself.[17]

Shortly after his defeat in 1911, Merriam received an invitation from Frederick A. Cleveland to join President Taft's Commission on Economy and Efficiency.[18] Merriam refused. He had no desire to leave either the university or the city. When, during the first Wilson administration, he was invited to join the Tariff Commission, he refused again. Merriam's commitment to Chicago and its university was the result of a happy combination of elements which could not, he felt, be reproduced elsewhere. And it is likely that he was right. These elements, however, were facets of the era of which Merriam was himself the product. While the elements were not unique, their particular combination is an interesting study in transition from the nineteenth to the twentieth century in American intellectual life.

Charles Edward Merriam Jr. had been born in Hopkinton, Iowa, in 1874. With a population of something over 600, Hopkinton scarcely qualified as a city, and, if it had any shames to speak of, the Merriams, a family which included at least three local politicians at any given moment, would have known about them. C. E. Merriam Sr., storekeeper, banker, sometime postmaster, and faithful Presbyterian elder, was a leading citizen of the town, a politician, firmly Republican and wedded to the platform of his party, whatever it happened to be. Like church organization, party organization was a commitment to order, not beyond reason by any means, but well beyond rebellion. Merriam Sr. had fought for the union during the Civil War, and afterwards had migrated from Massachusetts to Iowa. His wife, a Campbell born and bred in Scotland, was a schoolteacher who considered one of her responsibilities to God and the world to be the rearing of a son for the ministry. She failed; but the loving ardor of her attempt marked both of her sons with an awful respect for Calvin's God and a sense of responsibility which no amount of labor ever satisfied.

John Campbell, the eldest, became a natural scientist and ultimately director of the Carnegie Institution. Charles Edward became a teacher. Both showed a hostility to business which their father failed to understand. When, in answer to his father's urgings, John informed him that he had no interest in making money, his father snapped "well, in that case, you're already a great success." [19]

In 1896, after graduation from Lenox College and a brief apprenticeship as a teacher of Latin and mathematics, Charles went to Columbia for graduate study. The classes of William A. Dunning and the study of political theory became the center of Merriam's attention, academically speaking, but the city of New York provided ample competition, particularly in the fall of 1896. Bryan and McKinley were battling for the presidency, Tammany was at the peak of its power. Theodore Roosevelt, not yet forty, was Commissioner of Police, and although hardly the heroic figure he would later become, still a model of action and a colorful kind of public virtue. Merriam's fellow students, already immersed in their own investigations of slums, labor conditions, and city politics, introduced

Merriam to aspects of contemporary life which made Hopkinton seem ever farther away. In Iowa there had been the railroads, but if that was corruption the order and legality with which it was carried on in the formal confines of the state legislature were no match for what one could find in the city. For Columbia professors, railroads were a noise with which they competed in their old quarters in the heart of Manhattan as they shouted methodical analysis and ordered doctrine above the chaos of a city which seemed to know little of the paths of logic. Germanic methodology, precise and historically compact, no longer really new in American higher-learning, seemed pale alongside the bright, electric excitement of the city. City politics, the students were told, had no place in the classroom, but Merriam, on his own time and with his classmates, tried out tailgate speechmaking, shouting above traffic rattling on cobblestones to audiences who, if they could hear him, probably did not understand the language he spoke.[20]

In 1898 Dunning left on sabbatical and Merriam took over his classes for the year. He had an opportunity to experiment with historical aspects of American political theory. And in 1899 Merriam left Columbia for Berlin and the lectures of Otto Gierke and Hugo Preuss.

In retrospect Berlin seemed somewhat disappointing. He found he had come to hear the teachers of the men who had been teaching him at Columbia and even, to some extent, at Lenox. He admired the German preoccupation with historical method, but he had no more lasting patience with the details of historical scholarship in Germany than he had had in America. There seemed little point in going through it all again.

There were compensations, however, over and above his high regard for Gierke and Preuss. The government of German cities exercised the same fascination for Merriam that it had for other American travelers. He organized a study group among the students to examine German city government with its emphasis upon trained officials appointed for long terms.

And he applauded the dogmatically liberal Preuss who, as a member of the city council, exemplified the combination of theory and practice which Merriam would later adopt as his own ideal.[21]

At several stages in his life when he re-examined the bases of his education, Merriam sought the origins of his concern with the interrelations of theory and practice. Sometimes he traced it to Plato, the governing citizens of whose republic spent an apprenticeship in the "den" of reality. He vacillated about attributing it to Preuss, with whose concentration upon historical method and constitutional theory Merriam disagreed. He often called his brother John and Professor Dunning his two great tutors. And at times he seemed to deny all influences except the rough-and-tumble of politics which had, presumably, educated him to the limitations of theory in the daily political process. As he grew older he made increasingly cynical and increasingly cryptic remarks to his students about the function of "principles." But his first broad work, following his thesis and left unpublished on the advice of Dunning, and his last major work were concerned with the same problem—the study of systematic politics. The career which these parenthesized had been a major one in a time of major change; but in many fundamental respects the ideas which that career represented had undergone less in the way of transformation than one might expect. It was their shifting application which mattered.

The development of a science of politics was the fixed center of Merriam's thought throughout his career. His earlier writings are full of efforts to define what he meant by "science." His later work seems to take the problem of definition less seriously. To the consternation of his critics and the frustration of his friends, he used the term as an ideal, a goad, as an attitude they were expected to achieve for themselves, but never with the precision which he himself seemed to insist that it had. In his last major work, *Systematic Politics*, he defined it for them again; but by this time there seemed little point in noticing that in over twenty-five years he had not changed his mind in the slightest. "Science," he wrote, "is intelligence in human affairs and must enter into any emerging pattern of values and institutions." [22]

Merriam's definition of science had a simplicity to it which was both deceptive and disagreeable to those who sought positivistic rigor in it. Indeed, it was confusing to read in his writings such negatively answered rhetorical questions as "must we conclude that it is possible to interpret and explain and measurably control the so-called natural forces—outside of man—but not the forces of human nature?" [23] What Merriam meant by "measurably control" was not what it seemed to mean, apparently, because he continued to insist that the control of society by science and scientists would only be a new form of tyranny. Again, Merriam, who sought more refined techniques of social measurement as the sure road to the ultimate improvement of society, was deeply offended when, after an absence in Europe, he returned to Chicago to find that a colleague, William F. Ogburn, had had engraved on the walls of the new social science building which Merriam had built the quotation from Lord Kelvin: "When you cannot measure your knowledge is meager and unsatisfactory." [24] The words, cut in stone, are a monument to the ambiguity of his faith in science and democracy as correlatives of the new world. One could find innumerable paraphrastic versions of the same thought throughout Merriam's published statements, yet he disagreed, as he always had done, with the blunt versions of what often seemed to his students and his critics a fundamental assumption of his thought. As he grew older and watched students turning either to the right or to the left of his own democratic commitments as they calculated and measured the results of "empirical" researches suggested to them by Merriam himself, he appeared to condemn their lack of faith at the same time that he continued to call for more empirical investigation.

Earlier in his writings he had quoted Le Conte's statement that "science must be introduced into politics only as suggesting, counselling, modifying, not yet as directing and control-ling." [25] Science "ought to be strictly subordinate to a wise empiricism. She must whisper suggestions rather than utter commands." Late in his career, again in *Systematic Politics*, he had repeated the injunction in his own words, in effect, when he wrote "science is not ambitious for government and does not threaten the position of the political power. Theories of the rule of the philosophers may be evolved from time to time, as in Plato's 'guardians' or the modern picture of the techno-crat's state; but, on the whole, these do not seem a serious menace to the sovereign state." [26] This idea—that in the rela-tion between science and politics it was politics which governed and science which served—was, from the beginning of Mer-riam's interest in a science of politics and throughout his life, the key to his fundamental position. He supported the suprem-acy of politics, the view that the information received from research was only information, only material for use in the making of political decisions, the "commands." There were, for him, two politics: one the science of politics which was objective in its study of political facts, the other the practice of politics; but, paradoxically perhaps, the democracy of the practice of politics depended upon the willingness of those who commanded to listen to the "whispers" of the science. This belief would form the basis of Merriam's view of planning in government. The role of social science was advisory, not commanding.

The enemies of science, for Merriam, were political in the sense that the exercise of power could lead to the domination of scientific objectivity by political purpose. In an earlier work he referred to such enemies thusly: "The advances of science were not fully reflected in the domain of social phenomena where the earlier doctrines based upon tradition and the in-fluence of class and group interpretation continued to be domi-nant. The cultural groups were more closely related to the religious and authoritarian forces in human life, more control-led by precedent, less familiar with the measurement, comparison, and standardization of the natural scientist." [27] It is clear that if science is the application of intelligence to human affairs, anti or nonscience is the application of "precedent," "religious and authoritarian forces," or "tradition," the non-rational methods of guiding human events. In addition, he uses terms like "efficient spirit," "class and group interpretation," "struggles of interest for power," and other arguments directly traceable not only to the tradition of liberal rebellion in western society but to progressivism and the Wilsonian era of the New Freedom. The rhetoric with which he concluded the above statement is interesting in the side light it casts on other influences in Merriam's thinking. "Of scientific social studies it might truthfully be declared that 'not every one who saith, "Lord, Lord," shall enter the kingdom.'" [28]

Merriam was aware that there were alternatives to his definition of science, but he denied that they were as scientific as they claimed to be. He considered determinisms nonscientific to the extent that they denied the effectiveness of human intelligence. Too, while science was the ultimate liberating force, it was not the ultimate moral force. "The scientific attitude is itself the most revolutionary of human forces, for it respects neither law nor morality. It involves the substitution for the older traditions of the modern types of adjustment to changing conditions, an open-eyed rather than a blind adaptation." [29] While Merriam freely recognized limitations in knowledge, and sought science to eradicate them, he saw no ultimate limitations on intelligence. Ultimate perfectibility of human intelligence is the theme which runs throughout his writings, at times with a disturbingly optimistic abandon. Yet, even in his ultimate world, science and the scientist would not replace politics and the politician. "There will always be a margin of alternatives—a margin where human values and choices will be important and conclusive. The broadest outlines of political policy will remain subjects for general decision. The alternatives will be more carefully considered, and the elimination of unchecked impossibilities may follow; but the final decision will be generalized rather than specialized." [30] Politics the science would never replace politics the practice. But it would take "faith" to combine them: "It is a long road out of a slavery to inanimate nature, out of a slavery to human nature, up to the mastery of the dark and fateful forces around us and within; but the race is on the way. The future belongs to those who fuse intelligence with faith, and who with courage and determination grope their way forward from chance to chance, from blind adaptation to creative evolution." [31]

Merriam's vibrant optimism in a world gradually coming more and more to understand the destructive horrors which the efficiencies of science could produce became more isolated as the world he represented gave way to the world he had helped create. Merriam began as a Progressive. He remained one in a society which seemed willing to utilize his energy without sharing his faith. It was partly for that reason that he dedicated so much time to the problem of developing a systematic theory of democratic government.

Merriam's academic career was spent in the study of political theory. Most of the courses he taught were concerned with some aspect of the theory of government, and the vast majority of his writings, beginning with his doctoral thesis, *A History of the Theory of Sovereignty Since Rousseau*, dealt with political theory.[32] Despite the persistance of his efforts, one would be hard put to find for him a place in the history of his subject matter. Like the unfinished autobiography which occupied the last ten years of his life, the reformation of American political theory was an ideal sufficiently lofty in his conception of it to prohibit virtually its accomplishment. One could see the ideal in the manner in which he described his intentions. That the results often fell short of the intention was as obvious and as disappointing to him as it was to his audience.

Merriam's concern with theory began in rebellion against the legalistic, constitutional, political analysis which he had been taught at Columbia and in Berlin. The historical, "formalist" approach was characteristic of German-trained historians like Herbert Baxter Adams at The Johns Hopkins and Ernst Freund whom Merriam came to know at Chicago. While Charles Beard became one of the leaders in the revolt against old-fashioned constitutional analysis, the opposition touched even older roots in American thought.[33] Pragmatism as a philosophy, the developing social realism of Holmes on the Supreme Court, the Brandeis brief, all pointed toward the necessity of viewing reality in "factual" terms, not from the point of view of tradition or precedent or fixed and immutable principles. Objectivity and liberalism met on the common ground of factual analysis once facts were freed from past preoccupations with outmoded doctrine—or so the argument seemed to go. This was the social implication of John Dewey's methods of inquiry and the political implication of Woodrow Wilson's article on administration which had in 1887 suggested the need for looking at the methods and operations of government rather than solely at its forms. Wilson had opened that article with his supposition "that no practical science is ever studied where there is no need to know it." [34]

The revolt against constitutionalism was a logical one for American thought at the turn of the century. Most forms of post-Civil War progressivism had, by the 1880's at least, run into opposition from the Supreme Court whose interpretations of the Constitution forbade the developing trend toward regulation by state and federal governments of various forms of economic activity. American liberalism at the turn of the century, while it lauded and preserved the Constitution of 1787, found itself in the position of fending off a rigorous constitutionalism in the form of overly legal court interpretation. By contrast, liberalism in Germany during the same period had developed its thinking along lines similar to those familiar in France a century earlier. Constitutions and legal structures were viewed as bulwarks against arbitrary government, as a means of instituting and preserving democracy. In America there were those who saw constitutionalism and legalism as the destruction of democracy and the preservation of the evils of trusts and their makers.

Americans like Merriam and, more popularly, Herbert Croly found themselves attempting to voice a theory which would be consistent with the tradition of European theory without containing some of its most crucial elements. Since the eighteenth century, certainly, the major oppositions in European political theory had been based upon rebellion against or preservation of governmental form. American progressives seemed to be trying both to protect and to reconstruct rebelliously. It was difficult to tell the difference. It was even more difficult to describe a "new theory" of government which defended an old constitution as though it were a religious relic.

The argument seemed to be solely and completely over methods and operations of government, not principles or theories in any accepted sense. It would be another twenty years before the term "administration" would be resurrected from Wilson's early writings and given wide usage. But it would become the one real repository of all such arguments. Administration, admittedly a practical affair, had latent in it the potentialities of becoming a science, of having "principles," of embodying, somehow, theory.

It was only in his later years that Merriam himself came to use administration as a central element in the kind of political theory he was attempting to define. For most of his career the key term was "science." His efforts to construct a theory of politics were lifelong, however, and seem full of contradictions and paradoxes. He wanted to be systematic without being dogmatic. He wanted to construct a politics which would be based upon principles, but not restricted by legalism or constitutionalism. He wanted leadership to be powerful and authoritative, but he maintained his allegiance to old-fashioned liberalism and its individualistic ethic. He wanted government to be "planned" and "scientific," but he denied socialism in all of its forms and insisted that prediction in politics was not only impossible but dangerous. Merriam retained throughout his life his conviction that there could be planning which did not violate individual liberty and science which did not threaten a democratic belief in equality. Some of his contemporaries found his faith difficult to justify, let alone to understand. The same was sometimes true of his students. Those who shared his convictions often found, as he had found, that the language of a more scientific study of society did not admit such commitments into the new vocabulary. But for many of them a commitment to science supplanted a worn-out commitment to faith. This was, in fact, the point of Croly's new "promise" in American life—the rejection, presumably, of past faiths and assumptions and the conscious exploration of new avenues of knowledge and new understanding of society. Merriam's progressivism looked toward an exciting "newness" in all realms of social endeavor, but there was little of the sense of rejection.

It is as difficult to get a clear and precise image of the "faith" in Merriam's writings as it is of the "science." Both, however, stem from an understanding of reason and rationality which came more from the atmosphere in which he was raised than from that in which his professional education had taken place. For by the time Merriam reached college age, the schools of America were teaching the exciting determinisms and inevitabilities gleaned from the new sciences. Merriam had copied in his notes from E. R. A. Seligman's course at Columbia the motto "il y a peut-être autant de distance entre un cerveau scientifique et un cerveau théologique, qu'entre le cerveau d'un homme et celui d'un gorille." [35] This may, at the time, have stated adequately or even enthusiastically the rebellion he felt against the theology of his childhood; but it was a rebellion which time and experience would both modify and utilize in interesting ways.

For men like the Merriam brothers, raised with the doctrines of a firm and uncorruptible theology, the warfare between science and that, or any other, theology was never a battle between forces in rigid opposition. This is not to say that the transition from the hand of God to the methods of science was easy for either of them, quite the contrary. It is rather to suggest that the difficulty arose more from the rapids and eddies which lined the course of the transition than from the nature of the transition itself. Science supplemented religion. It corrected the weaknesses and superstitions which plagued understanding; but it illuminated and glorified the mind of God, if anything revealing Him more fully, but never replacing Him. The question of degree was a difficult one; and the requirements of doctrine and creed could be too immediately demanding to admit of a sufficiency of rational calculation. As a boy Merriam argued with his parents over questions like infant damnation. In questioning the creed his parents revered he came ultimately to drop most of it; but certain broad outlines remained.[36]

His brother John turned to science not simply out of a boyhood fascination with rocks and animals—although that was obviously part of it—but because he had failed to receive the "call" which he and his mother had dutifully prayed would be his. In the absence of that, science had a dignity and a meaning which could be respected. Most important, he felt a sense of "call" to the study of nature which he could equally identify with the will of his mother's God.

The traditions which guided both Merriam Sr. and his wife were not of necessity hostile to science and learning as separate from, if adjunctive to, the ministry. The dissenting academies of Scotland had contributed much to English science in the early part of the nineteenth century, and New England Congregationalism had always looked upon learning as necessary to an appreciation of God's works. Those who fought against the pursuit of learning did so only because their lack of faith forced them to view fresh understanding as a threat. True faith lay in the willingness to pursue all knowledge with an awareness of the fact that it would substantiate one's faith. Firm as that faith was, however, there were aspects of the new sciences which were difficult to reconcile with it.

Charles Merriam's insistent rejection of determinisms in any form, his antipathy to Marx, his guarded approach to Darwin and Freud, were based upon a firm conviction that a science of society could not contradict the history of moral intuition which prophesied hope for the future of man and continuing respect for his powers of reason. Science, the product of man's reason, was subject to reason. Science could not reveal any shockingly disturbing mysteries about the nature of man. It could, however, provide sharper, more efficient tools for dealing with those aspects of man and his society which had been known for centuries. Science could refine morality infinitely, but it need not destroy it. Society, in Merriam's terms, possessed an inexorable, forward energy, moral in the extreme, constantly harassed by ignorance, but irreversible in its direction.

On the eve of World War II when the inevitability of that conflict was as obvious as its horror, Merriam could write, "Man is a rational animal; and I observe that the animal rules from time to time, but not forever. I am no more alarmed at the outbursts of the animal than at those of the rational. . . . But in a moment when the world rushes forward perhaps to its most terrible, titanic, and destructive war, I see somehow an end of violence. . . . In a moment of widespread treason to reason I seem to see the inexorable and inevitable triumph of intelligence over ignorance and error." [37]

The contrast between Merriam and those of his contemporaries whose science led to less optimistic views of the prospects for human society, lay partly in the differences in their definition of the role of science, as well as in the choice of those aspects of science which could conceivably have social applicability. For Merriam, politics and ethics, regardless of any judgment one made about their methods, remained prior in power and importance to any other sciences in that the principles of politics and ethics governed the uses society could make of any science and its methods. Thus, if the study of politics resulted in information which was not accurate or precise in accordance with the best known standards of scientific methodology, then it would have to be made more so. The alternatives —labeling politics an "art" and hence incapable of scientific understanding, or substituting for politics some other more precise study—were inconceivable. True, there might well be limits to the precision which a science could achieve. Man's reason set him apart from the other animals science could examine, and while science could, practically speaking, analyze the animal nature of man, the reasoning, creative aspect of mind would always remain a step ahead of any science it could construct. Man's endowment of reason produced the sciences. Science could hardly deny the reason which had produced it. To Merriam the tautology seemed too obvious to require explanation. Limitations on precision did not imply limitations on validity.

It was possible, however, to view science as the source of answers to the hitherto insoluble problems of ethics and politics and hence the logical successor of those antiquated pursuits. Even in the hopeful years at the turn of the century one could not compare the successes achieved by the study of ethics and politics with those achieved already through physics and biology. That the prominence of the latter two might have, in some respects, depended upon the long history of the former two was possible, perhaps, but such a view required the sort of leisurely philosophic speculation which rapid new social developments and technical advances could not wait upon, let alone regard as a source of answers to problems so excitingly unique. The rigors of necessity made systematic approach to the measurable factors in human experience the only hope for the future welfare—if not total preservation—of mankind. A social science in these terms could dedicate itself to the basic problems which underlay and controlled political debates and ethical dilemmas and which had, in the past, made solutions impossible. Economists, sociologists, psychologists, each could seek some form of analysis of a basic nature of man which could be subjected to the rigors of laboratory-like observation.

The implication of such argument would indeed be that politics and ethics could not be the source of scientific principle, but that the principles applied to them would come, of necessity, from elsewhere. If the examination of the human psyche revealed hostilities and sources of aggression which were controllable but unchangeable, then an idealistic politics which attempted to ignore such acute observations would obviously lead nowhere. The study of man's behavior would thus have to be distinguished from the study of his ideals, since behavior produced data which could be subjected to analysis. Just what ideals had produced was difficult to say, but certainly the history of the political theories which Merriam and Dunning taught provided an extensive catalogue of broken dreams and trammeled aspirations.

In America Charles Beard's analysis of the economic motivations of the founding fathers was symptomatic of the sorts of increasingly skeptical questions being asked. Important, too, was the sense of need which such questions implied—not only to question historic motivation and ideals, but effectively to destroy them by substituting for them a new kind of "reality" which was both above and beyond the fantasies of politics and ethics. Earlier crusaders for the new study of society in America, men like Lester Ward and William Graham Sumner, had debated, in effect, the quality of the scientific analogy—whether biological evolution perpetuated the optimism of the American dream or substantially destroyed it, substituting in its place a realism which forced man to view the struggle in which he and his fellows were engaged. Veblen carried the analogical technique to the loveliest of extremes where the line between microscopic detail meticulously limned and caricature lavishly painted was sometimes impossible to find.

In any case, placing man under the microscope was not likely to reveal such beauty as he might have, any more than a retailing of his past record would necessarily lead to a faith in his ability to realize his ideals. The answer to the question "what is man?" would ultimately depend upon who asked it; but that in itself could be viewed as a flagrant denial of the whole history of scientific method.

The sense of science not simply as a means of organizing knowledge or wisely viewing the universe but as a method for getting things done, exploring the practical problems of human experience, was central to progressive thought. Wilson's concern with a transition from constitutionalism to administration, like Taft's interest in organizational structures of government, make it unnecessary to emphasize Theodore Roosevelt and the Progressive Party as the sole or unique repository of progressivism. But it was the progressives of the party who provided a much needed sense of rebellion, and, as a consequence perhaps, an intellectual voice for growing concerns with the relation between science and democratic society. Men like Croly summed up much of the sense of change. But despite the newness, the promise inherent in the application of system, science, and conscious technique to the problems of government, there was still apprehension lest these new ideas be inimical to traditions of American government. Older ways, seeming more secure, were being superseded by new methods which seemed threats to the principles the older ways had presumably embodied.

From 1901 and the succession of Theodore Roosevelt to the presidency, there was, in theory as well as in the rough-and-tumble of practical politics, a need for justifying federal action in various fields to a community inured to ideals of local government; economic regulation to a public which had for years been feeding comfortably if not happily on laissez faire; technical skill and the "expert" in government to a society which denied the necessity of elites.

Merriam, among many others more widely read, answered those who attacked the new developments as "undemocratic" with his insistence that the new methods were really the only true democracy, that they fostered and preserved democratic ideals within the context of a new industrial society. Merriam's reply to the charge that regulation, colonialism, and concentrations of power and wealth were destroying American democracy was not to deny the criticisms but to include them in his own generally positive view, a technique which would become central to many of his later arguments. He began speaking of "tendencies," just as he and his colleagues would later speak of "trends," Croly of "promise," and those before them of "destiny." "Tendencies," like "trends," could be looked at in groups. Individual tendencies might seem "undemocratic," or whatever other pejorative was current, but only because they were being looked at individually rather than in logical relation to one another.

"When we consider as a whole the numerous tendencies of which democracy is made up," Merriam wrote in 1903, "it is found that there are often other and counterbalancing influences, equally important and significant. Hence, it cannot be said that the broad tendency of American political life is away from democracy." [38]

The use of the broad view, the collection of tendencies or trends or promises, made it possible to project a future, to make limited predictions, just as science had always intended to do. But, equally important, the method allowed for the inclusion of the rough spots which did not fit the trend. No government was perfect. Multiplicity was inherent in the nature of political life. Faults threatened only the security of those who made too frightening a prospect of them, thereby ignoring the broader tendency in favor of the less relevant detail. And the broader a sweep one could see in history, the more details one could afford to ignore.

This is the sort of argument which would continue to subject Merriam to criticism and which would ultimately leave those who sought positive, systematic justification for his kind of scientific, democratic government in something of a fog. But it was a fog which would continue to fascinate them with the promise of lifting to reveal new answers. Merriam invited everyone to penetrate it, but he could not help them do it, and he often disapproved of what they thought they saw. Merriam liked to distinguish between what his students would call "facts and values"; but he never was quite willing to tell them which he thought was which.

Fundamentally, Merriam's basic distinction between a science of politics and the other of the social sciences rested on his faith in the primacy of politics as the controlling science among them. Political science dealt with the realm of the possible, and the exactness of aids from other sciences could guide politics toward a better understanding of what constituted the possible for any given moment; but they could not control politics any more than they could control what was possible. Merriam lumped together Bodin, Montesquieu, Bluntschli, Comte, and Coker as examples of "the danger of advancing beyond the lines of strictly authoritarian or tendential and prudential politics," while at the same time praising "the surprising practical advances made by criminology and penology, and the daily practical applications in social and industrial relations of information and methods drawn from the newer disciplines." [39] But it is the combination of "tendential" with "prudential" which has particular importance for the kind of thinking which Merriam represents.

Merriam sought to reintroduce the term "prudence" into political discussion. His definition of the term suggests the distinction among sciences which he sought to make. "By political prudence," he wrote, "is meant the conclusions of experience and reflection regarding problems of the state. This constitutes a body of knowledge which, though not demonstrably and technically exact, is nevertheless, a precious asset of the race." [40] Merriam could not define this "asset" any more precisely than that. Like "tendency" and "trend," "prudence" was a term which represented an attempt to find a descriptive language which would be sufficiently acceptable to the methodological demands of science, but which would not, at the same time, present unjustly the history of political speculation and its insights. While it is possible that the effort itself was beyond the demands of all participants to the debate, scientist and politician alike, Merriam's life work revealed a dogged insistence on the fact that there were no irreconcilabilities in the relation between science and politics. Both, he continued to reiterate, were part of the democratic tradition in western society.

### III

To whisper suggestions rather than to utter commands was the keystone in the arch which Merriam sought to build between the social sciences and the administration of government, planning and politics, theory and practice. All of the disjunctions which seemed to him threatening to the utility of knowledge in modern democratic society had to be brought together by advice rather than by control. Control by sources of knowledge, however reliably scientific they might be, could subvert the proper functioning of democracy. Elsewhere in the world, Soviet Russia, for example, planning and power were considered essential correlatives in the production of the good life. There the authority of knowledge, whether scientific or not, demanded the authority of government for the execution of its plans.

What Merriam seemed to be arguing by refusing to unite political knowledge and political power in the same hands involved several premises which were not readily reconcilable. First, social knowledge was in no state at present to consider itself absolute and therefore more research was needed, presumably to give it more "scientific" validity and hence more absoluteness. Secondly, however, social knowledge would never be absolute in the sense of holding the undeniably ultimate answers to political problems. Thirdly, even in those areas where social knowledge would from time to time appear absolute, it could hold no claim to political power without endangering the health of the society.

These arguments seemed to imply that absolute scientific knowledge required democratic approval in order to be truly absolute, that only when such knowledge was acceptable to the community as a whole could it be considered true. Two standards of truth, scientific and democratic, had ultimately to be reconcilable in order to be absolute for the moment in time when the conjunction occurred. To produce that conjunction as often as necessary was the function not only of a science of politics which had as its aim the objective investigation of all possible problems within the realm of social behavior but also of the democratic practice of politics which had as its aim the fulfillment of the ends desired by the people as a whole. Merriam's faith lay in his insistence that the ends sought by both the science and the practice of politics would ultimately be identical if each pursued its separate course with the best methods available to it, the one listening to whispers and uttering commands, the other obeying commands and perfecting the content of the whisper. What was most important was that science not be in a position to limit dogmatically the range of its own investigation or politics to command such a limit. Where ignorance might flourish, multiplicity was the only safeguard of future enlightenment.

Merriam's discussions of politics, political theory, and democratic theory in western society, undertaken at intervals throughout his life and never to the satisfaction of himself or his critics, seemed always to begin and end in an attempt to analyze the relation between knowledge and power. That somewhere behind the complexities of the study of the "possible" lay standards infinitely more immutable than those suggested by day-to-day maneuvering was both obvious and obscure in everything he wrote—obvious in that ethical standards were clearly presupposed by any political system he might construct, obscure in that the stated ethical beliefs were always of such a simple, "love-thy-neighbor" variety that they seemed scarcely capable of supporting the weight of so complicated—and realistic—a view of political operation. The contrast between simplicity of ends and complexity of means in politics was less of a problem for Merriam, given the solid tradition of his faith, than for those of his students and contemporaries who demanded more precise relationships in an analysis of means and ends.

High school essays written perhaps in his senior year reflect

Merriam's early conflicts between a sense of politics as a free-wheeling activity, undertaken by all men for all reasons but by moral men for moral reasons, and the definitions of morality which balanced sin and its punishments on a razor's edge. God's justice was inevitable and immutable, but man's justice, political justice, erred on occasion, if only to prove that men had their difficulties with sin. It gave a man room in which to move.

Merriam read the novels of E. P. Roe, and in his own attempts to write short stories, reproduced them with moral, if not artistic, accuracy.[41] Over and above the question of political justice and its flexibilities, virtue in the individual was a reward bestowed as surely as were the pains and stripes of the punishments for sin. Merriam's heroes and villains went to the city to do battle, not because the city was inherently vicious, but because it was the theater of opportunity, the completely equipped stage on which moral struggles could take place. In Roe's sagas, just as in Merriam's little imitations of them, one could tell the difference between a hero and a villain equally well in city or country. All one had to do was look at them. Heroes were blond, bright-eyed people who smiled. Villains were dark, sullen people who scowled moodily. Their actions, the unfolding of the tale, were relevant only to the extent that they exemplified the character defined at the outset. As a setting the country town may have been, perhaps, more "moral" by nature, but it failed to provide sufficient test of the nature and character of the individual. One could scarcely demonstrate one's election until one had been faced with temptation. The city called with the voices of both saint and siren. One could prove one's worth by the answer one chose to give. It was the only test of a will which sought the freedom to execute God's plan.

Calvinist doctrine and the debate over the relation between free will and predestination were lifelong concerns which played no obvious role in Merriam's published work but which underlay much of his private speculation. His rejection of a rigid Presbyterianism, however, did not preclude reasonable shadows of doubt as well as influences resulting from what was perhaps a necessary, if unconscious, translation of Calvin into the language of liberal, democratic government. Planning, the central interest of Merriam's career, meant for him things which reflected older paradoxes, resolved in a deeply personal and often uncommunicated fashion. To some extent, planning was a highly and privately reformed Calvinism which made gods of men who learned to precast destinies for the future of their race. But planning for Merriam involved—indeed produced—freedom: "The fear that planning will interfere with the development of free industrial society is groundless. The very purpose of planning is to release human abilities, to broaden the field of opportunity, and to enlarge human liberty. We plan primarily for freedom; the ways and means and instruments are secondary to the main purpose. The right kind of planning—democratic planning—is a guaranty of liberty and the only real assurance in our times that men can be free to make a wide range of choices." [42]

Merriam debated with those who argued that planning, presumably a step toward socialism, would limit freedom of choice; but he also fought against those within his own profession who wanted to turn planning into a science separate from and not responsible to popular government. Such arguments read like those among medieval scholastics over the limitation or lack of limitation which predestination placed upon free will. But Merriam's reformation—or his heresy—depended upon the particular role given to planning within the system of government he understood to be democratic in its traditions.

"National planning," he wrote, ". . . cannot be imposed from above by a few officials, but must involve the cooperation of many men and groups and rest upon free and general discussion by the public of what is involved in decisions of this kind." [43] The operation of planning, properly conceived, was advisory, "staff" in the language of systematic administration, not "line." Command positions were positions of political leadership and political leaders were not to be confused with planners, although the relation between them would, ideally speaking, have to be based upon mutual appreciation, respect, and the understanding that political leadership would always be the controlling, prior position. But the essential democracy of Merriam's view rested on the distinction between political leadership and "scientific" planning, the practice of politics and the science of politics, a distinction which could be maintained despite the dependence of one upon the other. As long as planning remained a public matter, utilizing both general and particular knowledge which could be related directly to public need, then leadership as the responsible expression of public will would always have over it a control which was not internal to itself and the government it administered. While government, from Merriam's point of view, could incorporate planning and planners, the final responsibility would have to rest with those who led, not those who advised. For the utilization of many sources of advice and many kinds of knowledge was a function of responsible leadership. Where planning and leadership were identical one found totalitarianism in one of its many forms. Where leadership and planning were totally separate, one found chaos or inaction. In terms of the complexities of modern industrial society, planning was the key, not to political power alone, but to the continuity and stability of whatever political power there was. To continue to exist modern governments would have to learn to plan, to understand public need as well as to respond to public will. For wherever public need remained unsatisfied, that government which fulfilled that need would, for the time being at any rate, be responding to public will. Merriam could not and did not argue that Hitler and Mussolini were not responding to needs or failing to represent public will. What he could argue was that this promised no continuity of power for them, that the only such promise lay in the direction of what he called "democratic planning."

Democratic planning involved the separation of means from ends and the retention by the people of their control over ends. What they delegated to government were means. The "plan" served a uniquely modern function here, for it formed the link between ends and means, operating, in fact, as a systematic means of describing ends, specifically, concisely, scientifically. Thus a concept like public welfare could mean many things to many people at many moments in a given historic period. The problem of the planner was to discover what, at a particular time, the term meant with regard to specifics—housing, medical care, wages, etc.—and what it was likely to mean within a for-seeable future, i.e., the "trend" it represented. On the basis of this description and projection, specific courses of action could be devised. But what the planner was not to do, ideally speaking, was to determine the end by the kind of analysis he under-took or the kinds of action he proposed. The unlikelihood of the fulfillment of such an ideal was what necessitated the separation between planning and leadership and the priority of the latter. Planning would be valuable to the extent that it could be multiple—many planners and many plans. The political choice among them would ultimately be univocal and authori-tarian, perhaps, but the investigation delegated to planners would not be. For political leadership depended upon balancing the edge between public need and public will; and planning which moved so far beyond public understanding that it destroyed itself could be curbed by the political sensitivity which science so notoriously lacked. Thus, central to Merriam's whole way of thinking was the belief that science, plans, the entire structure of specialized thought and analysis did not determine ends, but only described them from every conceiv-able standpoint. Ends were determined only by public need, and the speed which could be made toward them would have to be determined by public will. "Trends" and "tendencies" were a means of describing the emergence of purpose in the patterns of life being lived by a democratic society. But the choice of methods of producing those ends was a problem for politics alone.

Opposition to Merriam's point of view was often central to New Deal dispute. It tended to follow two lines. There were men like Rexford G. Tugwell who believed firmly that the place of planning was not only in government, but immediately in, as a fourth branch, quadrisecting the traditional distribution of powers.[44] And there were those in some academic circles, in the governmental and municipal research institutes and bureaus, in the camp of traditional reform, who felt that advice and technical advisory agencies had to be kept pure and apart from politics, that they should be free, according to the standards of their sciences, to advise either the President or the Congress, the courts or the public, as nonpartisan observation necessitated. The course through which Merriam's view came to prevail is interesting to follow.

On the 20th of July, 1933, Harold Ickes as Administrator of Public Works, appointed a National Planning Board, consisting of three members, Frederick A. Delano, chairman, Charles E. Merriam and Wesley C. Mitchell. Some of the duties of the Planning Board are worth noting here:

Its functions are (1) To advise and assist the Administrator in the preparation of the "Comprehensive program of public works" required by the Recovery Act, through—

1.  The preparation, development, and maintenance of comprehensive and coordinated plans for regional areas in cooperation with national, regional, State and local agencies; based upon

2.  Surveys and research concerning (a) The distribution and trends of population, land uses, industry, housing and natural resources; and (b) the social and economic habits, trends and values involved in development projects and plans; and through

3.  The analysis of projects for coordination in location and sequence in order to prevent duplication or wasteful overlaps and to obtain the maximum amount of cooperation and correlation of effort among the departments, bureaus, and agencies of the Federal, State, and local governments.[45]

By Executive Order of the President, June 30, 1934, the National Planning Board became the National Resources Board, and in passing submitted to the Administrator of Public Works a "Final Report," written by Merriam, and a document, also prepared by Merriam, entitled "A Plan for Planning." [46] The latter recounted the history of planning, or what Merriam chose to call planning, beginning with Hamilton's "Report on Manufactures," and moving through Clay's "American System" and touching upon all American efforts to organize or construct national or local policy in any form. Merriam sought to suggest, if not to prove, that the concept of planning was as old in America as the Constitution itself. In that document his most important evidence was the preamble with its references to "general welfare," and the securing of "the Blessings of Liberty to ourselves and our Posterity."

The immediate origins of the National Planning Board, however, were in the introduction to the report of President Hoover's Committee on Social Trends. Merriam, Mitchell, and their fellow committeemen had there suggested the formation of a "National Advisory Council," modeled along the lines of the Social Science Research Council, and possibly growing out of it. It would include "scientific, educational, governmental, economic (industrial, agricultural and labor) points of contact, or other appropriate elements, able to contribute to the consideration of the basic social problems of the nation." [47] A comparison of that statement with the functions of the National Planning Board points to the obvious elements in continuation of the original aims. What could not be made clear was the relationship between such an advisory council and the federal government. The appointment of such a committee or council under Public Works did not make the relationship clear; and the transfer of the committee to the status of an executive board in 1934 also left the question in abeyance, since the members of the original NPB became, by that order, advisers to a cabinet board which advised the President. But the original mandate of the NPB, in addition to its "social trends" function

[ 77 ]

mentioned in point 2 above, was, under point 3, "the analysis of projects for coordination . . . to prevent duplication or wasteful overlaps and to obtain the maximum amount of co-operation and correlation of effort among the departments, bureaus, and agencies of the Federal, State, and local governments." Such a mandate was consistent with the by then ancient cries of economy and efficiency in the federal government, but as part of the Planning Board it tended to take on new meaning.

Under the name, the National Resources Planning Board, the unit became part of the Executive Office of the President in 1939 when the Reorganization Act of that year created that body. The Reorganization Act had been based upon recommendations made by the President's Committee on Administrative Management, of which Merriam was a member. "Administrative Management" was his term. It replaced "economy and efficiency" and "reorganization," giving to the endeavor a new cast which, in part certainly, it deserved. In 1935 Merriam, at the request of the President, had prepared a memorandum in which he sought to point out the relationship between planning, leadership, and administration and to separate the older ideas of executive reorganization from those to be advanced by the Committee on Administrative Management. In that memorandum, Merriam referred to the "executive skill" which he termed "one of the greatest assets of America." From executive skill came leadership, he continued; and he included "management and administration" among the nation's most important "resources." "The National Resources Committee is conceived as a general staff to the Executive and in order to be most useful must be adjusted with the greatest pains to the other technical functions and agencies of the going concern known as administration." Merriam went on to distinguish between the "political relations" of the Executive which he felt would "go forward with relatively little change," and "the technical services" which he felt presented a different problem. "Steps have already been taken on the personnel side in the establishment of the merit system and the civil service commission; on the fiscal side through the establishment of the budget director and the comptroller general; and in the coordination of long-time planning policies through the National Resources Committee." [48]

These three points—personnel, budget, and planning—formed, from the beginning, the basic framework of the new concept of organization. They set the basic problems and basic structure of the report of the President's committee. They continue, today, to shape the movement of executive reorganization; and, as we shall see, their statement in the mid-thirties consolidated a history of at least sixty years of argument and projected into the future the major categories of American executive government.

When congressional hostility in 1943 succeeded in liquidating the National Resources Planning Board, Merriam could still point to seeds of planning growing steadily not only in separate agencies of the executive branch of the government but in congressional committees as well. Merriam, nonetheless, continued to insist that planning was fundamentally a responsibility of the executive. He called for a central office of planning "to be set up as part of the Executive Office of the President alongside the Bureau of the Budget and Civil Service." Its functions would be purely advisory and subject to the will of the President, the members of its advisory committee to serve at his pleasure for unstated terms. [49]

Whatever planning and administration meant to Merriam and his career, their relation to leadership was clear. Leadership, the politics of democratic government, would always be prior to and independent of planning, administration, and the sciences of society. The latter group must always be subject to the leaders chosen by the people as executors of their will. Their dependence upon one another was, however, a joint responsibility of both to be accomplished only by their free willingness to relate themselves to one another in the common enterprise of American life.

Late in his career, and, interestingly enough, in the final report of the Spelman Fund, Merriam described administration in what seemed to him to be its contemporary context:

> The weal or woe of mankind in the coming years rests very largely with administration and administrators. Administrative agencies and activities are moving to the front all over the world more rapidly and powerfully than judicial or representative bodies. Sometimes the new administration is that of dictators, but I am referring to the administration developing in a free society.
>
> It cannot be forgotten that administration is not an end but a means—a means of realizing a purpose and determining direction. If the means becomes the end, we are back again in the old groove of despotism under some newfangled name.[50]

This was the "new administration," a prospect of a kind of executive authority consistent with modern problems and traditional democracy. Like planning, like science, like all of the interests which had moved Merriam from one concern of his career to another, administration was a "means" and means were, more and more, of the future. But the "ends" were old and much beyond the necessity of reform, just as they were beyond the necessity of definition. The "new administration" could be misused, but not by those who recognized that knowledge, whatever it reveals, is the servant of mankind, not the scourge, and that the revelations of knowledge, regardless of the darkness they may represent, are a public responsibility.

Merriam sought to reform politics by making it a body of public knowledge to which any man who could learn could aspire. This was not to make wise men politicians or politicians wise men but to increase the general store of knowledge which the whole system of American democratic government could have of itself, and thereby to lay the foundation for a wiser society. The technique was an old one, the construction of the liberal community in which knowledge—one of the "mass gains" of which Merriam so often spoke—could be distributed more evenly, more liberally. The Social Science Research Council was one step in the general direction of getting men to teach one another, to pool their separate wisdoms. The Social Trends Committee put new techniques at the disposal of government. The Committee on Administrative Management sought, in part at least, to prepare government for the more effective use of its new services.

Merriam's view of government discarded the philosopher-king although this was not a conclusion which came to him easily. He had himself wanted to be both philosopher and king, and it is likely that his failure to succeed at it was a greater education than any he had received from more orthodox sources. To reconcile theory and practice, to teach Machiavelli by day and fight the ward bosses in city hall in the evening, to formulate a theory of government which could be observed in practice, these were ambitions rarely, if ever, achieved—but if ever achieved to his own satisfaction, then in the years of the President's Committee on Administrative Management and the reorganization it entailed.

To be known as an adviser to Presidents became to him the highest of accolades; but it was never quite what being President would have been. Yet he found his greatest satisfactions in the quiet conversations he had with Franklin Roosevelt, a man who came close to fulfilling his basic image of political leadership. No doubt the closest approximation in his lifetime to the ideal relationship between theory and practice, planning and leadership came in those moments when Charles Merriam gave advice to Franklin Roosevelt, who in turn revealed to his adviser sides of prudential politics which the professor, with all of his wisdom and all of his experience, would not otherwise have known. This was in practice the life of science which Merriam had attempted to live. He had institutionalized it hopefully in the SSRC and watched it develop in the Committee on Social Trends. To bring it permanently and effectively into the institution of the presidency became an ambition made possible now by the appointment of the Committee on Administrative Management.

## The Professionalism of Service and the Practice of Administration

I

IN THEIR later years neither Louis Brownlow nor Charles Merriam could remember either the date or the specific circumstances of their first meeting. The closeness of their friendship and the comparative lateness of it in their careers made the questions something of a curiosity both for the two men themselves and for those of their companions who were privileged from time to time to observe the effective and affectionate dialogue which took place between them. It was a working friendship as well as a convivial one. Each had known of the other's work long before 1931 when Brownlow came to Chicago to direct the Public Administration Clearing House, the founding of which was largely the result of Merriam's efforts. They had not previously met one another, but the community of their interests was immense. Brownlow had been a city manager and had been instrumental in the founding of that profession's permanent secretariat during his tenure as president of their association. Merriam had been much interested in the development of associations among public administrators and practitioners of government for the purpose of the interchange of ideas and the expansion of useful research. Brownlow had instituted a research body within the city managers' professional group and had sought continually to expand the professional self-consciousness of all public administrators. Merriam, as a result of his years of direct activity in Chicago politics, could walk among the practitioners of government as few other academics were privileged to do. Brownlow's move to Chicago was his first professional experience in the academic world.

This last point marked a major difference between them. Brownlow's childhood education had not come through the schoolroom, despite the fact that both of his parents had, at one time or another, taught school. Childhood illness had kept Brownlow at home, but not away from education—quite the contrary. He was free to wander about the little community of Buffalo, Missouri, sampling the many lives of a country town. As a result, his early recollections are filled with childhood images of adult responsibilities, of politics, of religion, of family and neighborhood gossip. What he did not share with his contemporaries as schoolchildren he shared with them as members of a larger, ageless community. All ages were contemporary with him and he with them, a quality which stayed with him throughout his career.

His appetite for the printed word was immense. It was also virtually without direction. He supplemented the standard childhood fare with the gleanings from attics and front parlors, thereby adding to the staple McGuffey material which included the ubiquitous dime novel, back issues of *The Century*, religious periodicals, and the household library "set"—a range which could as easily contain the works of Dickens as Josephus or St. Augustine.

When he left Missouri to become a newspaperman, first in Tennessee, then in Washington, and finally around the world with the Haskin newsletter, he took with him habits of self-education which he would often describe himself as those of a badly trained bird dog which bounded off after every passing rabbit instead of sticking to the quarry. Even so, he managed more often than not to catch his prey; and if the achievement was not always what he or others intended, it was achievement nonetheless. His articles for the Haskin letter, syndicated throughout the country, were often models of detail artfully woven into miniature designs; but the subject matters, naturally dependent upon where he happened to be at the time, could range from the daily habits of a Manchu princess to the early experiments with refrigeration in Florida.

In 1911 the Haskin syndicate printed and marketed a volume entitled *The American Government*. Published under the authorship of Frederic J. Haskin, and a rather extraordinary best seller, it was in fact written by Brownlow. The structure of the book is particularly interesting. Intended as a popular tour through the workings of American government, its organization completely by-passes the traditional emphasis upon the tripartite separation of powers. Of the thirty chapters, one is devoted to a discussion of the President, three to the houses of Congress, and two to the courts. The other twenty-four deal in turn with the separate departments, but again without any particular structural design. The Patent Office and the Bureau of Standards are given a chapter each, equal in length to those covering the State Department and the Treasury Department. Public Health and the Smithsonian Institution, the Panama Canal and the Government Printing Office follow one another or are interspersed with chapters discussing the Senate, the House of Representatives, and the Library of Congress. All in all, the book avoids completely any attempt to cope with rationale. Instead, after an initial paean to "the land of the free and the home of the brave," it proceeds to a chatty and descriptive tour of government, concentrating upon offices and functions wreathed in the fascination of statistics (the number of patents granted, pennies coined, letters written or handled, etc.). All of this is presented in a style characteristic of the Haskin column, combining a shrewd and often subtle eye for detail with the enthusiasm of a child dismantling a clock. Brownlow wanders around the official sights of Washington the way he strolled through Tokyo and Peking, pointing out the interesting facts in a manner which was not too relaxed to conceal the attitudes and preconceptions that gave continuity and selectivity to the bright masses of detail. Government would always be to him something which *people* did. Staffing and organization would always be oriented more toward individual minds and human capacities than toward principles or charts, however rational and logical they might be.

While Brownlow's freedom from the academy was also a freedom from its then current preoccupation with scientific method and philosophic principle, his background in newspaper work and as an observer of the turn-of-the-century political scene brought him into contact with the same problems and the same materials which were beginning to fascinate the new generation of social scientists. But the fact that Brownlow had not been forced by training to take a stand either for or against any school of social science made him a useful figure wherever methodical doctrines disputed courses of action. The politics and protestantisms of his youth could be debated within the family circle and within the community without damaging the essential affection which constituted the real society. Awareness of common purposes served as a fundamental tie as long as purposes were defined as ideals to be achieved rather than as methods to be imposed. There were many doors to the kingdom and many mansions in it.

Brownlow's lack of doctrinal commitment gave him an extraordinary mobility among men of various intellectual persuasions. But if he moved among his teachers without being burdened by what they might sometimes have considered their best teachings, he shared one of Merriam's constant observations about his own career: that he had learned more from men than from books. That Merriam and Brownlow learned much from one another can be documented largely by the harmony of ideas expressed in the projects in which they were jointly engaged. Yet they approached administration and government from opposite poles of experience. Where Merriam had spent his career seeking ways to bring knowledge of government to bear on the practice of it, Brownlow continually sought knowledge which could clarify and explain his constant involvement in the practice of administration. The harmony was often a harmony of useful opposition.

Brownlow and Merriam shared much in background and ambition. Both were sons of post-Civil War families migrant to that part of the settled west which lay just across the Mississippi. Missouri, scene of compromise and embattlement prior to the war, had, by the 1870's and certainly the eighties, outlived its frontier tradition, cleared its land, and set about the fulfillment of its solid agrarian responsibilities. But where the Merriams had moved westward from Massachusetts in satisfaction of the older motive of new opportunity in its more or less pure form, the Brownlows, while seeking a new beginning, were seeking it from the experience of defeat in the nation's most devastating conflict. While it is difficult, certainly, to trace the effects upon attitudes which that defeat engendered, men like Woodrow Wilson would remember and perhaps be irrevocably marked by the childhood recollection of pride in state and family reduced to bitter defense which transcended the claims of reason or justice. For many, defeat was more than the loss of a cause, whether or not they believed in it all. It was the defeat of a community of honor sanctified by blood and the ancestral authority of state citizenship.

The Brownlows of Tennessee had not moved westward to Missouri as pioneers building a new world out of a wilderness or as ambitious entrepreneurs seeking greater wealth, but as war-weary suppliants to a settlement which might help bind the wounds and make living possible.[1] Adherents to the southern cause, they acknowledged freely to themselves and to their children that it had all been a mistake, but one which in loyalty to family and the state of Tennessee had been for them unavoidable. There was in the new household a reverence for the ultimate justice and honor of American politics, a strong faith in a democratically Protestant God, but little agreement and endless debate on the proper approaches to politics and the appropriate doctrines of religion. Robert Brownlow had a shifting addiction to third parties and the dissents they voiced, while his wife was firmly and finally a Democrat. The rest of the Missouri county in which they lived was solidly Republican.

The Brownlows' attitudes toward religion, a matter of some dispute between them, were generated out of the schisms which, during the Civil War period, tore American Protestantism into even more numerous sects than traditional liberalism had produced. Baptists and Methodists had divided north and south when slavery dissolved the distinction between theology and politics. Other groups, such as the Campbellites or the Disciples, joined with the dissenters in arguments over infra- versus supra-lapsarianism, pipe organ versus non-pipe organ, infant versus adult baptism, and the numerous versions of historical criticism of scripture. Many a small midwestern community of population under a thousand souls could boast of its bank, its jail, its schoolhouse, and its five Protestant churches. In many families, as in the Brownlow family, mother and father debated the separate virtues of doctrine, political and theological, without undermining a basic faith in either. Above all, there was an acceptance, too deep to be debated, of the southern sense of family which included the community at large with infinitely remote kith and kin providing bloodlines of endless complication but irrefrangible cohesion. The Brownlows of Missouri were a tightly knit family group, but Sunday morning was apt to find Father Brownlow with the Disciples, Mother Brownlow with the Methodists, and son Louis off in one of the other three possibilities.

Louis Brownlow's introduction to politics, journalism, and government, like his introduction to history, religion, and morality, was based upon the realities of a small, midwestern town of the late nineteenth century, to which were added the traditions of the Civil War and pre-Civil War middle south. What this seemed to mean was that local government had and would continue to have for Brownlow a dual nature. It would, on the one hand, be dependent upon a certain unstated homogeneity of purpose, a communal sense of shared traditions and

[ 87 ]

attitudes which could override most internal dissensions. But the community would, on the other hand, have a multiplicity of interests of which politics and government would be only one. The interest of the citizen would be centered upon government, locally speaking, only to the extent that from time to time such matters required his attention. Otherwise, his interest would lie in his occupation and his family.

While stating the duality in this form points rather obviously to the Jeffersonian-Jacksonian origins of these attitudes in the agrarian background of a large part of the country, the generality itself scarcely begins to describe the reality of the small-town community in which these beliefs were realized. In such instances the working of "principles" makes of them a practical reality which removes them from the realm of systematic statement or description. Buffalo, Missouri "worked." It utilized no systematic schemata or philosophic debates in its achievement of a homogeneous community in which government was conducted by the citizenry for its own benefit. While Brownlow's childhood recollections are, as he recounts them in his autobiography, full of politics, it is national and occasionally state politics; but the "government" of the town of Buffalo is a subject neither of discussion nor of concern, chiefly because in the sense of the term characteristic of all forms of modern government it did not exist. His description of the workings of the community as a practical sharing of interests and concerns is, in all its detail, the image of community life which he would carry with him throughout his career.

It is interesting to contrast this image and its background with that of Lincoln Steffens who shared with Brownlow many concerns with the course of American social and political life. Steffens, born thirteen years earlier than Brownlow in California, was the son of an English mother and a Canadian father. Unlike Brownlow's parents, Steffens' had gone west to start their lives, not to salvage them. The war had little or no real meaning for them, at least nothing which was of importance to their son. But Steffens was taught that politics was evil and business an occupation for those too weak to work an honest living from the land.[2] Steffens came ultimately to his appreciation of Marxism because, in his particular view of it, it identified politics and business for the practical purpose of doing away with both.[3] But where Marx treats industrial society and technology as valuable assets which are an evil presumably only when evilly used, there is in Steffens a Luddite streak which mistrusts technology and looks to the agrarian past with something more purposeful in mind than nostalgia. That past and its possibilities for the future realize a vision born in a California small-town childhood.

Where Steffens was prepared to suspect politics, Brownlow had an almost primal faith in it. Both men came to the conclusion that politics had a smaller and smaller role to play in the necessary services which government could render the citizens of a community, but Steffens' total removal of politics from the realm of human welfare was, in Brownlow's terms, not only unnecessary but wrong. Brownlow's experience as a boy growing up in Missouri was of the community as a whole, with politics and business vital elements in it. The apparent impossibility of transferring the small-town communal sense to large and complex urban, national, or international agglomerations did not destroy his belief that some part of his image could be retained and that the successful transference of whatever that partial image was would be necessary for the continuance of democratic society in an industrial age.

Even as a child Brownlow's sympathies had never been agrarian. He admired the city; he looked hopefully toward the east when most of his young Buffalo contemporaries looked west. But he did not go east to reform the city and send its sinners on the paths of righteousness. In his years as a journalist, even in the days when, like Steffens, he would have been free to speak his mind in his own name, he raked no muck, exposed no evils, documented no abuses of public trust. Yet City Manager Brownlow informed his fellow managers at their meeting in 1922: "I look upon my profession as city manager in exactly the same way that a minister of the gospel looks upon his mission, and believe that as a city manager endeavoring to make the city for whose administrative affairs I am responsible, better in every way for every boy and girl in it, I am doing on earth the work of the Master. I have that feeling and I am not ashamed to confess it." [4]

This was a kind of zeal which predated the reform and progressivism of the turn of the century. This was the reform of the constant improvement and infinite perfectibility preached by Emerson. It was the reform of post-Civil War agrarian discontent. It absorbed such concepts as the city manager, industrialism and technology, indeed the whole gamut of progressive reform, but it absorbed them as useful devices for an end which was traditional in America, not as examples of revolutionary new theory, new promise, or the like. Brownlow's intense traditionalism could scarcely have been less threatened by the twentieth century.

That the experience of the traditional community should have been transferred to the problem of urban industrialism in America would not be so unusual were it not for the virtually innocent enthusiasm with which it was done. In England and in Europe industrialism and the subsequent growth of cities served as the dual trigger mechanisms for revolutionary political doctrine. But the Benthamite political persuasions of early nineteenth-century England sought to bring the voice of the individual to the problems of the nation as a whole, while Jacksonian reforms in America were efforts to turn government back to ultimate local units. Yet both looked to individual will, regardless of birth, occupation, or economic position, as the basic unit of government. Part of the difference lay in the fact that the tradition of government in England had been national government with democratization bringing local government into existence; in America almost the reverse was true, traditions of government having sprung from generations of local autonomy, with democracy, through the nineteenth and into the twentieth century, seeking national government as its instrument.

Jacksonian reforms, generated by the desire to create genuinely democratic government in America, produced problems with which the post-Civil War generations would have to cope as the foci of their own reforms. Two of these formed the heart of the newer movements. The Jackson era had emphasized the legislative process in local government as a means of removing government from the hands of special groups deemed dangerous to enthusiastic democracy. This had obviously and seriously weakened the role of leadership by taking power away from the executive and turning it over to expanded legislatures and committees. Whatever virtues this may have had for cities of the prewar years, the rapidly growing urban complexes of the seventies and eighties suffered under the dispersion and confusion of large legislative bodies attempting to run government by themselves. Thus one prong of the reform offensive moved into the area of executive government. Another prong was not unrelated, although its manifestations were quite different. For the Jacksonian concept of rotation in public office, branded "spoils system" early in its youth, was a response to the needs of representative democracy which, in the growing technological complexities of urban and industrial operation, placed in public office men whose background and training were frequently totally unsuited to the simplest technical requirements of the jobs to be done. If legislative government led to hopeless and appalling confusion, its coupling with ignorance and inexperience led even more inexorably to the practical necessity of corruption as the only means of getting the work done.

The search for an effective executive and the movement for training and professional job security for personnel to assist him created a center around which numerous reform organizations could develop toward the end of the nineteenth and well into the twentieth century. In local government the city manager became the symbol of the new movement even before Theodore Roosevelt dramatized the presidential possibilities of the strong executive. And the business executive as the dynamic source of power and wealth undoubtedly served as a model for both. While Civil Service reform carried much of the public burden of concerns with trained and effective personnel, the development of training schools and the growth of associations of professionals with interests in particular aspects of government had, in more quiet fashion, begun to debate the determination of standards and the definition of quality as well as the recruitment of talent.

Louis Brownlow's career in public administration was intimately involved in the search for solutions in both areas—the effective executive and the growth of professional identity in public service. From 1915 until 1931 he was actively engaged in the running of city government as Commissioner of the District of Columbia, City Manager of Petersburg, Virginia, and Knoxville, Tennessee, and in the experimental community of Radburn, New Jersey. In 1931 he became Director of the Public Administration Clearing House and spent the years until his retirement in 1945 founding, guiding, and introducing to one another various organizations of professionals in government and administration. His own background and that of the movements with which he identified himself combined to produce methods of approach which could ally the newer problems of government in modern society with the democratic tradition.

II

In the beginning—which is to say, from 1908 until 1912—the city manager was as mythical as any creation dreamed up by the social science fiction of Edward Bellamy. 1908 is the year the city managers celebrate as their first;[5] but the name itself did not come into existence until 1911 when Richard S. Childs put it in the Lockport Plan.[6] And not until 1912 when Sumter, South Carolina, adopted the commission-manager plan did a legally constituted office by that name appear on the American scene. Yet the idea can be traced back at least as far as 1894;[7] and for those engaged in civic reform, the ideal was a fighting reality before it had even been seen in the flesh and properly christened. The symbol preceded the fact.[8]

The ideal was much clearer than the fact, even though it embodied confusions which were already a tradition in American government. The relation between the efficient executive and popular sovereignty had never been marked by either clarity or comfort in American governmental history; but by the turn of the century, the increased burdens on local government had made a chaos of older, formalized institutions for the direct expression of public will. To the National Conference on Good Government, called in 1894 by the City Clubs of New York and Philadelphia, the answer lay in the creation of strong mayors by the reformation of local charters. The conference led to the formation in 1895 of the National Municipal League. From the beginning the League devoted itself to reform in local government through the streamlining of institutions and forms. This concern with forms tends at times to run counter to the institutional conservatism characteristic not only of the traditional American view of constitutional government but also of the antiformalist bent of the period. Yet it preserved a relation to American traditions by rigorous separations between problems of local government—essentially practical, technical and more subject to knowledge than to democratic debate—and those of the federal government with its concern with the formulation of policy and the open battles of national politics. With this distinction as a basis, men like Woodrow Wilson and Charles Beard could be thoroughly opposed to formalistic, institutional approaches to politics and history, but also crusaders for charter revision as the key to reform in local government. For such men "politics" was a word with two distinct meanings: synonymous with corruption at the level of local government, but on a national scale the central term in the traditional moral ideals and historic realities which governed the world of men. It was a distinction with a troublesome difference.

Two approaches dominated reform solutions to problems in local government. The first was characterized by some attempt to construct a unitary, powerful executive whether in the form of a refurbished office of mayor or in that of some new, modern executive with technical skills and responsibilities. Independent of such plans, however, and in contrast to them, were ideas favoring a multiple executive or commission. The Galveston plan, formed in 1901 under emergency circumstances, became the practical model. A devastating flood had all but destroyed the government of Galveston. In the wake of the disaster, five local businessmen were given control of the city's services, dividing among them the various administrative responsibilities. It was not long before city reformers throughout the country would look to multiheaded boards of specialist-businessmen as the answer to local corruption and inefficiency. But those who favored either a strong executive, or the strict separation of executive from legislative power, or some combination of the two, looked upon the commission plan either as a danger or as a reshaping of inefficiency and confusion.[9]

The city manager plan, like the commission plan, was initially the product of a practical solution to a near-catastrophe. C. E. Ashburner's appointment as general manager of Staunton, Virginia, in 1908 was the result of the city's desperate need for a good engineer, not of a reform attachment to an ideal. While it was true that many interested men had been arguing for something in American local government which could imitate the practical efficiency of the German *Burgemeister* with his political independence and his tenure of office—Charles Merriam had suggested such a possibility to the Chicago City Council in 1904—Ashburner's appointment was in response to an obvious and urgent need. Parts of the city of Staunton were in danger of collapsing into an underground system of natural caves. The city needed an engineer, not a reformer.

For those concerned with problems of city government, however, the new methods, regardless of the spontaneity which may have seemed to characterize them, provided a new and exciting opportunity for reform. Even more striking was the fact that Richard Childs and the National Municipal League could see in the engineer-manager and the businessman-commissioner a possible relationship which could transcend the fact that there had been a real opposition between them as competing methods of executive power.

Despite what would seem a clear opposition between the proponents of the strong executive and those of the commission plan, the National Municipal League found in the commission plan some rather interesting possibilities for the furthering of its own aims. Election of commissioners on a nonpartisan ballot, thus abolishing ward lines and party labels—i.e., machines—was a particularly effective undercutting of politics in local government. For Richard Childs and his newly formed Short Ballot Organization—to which Woodrow Wilson, President of Princeton, had given much aid and support—the destruction of local partisanship gave the commission plan an obvious appeal. Too, Childs's interest in the short ballot reflected his interest in British voting and party procedures; and the fact that he thought he could see cabinet-like qualities in the commission enhanced that interest.[10] Equally important for Childs was the connection between the businessman and the commission arguments. For despite the great concerns over trusts and "malefactors of great wealth," business in an age of expansion was the center of innovation, inventive technology, and skill. Equally important was the professionalism it was coming to represent. For a society which rejected the idea of a class of professional governors, the businessman, morally reconstructed, provided an ideal image of the man of skill who was also, in the broadest sense, a public man. Business, with its developing sense of efficiency, management, and even planning, provided the public picture of the democrat governing himself. Professional self-government was a difficult concept to define in America except by analogy; and for the moment the businessman could provide the analogy.

The relation among the three images of executive authority

current in discussion from 1885 through the progressive period —strong mayor, businessman-commissioner, and manager-engineer—is interesting in that it focuses attention on the continuum of relations between politics and the administration of government. The strong mayor retains the older reform tendency to replace "bad" men with "good," adding the one fundamental change—the strengthening by charter of the executive position—required to redress, presumably, the old balance. Such a change called for not simply a good man, but a good man empowered by legal authority. This point of view could continue to identify politics and administration, distinguishing only between proper and improper politicians.

The businessman-commissioner moves a step further, adding "nonpartisanship" as its central factor, calling for a change not only in the nature of politicians but in the nature of politics as well.[11] For from this point of view the character of administration was defined as an accepted professional activity, separate from politics but identified with business as a recognized occupation. Administration and politics were both a responsibility of the citizenry, and specialization, while important to the argument, became, through identification with the businessman, a matter of degree.

The manager-engineer, however, evoked a sharp separation between politics and administration. His skills, a matter of training and knowledge and distinctly separate from the debates of politics and related to business only by analogy, were not even subject to questions of public morality. Ideally speaking, he served the city as the city, through its political leaders, chose to be served; and he applied his skills to the execution of their will—whatever it might be.

The three images as described above were only images—ideals which in the course of time were blended with one another to form the practices of municipal government which characterized the new reform. The system which came to combine the supposed virtues of the strong executive and those of the commission became known as the commission-manager plan. But the oppositions were not discarded. They continued in the form of questions relating to definitions of the manager and his functions in the government of the community as well as in the community life as a whole.

For Richard Childs, who in effect performed the marriage between the commission plan and the central executive, inventing the name "city manager" as a promotion idea to utilize the public attraction to business management, the formulation of the three separate parts—executive, short ballot (nonpartisanship), and commission—provided a possible continuity which could be seized upon, despite conflicts in definition, and turned into actuality. Thus, Childs, as an expert public relations man, created a concretized myth of local leadership which could then become the reality in its many disputed forms. But the formulation of model plans and model charters did not succeed in doing away with the initial conflicts. Insofar as the commission was to be viewed as a more efficient, nonpartisan legislature, the commission was not an administrative, cabinet-like staff for an executive leader. It was a group of somewhat more qualified citizens exercising Jacksonian self-government and engaging in—whether it liked it or not—politics. The centralized executive, in keeping with the tradition, provided a Jacksonian corrective to a Jacksonian excess by establishing itself as a single figure of public leadership which could, in an era of massively decentralized corruption, put public authority back in public hands. The paradox of the Jacksonian ideal—that it used an image of strong leadership to create and enforce decentralized public authority—was retained in the debates which continued to split the image of the city manager into numerous subimages, each with strikingly different characteristics.

In 1927 when Leonard D. White published his study of the city manager,[12] he included a carefully selected bibliography of four pages, only a fraction of the material in print. White's book was the first full-scale academic work on the subject and is interesting not only for the ground breaking which his colleagues in political science felt it represented but also for its relationships to the history it described. White, who had come to the University of Chicago in 1920 to study under Charles Merriam, followed Merriam's guidance, not only in his choice of subject, but also in the basic form of his exposition. His study did not emphasize the virtues of a "new" plan, the idea by then being something less than new. Merriam had concerned himself with the problem of democratic leadership,[13] and White, in viewing the city manager, chose the individual, leadership aspects of the plan, rather than the form of the plan itself, as his center of emphasis. As Merriam had done in his book on party leadership, White selected the significant figures from the twenty-odd years of managers and discussed the relation between their personalities and the plan. It was this, the personality of new leadership rather than the structure of charters, which absorbed his attention; and his description of that personality provides an important link between the older reformers and the new.

City managers according to White are men who *do* things and talk very little. They are straightforward, direct in their approach to problems, knowledgeable with regard to the methods and techniques of management, essentially opposed to political manipulation and public cajolery.[14] In short, they represent the absolute opposite of the nineteenth-century image of the politician but are identical with that of the twentieth-century businessman. White's emphasis upon their fundamental nonverbal quality is important, not only for its summation of past ideals but also for its forecasting of future problems. For managers, being nonpolitical, are also opposed to engaging in debate, preferring to convince the public—if convincing is ever needed—by means of actions rather than words. This poses problems for the future of city management, since that silence is apt to leave the manager open to political attack as public interest flags, and the flagging of interest is itself likely to be a result of the managerial silence. The silent managers have, however, some rather positive nonverbal means of communication, and here White's picture has a curiously repetitive quality.

They tend to have short tempers and to pound their desks as a means of emphasizing brief commands which are, invariably, "snapped." All have great physical energy, although a tendency to overwork subjects them to periodic breakdowns. They amalgamate the businessman and the engineer-scientist, Andrew Carnegie and Thomas A. Edison, drawing efficiency and management from business and a certain practical inventiveness from the inventor-engineer.

White's investigations did more than consolidate the image of the managerial personality. His book stressed the fact that the institution of a new form would not be sufficient without some understanding of the required personality of leadership which that form would have to have for its effective, and continuing, operation. While he saw in the city manager the hope for a developing trend in government—away from partisanship and its attendant corruption and toward more effective uses of government—he saw also that professional skill and technical knowledge would not, in and of themselves, provide the proper preservations for a democratic society in an industrial age. To put White's contribution into relation with the history described thus far, one could say this: the commission plan attempted to combine professional skill with the idea of the leaderless liberal community. The manager added to this the supposedly nonpolitical technician, operating as a consolidator of technical efficiencies. What White added was a statement of something which the managers themselves were already beginning to worry about: that the manager was a leader of the community, that perhaps he was not a "politician" in the pejorative sense of the term, but whatever you called him, he was serving a community function which brought him into contact with more than the technical problems of engineering. White preferred to state his view of the problem in the language of the nonpartisan reforms of the past, looking toward a combination of new forms of effective government and forms of leadership—executive business leadership—drawn from the same past he was quick to condemn. "Looking over the past," he wrote, "the manager movement shows a noteworthy record of achievements. These are most evident in the economy and care with which the business affairs of the city have been handled. There has been consistent effort to use the city money with the same intelligence and foresight which would be expected in a private corporation." [15] And White, in his concluding effort to describe objectively a new personality, succeeded in transmitting to his reader his—and their—best image of an old ideal.

> The managers have demonstrated a unique readiness to accept responsibility. . . They do not "pass the buck" but are forthright and straightforward. . . They have been wholly unwilling to deceive the voters about the real condition of public affairs and have frankly given the facts to the public. . . They have sought support for the larger interests of the city on the basis of the plain truth and have been content to let the record speak for itself without unnecessary advertising on their own part. They have been refreshingly free from the arts and wiles of the traditional American executive, and by their unflinching devotion to their job have furnished the American cities with a new and finer conception of official duty.[16]

The city manager, then, combined nonpartisanship, scientific skill, and the practical, realistic personality of the business tycoon newly infused with an old-fashioned moral sense. Inherent in this combination of characteristics were some real conflicts. Business and industry could provide a model of efficient, productive practice; but there were those who were quick to spot the fact that business was conducted for profits which could be calculated in precise financial terms and government in many important respects was not. As valuable as the business image was for purposes of proselytizing, of appealing both to the influential business community and the public's respect for the industrious entrepreneur, it led to confusions, not only in the proper definition of governmental functions but also in the minds of those who were appointed to carry out those functions. Engineers, to be sure, were free from the taint of the politician, but were they businessmen? The City Manager's Association did not want to discuss principles of government or politics.[17] Their province was efficient and economic management within, or in spite of, whatever limits local politics set. They considered themselves servants of the community, not leaders of it. If the political leaders failed to provide leadership, the manager's services to the community might be limited, but the community would have to take that complaint to the polls, not to the office of the manager. While men like Richard Childs attempted assaults upon this attitude from without, within the group of managers themselves there were manager-engineers who were dissenting from the rigid position taken by their colleagues; and there were beginning to be those among the city managers who were not engineers. They were coming to recognize, as White at least had implied, that the public might not understand with sufficient clarity the distinction between leadership of the community and service to the community. Moreover, the campaign for the new charter took place within the traditional arena of politics; and despite its disavowal of that tradition, the political intensity of the campaign gave the post of manager a heroic stature which its occupant might choose not to fulfill.

White's book beautifully describes the ambivalence, at times without the author's awareness. The city manager's silence had somehow to be more expressive and far more impressive than the politician's speeches had ever been. The businessman provided an ideal which had to be reconciled with that of the engineer. Above all, White did not describe the manager as a happy machine humming softly and efficiently in the background. He pounded, he shouted, and he snapped.

The meeting of the City Manager's Association in 1922 gave formal recognition to the growing transition in the profession's attitude toward itself by electing to its presidency a non-engineer, Louis Brownlow. Forty of the fifty-five members of the association were engineers. The closeness of the vote—a majority of one—indicates the extent to which the engineers were themselves willing to look outside their own professional training for leadership. Brownlow gave it to them by insisting as a condition of his acceptance that they approve the setting up of a permanent secretariat to conduct the association's business and to maintain contact with members in between yearly meetings. Brownlow's concern for the permanency of professional organization was motivated by a very practical sense of the value which such an organization could have for the interchange of ideas and techniques of management. This is a concern which he came to apply to the problems of public administration as a whole.

Brownlow had made the transition from newspaper work to municipal administration in 1915, the year Henry Toulmin published his book on the city manager, the first study of the subject to achieve genuinely general, public circulation.[18] The District of Columbia had once had a governor who had, in keeping with the traditions of municipal management in the 1870's, engaged in the sort of corruption which built American cities and kept them moving before the inefficiencies of the method became a moral offense in the eyes of the citizenry. The Board of Commissioners of the District of Columbia represented a modern method consonant with reform aims but, given the circumstances under which the nation's capital was governed, proved to be a peculiar example of the form it followed. Three men, one of whom was required by law to be an engineer, were appointed by the President with the advice and consent of the Senate. In 1915, when Brownlow became a District Commissioner, the body to which he was appointed exemplified more than any other governing group in any American municipality, the relationship between politics, policy, and administration coveted by those who were seeking to set up reformed city management. For in the District of Columbia the President, the Congress, and the Party politics they from time to time reflected constituted a policy-making body separate from but vitally interested in the local government of the District. The District Commissioners were, by the same token, responsible to the President and Congress but, in administrative duties, separate from them. Appointees of the President, they were, during the years 1915–1920, subject only to such influence and advice as a wartime chief executive had time to give, yet charged with the operation of the nation's capital. As an introduction to executive experience in American municipal government, the job was both a unique instance and a representative ideal.

Brownlow's relationship to President Wilson during the five years of District commissionership were similar to those envisioned by the ideals of city management. The President quietly oversaw and, when necessary, either bore or ducked responsibility for specific actions, but in any case supported Brownlow against such public criticism as occasionally arose. Brownlow cites several instances in which the tacit approval, or at least the equally tacit understanding, of the President backed actions which the President could not publicly acclaim. The arrest of the more militant suffragettes toward the end of the war was a subject of some embarrassment to the President, but he respected the necessity of it and quietly acquiesced. Again and more importantly the strict handling of the threatened police strike at the end of the war brought much criticism on Brownlow's head, but he was supported by the President whose knowledge of Brownlow's refusal to negotiate with the union had given the initial support to that refusal.

In short, Brownlow's freedom to act as an appointed public official was supported by the responsibility borne by the nation's chief elected official. This tracing of the course of responsibility from appointed officials to elected officials responsible for appointment and thence to the public charged with the election of its chiefs had been the heart of reform movements dedicated to the simplification and professionalization of the democratic relation between the public and its servants. That it worked so well in the District may have been due largely to that city's peculiar situation, but in any case the eminently successful instance and its connection with the faith in the process shared by Wilson quite likely made later failures bearable, if not explicable.

When Brownlow left Washington in 1920 to become city manager of Petersburg, Virginia, he found a community which presented to him not only the perfect environment for the new techniques of municipal government but also for his traditional faith. The history of Petersburg was the history of Virginia and virtually the history of the traditionalist's south. It had accommodated itself to the twentieth century just as it had to the three preceding centuries. World War I had shaken this stability a bit with the placing of Camp Lee near the city's borders. The resulting expansion and dislocation had aroused public concern; and the city government as it stood could not cope with the problem. The adoption of the new system was more a movement of preservation than of innovation, and its "newness" was well outweighed by the importance of the past it could protect. There was little or no entrenched opposition, particularly within the context of one-party politics. The proof of the value of the new system would lie clearly in its effectiveness; and Brownlow's tenure as manager was more than sufficient proof.

Brownlow's innovations followed procedures which were becoming the basis of the new management. He introduced a budget and accounting system, a step which can be seen in its proper perspective when one recalls that no American city had a budget prior to 1910, and that the federal government did not have one until 1921. At the end of his first year he could inform the citizens of Petersburg that his salary had cost them nothing because the new system of finance had accounted for savings more than equal to the cost of the new manager. Given the fact that managers were being paid at salaries considerably above those ordinarily paid to mayors, the news was particularly impressive to those among the public who had found the high cost of "specialists" unjustified. In addition the modernization of existing public services consisted in bringing new machinery to perform familiar tasks—motor cars for the police force, newer methods of road construction, more efficient water supply apparatus. These were aspects of innovation which required specialized understanding of the particular tasks involved and, because modernization frequently represented saving, justified further expenditure for expert advice and staff. Finally, the introduction of new public services—new medical and public health facilities, public libraries where libraries had previously been private or nonexistent, and expanded services in the schools as well as public playgrounds—all of these represented innovations which could bring to the smaller community the technical and progressive improvements which larger communities had been developing over the previous two decades. When Brownlow left Petersburg in 1923 he did so with general public acclaim and with the solid beginnings of a national reputation for himself and his profession. His presidency of the City Manager's Association had done much to identify his personal reputation with that of the methods and techniques which the name, City Manager, was coming to embody. Knoxville, Tennessee, his new post, was considered fortunate in getting not only city management but the best of the new profession.

The circumstances which brought city management to Knoxville in 1923 were considerably different from those which had brought it to Petersburg. In Knoxville the new charter was a revolution. East Tennessee had, by traditions almost as old as Petersburg's, been divided into factions, political, vocal, and well-accustomed to doing battle. The city manager came in not simply as a means of solving serious practical problems but as a symbol for some of political triumph, for others of defeat. Brownlow's solutions to the city's serious financial problems brought him nationwide attention; but they served as well to fuel antagonistic fires in Knoxville. Brownlow's career as city manager of Knoxville ended four years later in an illness which forced him to give up the job; but it is highly possible that events themselves, unaided by ill health, would ultimately have forced the same conclusion. The Knoxville episode, occurring as it did during the richest years of public awareness of the new plan, opened questions for professional men and cast new and disturbing light on previously unquestioned optimism. The very high quality of Brownlow's service in Knoxville only seemed to sharpen self-examination.

Comparison of the Knoxville and Petersburg experiences is important. In each instance the skill of Brownlow as an administrator was amply demonstrated, and in each the virtues of city manager government as efficient and economical government were objectively proven. Yet the personal and professional success of the first instance was, in the second, a distinct failure; while Brownlow's contribution to the modernization of city government was, in Knoxville, far greater than it could have been—or needed to be—in Petersburg.

A difference in the role of politics in the traditions of the community was, in each case, an important factor. While Petersburg undoubtedly had its partisan debates, as well as its traditional social disputes, these did not tend to be reflected in city government and its offices. The eastern, mountain section of Tennessee had a tradition of argument with the rest of the state, and indeed with anyone willing to argue. Fiercely independent, the embodiment of that atomistic liberalism which gave logic to the chronic opposition of Virginians like John Randolph and, later, a certain rationale to the Jacksonians, the citizens of east Tennessee—or a vocally significant portion of them—would have objected to any reform which seemed to threaten their own sense of political control and maneuver.

A newspaper, set up by the opposition in Knoxville as an organ for attacking the city manager, referred to Brownlow as "King Louis" and to the offices of city government as "Buckingham Palace." The peculiar alliance of an Anglo-French monarchy was an accurately confused generalization of the whole ugly idea of unified, secret, undemocratic control. For such people monarchy was as evil as corruption, if not more so, but in any case no cure for it. In ten years the American opposition to executive centralization would describe itself as fighting "dictators." Whatever their politics and whatever their particular persuasion, the voters could, if they chose, attack the city manager as a fundamental anachronism in their traditions of government. They had not elected him. He was not one of them. His insistence upon the professionalism of his task excluded him from their ranks just as it excluded them from their traditional rights and privileges.

The ideal of nonpartisanship could scarcely avoid being self-defeating in a community such as Knoxville where partisan politics could be pointed to both as a source of intense satisfaction as well as of corruption. The very acceptance of a measure of corruption as a part of politics was a recognition of certain traditional realities in small communities. The line between shrewd, smart business and corruption could not always be so clearly defined, any more than could the difference between a skilled, freely competitive entrepreneur and a "malefactor of great wealth." Size could be used as a limited standard, to be sure; but numbers alone could not solve the dilemma in moral attitudes. If amount were the major difference between clever, independent initiative and thievery, neither public courts nor public polling places could offer clear alternatives, let alone definitions.

Brownlow's defense, like that of his fellow managers who found themselves under attack, had to depend upon works, not faith, and certainly not politics. But the definition of works posed problems which were difficult to ignore and virtually impossible to control. Brownlow had found the city on the edge of financial crisis. He had skillfully floated the proper loans. He found the water supply seriously endangered by faulty machinery. He corrected it. But from the point of view of public opinion, a near-catastrophe was no catastrophe at all. Its prevention was, like all prevention, entirely without drama. The politicians who plugged leaks and juggled books could, when discovered, be replaced by more politicians who plugged leaks and juggled books, and so on ad infinitum. The transitions could be high-spirited moments of the exercise of public responsibility, political morality, and the like. One of the difficulties which the prevention of the cause of dramatic incidents was bound to occasion was a removal of the public from an awareness of the nature of its government, and hence a certain reduction in the factors which might, in case of attack, lead to proper public judgment. By removing the operation of the city from the category of "issues," the administrator left political oppositions to invent issues of their own. In communities where city government had long been an issue, the coming of the manager did not signal the withering away of politics.

Secondly, corruption had served more complex purposes than its enemies had ever been able to indicate. Corrupt city business methods were intertwined with the presumably honest practices of those citizens of the community who sold goods and services to the city. City government, too, often bore the burden of employment for members of the community whose sole means of support in effect was the ballot they were entitled to sell on election day. City government, casual and corrupt, was of value to many of the community who were not themselves engaged either in politics or corruption, but whose methods of dealing with city government gave rise to the things which the new reformers were seeking to obliterate. The city manager who by-passed the man who had been selling the city some commodity at a tidy little profit and bought instead from a more competitive supplier made an enemy of the first without necessarily making a friend of either the second or the community at large. Brownlow's fiscal and operational innovations in Knoxville drew nationwide attention from those interested in techniques of municipal reform, but Knoxville itself was less impressed.

Thirdly, the relation among honesty, economy, and efficiency—the three prongs of the reform offensive—was undergoing crucial changes. True, corruption meant expensive government; but technical innovation was never exactly cheap. City managers like Brownlow could pride themselves in having saved the city the amount of their salaries during their first year as managers, but the pride was rapidly becoming a fiction from the past which they shared with the citizens of their cities. After an initial and sometimes dramatic fiscal saving following the change-over, the demand for increased services, increased technical skills, and modernization and expansion of equipment meant that the city's taxes would not, in any case, go down. Efficiency could mean more government, economical to be sure, but in out-of-pocket tax costs, just as expensive.

Finally, technological innovation could never be in reality as dramatic as its exponents tried to make it seem. When Brownlow motorized the police of Petersburg it was an innovation only so long as the automobile remained "new" to the public. But that was at least something which could be seen. Most public improvements were less dramatic, less part of the general fascination with gadgetry. The public dreams its technological fantasies in terms of sidewalks which move—potentialities, but far in advance of current technical possibilities—not in terms of public utilization of improvements already privately in use. Public improvements were precisely that—improvements, corrections of defects which may well have required innovation, but innovation which the technician could appreciate in terms unavailable—or worse—uninteresting to the citizen. In short, the technology which appealed to the technician and which he could describe at times in glowing terms was likely to be so commonplace to the citizen that innovation could become daily practice as soon as it occurred. The citizen was dreaming dreams well beyond the immediate reality, dreams which the purveyors of popular technology were inventing at times to keep him interested in the reforms he had voted to institute. But it became difficult to get him to vote to protect them. The technician understood his work, respected it, and even admired it. In the context of a democratic community, however, the public would have to support its own advances or run the risk of losing them. And support was difficult where understanding was absent.

When, after the Knoxville debacle and during Brownlow's recuperation in Washington, David Lawrence suggested to him that he undertake a syndicated column on municipal government, he could not help being interested. The opportunity to inform the citizen about the city presented to Brownlow the possibility of combining his long-time experience in journalism with the more recent interests of his administrative career.[19] But his newspaper articles, like his experiences in the District, Petersburg, and Knoxville, were all concerned with specific problems. A syndicated column required the discussion of generalizations which could be applicable and intelligible to most citizens in most cities of America. While it was true that such specifics as schools, public utilities, welfare, public transportation, and other such items were common to all cities, the extent to which any one of them could be considered a "problem" worthy of attention—even to the extent of reading several columns of newsprint devoted to it—varied widely from city to city. Citizen readers, inured to reform as the center of civic attention, found anything less an unnecessary encroachment upon their time. The police department dealt with crime. If there was no crime, then the police were an uninteresting group of public employees. If there was crime and the police were coping with it, then they were public servants doing their duties. The public was grateful but uninterested. If there was crime and they were not doing their duties, then and only then could interest and appeal be raised. The specificity of it defeated attempts at generalization.

One could well ask, "why generalize?" In many respects the professional status of public office depended upon the capacity to generalize. If public management had techniques, if it aspired to inclusion among the sciences in any sense, it would depend upon the discovery of principles which could be reached through generalization which was appropriate to experience. Too general for the problem-minded citizen, the series offered to the professional no glimmer of the principles he was seeking as a foundation for professional justification.

The purpose of generalization was twofold. To the extent that it brought a given public to an awareness of the relation between its specific problems and the realm of knowledge and experience already dedicated to coping with them, it gave support to public understanding of the difference between the technical nature of many community problems and the sophistries possible in political debate about them. A valid political debate could take place over the advisability of building a new road or a new bridge, but once the decision was made, partisan debate over the awarding of contracts and the preferability of materials or methods could easily become sophistical, and thence corrupt.

Generalization served another purpose as well. Early in his career as a municipal administrator Brownlow had become aware of the need for giving shape and direction to the growing professionalism of public administration. His presidency of the City Manager's Association and his involvement with the development of other associations of administrators had indicated his view of the importance of association and intercommunication. Generalization as a technique of abstracting common problems from diverse circumstances was not only a means of increasing the understanding of methods, it was also, and more subtly, the means of building professional identification. For many in public administration, as in other professions being organized nationally (medicine and pharmacy, for example), professional identification tended to seek standards, certification, and the exclusivity characteristic of the guild-like motives often found in such organizations. For Brownlow, influenced in part perhaps by the circumstances of his own election as a nonengineer to the presidency of an association then largely comprised of engineers, public service was as much *public* as it was *service*. Association, professionalism, and individual identity were, like generalization, a means of being inclusive, not exclusive, a means of specifying the knowledge which could be carefully applied, not the individuals who could apply it.

Even so, Brownlow's interest in administration as a public

profession sprang from more than the results of his own immediate experience. It came from the method by which the Jacksonian concern for the relation between the individual and his
government could be made consistent with the demands of
modern technology and specialized knowledge. Public administration in a democratic society would have to remain public.
The separation between the administrator and the citizen was
untenable in the traditions of American government. Whatever
excesses and whatever errors the Jacksonians may have perpe-
trated in their effort to bring the citizen into his government,
the spirit was liberal. Whatever principles, whatever generalizations public administration discovered, the central element of
Brownlow's faith demanded that they be consistent with that
spirit.

Thus there was established in Brownlow's career a relationship
between professionalism and the personnel for public service
which made his appointment in 1931 as Director of the Public
Administration Clearing House not only logical, but in terms of
his attitudes, virtually unique. A professionalist in the sense of
respecting and encouraging the development of professional
identity he nonetheless served as a counterweight against centrifugal and elitist tendencies within professional groups themselves. Following his own methods he formed the Public
Administration Clearing House as an organization among other
organizations and within the community of public professions,
not as another force competing separately for the identity they
all were encouraged to seek.

By 1930 it had already begun to be clear that the revolution
in public administration was not solely a question of the
authority of the executive, but also of the tools which could
serve him. Industrialization and science were providing mechanism. Government could be motorized and budgeted and
bridged. But mechanism was not enough unless one were so
old-fashioned as to take the nineteenth-century image of the
executive more seriously than the circumstances of the twentieth century could allow. The executive was not simply a

singlehanded manager of machines. He needed staff, trained staff capable of providing him with the instruments of knowledge which he did not himself possess. That staff needed not only knowledge but an awareness of identity which could insure that modern technical efficiency be maintained in a manner consistent with the traditions of American democratic government.

Merriam had encouraged the community of knowledge and PACH was indeed the outgrowth of that encouragement, just as the SSRC had been. But what would be the method of that community? How could one counter the tendency of systems of knowledge to be hierarchical, even authoritarian, without damaging freedom of investigation and the logic of science? This was indeed the question of scientific professionalism in a democratic society. For Brownlow PACH provided the answer.

### III

On the last day of December, 1930, the Public Administration Clearing House was chartered as a corporation in the state of Illinois. To many, even those who knew it most intimately, its legal definition would be about as accurate a description as any. Attempts to write its history would all, in one way or another, remain unpublished. When, in 1955, the organization closed its doors there would be no more agreement on its basic character and utility than there had been throughout its life.[20] PACH had helped to erect the building on the University of Chicago's midway, the building which housed not only its own offices but those of the other organizations it had either aided in founding or had been instrumental in bringing to Chicago. The brass plaque which listed the building's tenants bore the name of PACH in proper alphabetic sequence, and those who mistakenly referred to the building as PACH, a seeming logical error to many, were usually informed that the building was known by its number, "Thirteen thirteen," and that PACH was simply one of the organizations it housed, no more, no less.

PACH was founded under the guidance of Charles Merriam,

[ 113 ]

Beardsley Ruml, and Guy Moffett in consultation with Louis Brownlow. Merriam, Ruml, and Moffett were all, in one way or another, connected with the Rockefeller Foundation. The Laura Spelman Rockefeller Memorial provided the funds, having itself been reorganized as the Spelman Fund, partly, no doubt, to take the name Rockefeller away from anything even remotely connected with politics. The idea of PACH could be summed up simply under two points: first, that a really practical and economic advantage might lie in bringing together under one roof the various agencies of officials concerned with public administration; and secondly, that the general field of public administration could benefit from the interchange of ideas and experience which a center for administration could provide. When PACH opened it assembled around itself the secretariats and administrative offices of the International City Manager's Association, The American Public Welfare Association, the American Municipal Association, The Municipal Finance Officer's Association, the American Legislator's Association, and the Governmental Research Association.

PACH developed out of the same motives which had produced the professional associations in the various areas of public administration, the most important motive of which was perhaps the need for the centralized and continuing exchange of information, ideas, and practical experiences. Just as the academics had, a generation earlier, recognized the values of professional association as a means not only of exchanging information over wide distances but also of consolidating the sense of professionalism, so had the city managers, the municipal finance officers, and others in the various fields in local government. But to the academics, a second-level professional organization—whether the ACLS, the SSRC, or the NRC—had a general logic to it which connected easily with the intentions of professional organization at the first level. Whether there would be one or two or three such superorganizations posed problems, as Charles Merriam had already discovered in his creation of the SSRC.

Such problems were minor by comparison with those posed

by the possibility of organizing administrative associations into a single group. The academic associations, regardless of their differences in subject matter, shared a common intellectual ideal, whether it looked like the Royal Academy or a German *gesellschaft*. Most of the associations of public officials shared a common original ideal, too, but calling it reform was as far as one could go in pinning it down. From there on it splintered and shifted with all the diversity and intellectual disorganization of nineteenth-century American reform groups. Much of the forcefulness of the original reform groups—and all of their hard-won pride—tended to be institutionalized in the transition from reform to profession.[21] Much of the new logic of further association raised knotty problems which were quite different from those which academic association had raised. The original idea for PACH was probably Charles Merriam's. With his advisory influence on the Spelman Fund, the organization was given financial backing. But the choice of Louis Brownlow as Director was the source of the method of organization, the unique and perhaps the only method whereby the complex association of public officials came to be.

The reform groups which produced many of the professional groups tended to be, originally, collections of public-spirited, philanthropically minded citizens who had banded together for purposes of the continuing reform of the abuses which had first enlisted their attention. In many instances such organizations faced, after the enthusiasms of the progressive period abated, the prospect either of gradual extinction or a gradual replacement of the citizen members by professionals in whatever field they had centered upon. The latter came to have less and less sympathy with reform methods and manners, and the former frequently objected to the "specialists" who often had been trained at their expense and who now sneered at their zeal while usurping the positions and utilizing the opportunities that zeal had won. That both, professional and citizen, were moved by the same fundamental motives did not help the debate which developed between them. Nor did the addition of a third party, the academic, make the solutions to disagreements easier to come by. It did, however, enrich the mixture considerably. The younger generation, those who had learned their politics at the feet of either Wilson or Theodore Roosevelt made interesting and sometimes individual combinations of the elements available to them; but most of them, in one form or another, worked to discard the image of reform which the public had developed. Some difficulty lay in the fact that it was possible to discard the public along with its images.

To gather the variety of associations under one roof would be feat enough. To do it without subjecting them to a single, unified control would be the point which would give to the feat its most spectacular quality. Unified control, or any hierarchical arrangement whatsoever, was the source of the one central objection to any form of "clearing house" association and of the one constant suspicion maintained by each of the separate groups. But the continuation for some of them of their separate existences was, by the late twenties and early thirties, already a waning possibility. Public interest had slackened. The transition from individual philanthropy to the foundation had left some of the groups in doubtful financial circumstances as professional directors of foundations looked carefully upon enthusiasms which a previous generation had indulged. The remaining individual donors found it difficult to see in the cities of the twenties any proof of the success of their previous efforts. For some of the groups the Brownlow-Merriam-Spelman Fund idea of centralized offices had a financial attractiveness born of necessity. But they continued to look at the arrangement as a matter of office space and little more.

For others the clearing house idea had definite appeal. But jealousies born often of naturally overlapping interests fed suspicions of centralized organization. The associations themselves had grown out of such diverse problems and such varied interests that though they were all concerned, in general, with various aspects of local government, as a group they demonstrated little in the way of logical relation to one another or even to the totality of the problems which, as a clearing house group, they might be called upon to serve. These continued to look upon the new arrangement as a quasi service organization which looked after the rent, lights, and telephones, to be sure, and handled the mimeographing. But again the desired image was one which spelled out limitations as clearly as the suspicions would allow.

The fact of the matter was that PACH was all of these, plus several things more. In assembling the group Brownlow skillfully avoided the identification of PACH as anything more than one of the member organizations. For purposes of group identification he stuck to the notion of a joint building, referred to by street number only. The first such building, an accident of available location, was numbered 850, and thus titled "Eight fifty." The second, however, was built with Spelman money and the street number was chosen—in confusing violation of the then existing arrangement of streets and buildings—quite deliberately for its dual use as number and name: 1313 on Chicago's East 60th Street, the famous "Thirteen thirteen." Thus, the assembly of organizations was not PACH, and PACH was only one of the organizations which gradually and collectively were willing to refer to themselves as part of "1313"—and that was not an organization but a building. The separation of PACH from any collective status or responsibility made its relation to the other groups virtually impossible to define, for attempts at definition were likely to be a violation of the individual integrity of each of the organizations, or at least to be taken as such.

The question, what did PACH do, has never been answered to the satisfaction of any of its participants, friends and foes alike. Indeed, the failure of any of its supporters to be able to explain its functions in such a way as to obtain continued funds for its existence led ultimately to its demise. To try here, therefore, to accomplish this task of definition is perhaps a bit foolish, but possibly worth the effort.

PACH did three things which can be described as distinct

from one another, even though their interrelations are the fundamental point. First, it established a working vocabulary, so to speak, for the field of public administration by founding a library with all of its attendant technical appurtenances—categories, subcategories, periodical listings, and the like—and by searching out and constructing a directory of organizations in the various fields which could be considered fields of public administration. These two efforts established connective linkages with old reform groups, new research groups, societies of technical agents in public work, universities with interested governmental groups, and civil service organizations throughout the world. The existence of PACH and its work laid lines of communication among innumerable nation and world-wide agencies simply by the device of making them aware of one another's existence. Secondly, this mapping out process revealed gaps in the existence of organizations in professional fields, gaps which could be filled by the encouragement of new associations and the establishment of secretariats through which members of such groups could communicate with one another. PACH "encouraged." Its connections with available foundation funds made its advice and encouragement a very real and very effective beginning. PACH always insisted that it had itself no money to distribute and that it thereby lacked, happily, hierarchic power. Certainly with Merriam as administrator of the Spelman Fund there was little doubt about the basically friendly attitude of the Fund to the advice of PACH. It is still true, however, that such advice was subject to consideration and review by a large group of knowledgeable individuals.

In addition to its function of identifying the field and encouraging new organizations PACH served a third purpose. As a general public relations agent, in a way, for the various organizations within the field, it kept them conscious of the efforts each was making to develop new techniques and perfect old ones. In addition, PACH worked to keep other areas of the intellectual community as well as the public at large aware of the work going on in public administration. The first function involved the expansion of intercommunication which Brown-low had sought ever since his early days as a city manager. The second—informing the public at large—was a far more complex matter which depended upon keeping newspapers and other public media aware of what was going on in the field. In both respects the efforts of Brownlow as a force for unity, generality, and encouragement kept information moving and sustained in all endeavors of which he was a part an almost electric sense of the possibility that something usefully new and different was afoot.

Partly the sense of novelty was true, for PACH gave prestige to research in areas where practical professionalism sometimes looked askance on such endeavors. But partly the sense of novelty was a brilliant illusion, for the content of the newness lay in the associations and organizations themselves, if only potentially. PACH and the personality of Brownlow were a brighter, newer reflection of what they themselves had been doing all along. Disillusioning as that realization may have been to those who glimpsed it from time to time, the fact of the reflecting object was a great thing to others who saw in it what they were and what they were not. If they sometimes appealed to it for oracular advice—as did the Queen to the mirror in the fairy tale—they could not help being surprised or amused or even disappointed to find smiling back at them the face of Louis Brownlow recounting some tale of southern politics after the Civil War.

The functions of PACH were a Brownlow invention and so infused and suffused with the Brownlow personality as to be, or at least to appear to be, inseparable from it. This, too, was a con-venience which allayed questions of relative status, and it was partly true. But there is an element of greater importance in PACH which can be described apart from Brownlow, though it was undoubtedly the invention of his personality. In a sense, PACH was the "antiorganization" of the group. It provided a centripetal force to oppose the centrifugal characteristic which the others had developed in their years of separating themselves as professionals from amateurs, technicians from politicians, practical specialists from general theorists, and ultimately from one another and the community they were dedicated to preserving. Like the classic image of the liberal community their individualism—whether they chose to call it professionalism, science, or what—was threatening to undermine their effectiveness as part of a community which was not only liberal in principle but republican in fact. Nonetheless, their professionalism and their respect for technical knowledge and skill was itself a modern reality, necessary in a modern world; and the preservation of it was essential to the continuation of the successes which their work had achieved up to that point. What was needed was something which could respect their inherent egocentricity—indeed preserve it—while encouraging their communication with and support of one another. In effective denial of the most ancient of logical laws, that "something" would have both to be and not be, exercising authority only with the consent of a group inherently opposed to authority and unwilling to recognize any need for it.

While the creation of such an institution might have seemed to some an impossibility, Brownlow's background and temperament were ideally suited to the task. In a world of practical specialists and general theorists, he found himself a practical generalist with a chronic inability to specialize and an insecurity about theory which overpowered his respect for it. His habits of self-education, the product of a bright child allowed to indulge himself as he saw fit—and thereby undisciplined habits from the point of view of rigorous training—were nonetheless a source of infinite and endless enjoyment for him. Utilized to their fullest during his newspaper days, they found their most important employment in PACH. Professional public administrators, proud of specialization and its contribution to the knowledge of self-government, might have had difficulty communicating to one another. But they could all communicate with Brownlow.

The work of PACH was to institutionalize as effectively and

as rapidly as possible the communication of the groups with one another. The Spelman Fund paved the way by generous grants; but the idea of the external source of income for PACH was fundamental to the whole arrangement. Since none of the organizations was or should become dependent upon any other, PACH, too, would have to maintain its independence. Thus, PACH could not accept support from any of the organizations of 1313. At first this was scarcely a question, since the financial condition of the organizations was such as to make doubtful their continuing support of themselves, let alone any other organization. On recommendation from PACH, money was given by the Spelman Fund to those organizations in need of support, either for sustenance or expansion or both. At the point at which support from their members enabled the organization to be self-sufficient, support from the Fund ceased, in the sense of the basic problem of existence, but continued in a subtler way by the provision of support for experiments which would, of their nature, affect the organization's work. Here Brownlow had considerable leeway in suggesting projects, although for the most part these remained the work of the organization, not of PACH.

The creation of interorganizational services, like the suggestion of individual projects, was another of the self-liquidating operations of PACH, although here the identification with PACH was initially more obvious. The setting up of such units as the library, personnel files to which those concerned with filling governmental vacancies could appeal, publicity, public relations, news agency work, and the like began either within or with the direct support of PACH. But in each instance either the project was turned over to an organization which could support it or was reorganized as an independent member of the group providing services paid for by members using it.

Through such means PACH served as channel through which information, ideas, and methods flowed within and among the organizations themselves. It encouraged new organizations where it saw the need for them. It provided opportunities for

conferences among officials of different groups in various areas
—education, social welfare, and the like—but it carefully maintained control over its dealings with the outside world, preferring to arrange contact with the particular organization most
suited to handle the problem raised. In this sense, it developed no
ideological existence in and of itself, deliberately avoiding competition with organizations of public officials. The preservation
of the clearing house principle—the channel rather than the
source—did not preclude the origination of ideas; but it did
preclude their identification with any institution but that im-
plementing the suggestion.

Those who have attempted to describe the Clearing House
have tended to insist upon one point: the Clearing House was
the institutionalization of the personality of Louis Brownlow.
The truth of it may well be undeniable, but obscures some
important observations. True, most of the organizations would
have been unlikely to have accepted advice from anyone other
than Brownlow at the time the whole assemblage came into
being. It is also beyond question that Brownlow's awareness of
the technique required to make a go of the venture was responsible for the success of it. But here the fundamental confusion
is revealing. What was the venture? Was it PACH? Or "1313?"
It becomes difficult when one writes of Brownlow to separate
the two, although sufficiently easy when writing of any of the
other organizations. PACH was the functional institution which
Merriam and Ruml had intended it to be. The personality of
Brownlow in a historic sense of the term is in 1313 itself. For
if the fact of communication could be assured, the substance
of it would take care of itself. Content would ultimately have
to come from the individual groups, but their relation to one
another could reveal the gaps which new ideas would be called
upon to fill. In this fashion the old reform motive of the liberal
community recognizing its needs and attending to them could
be preserved in modern, efficient form. The community of 1313
could be given voice and practical effect by PACH, but the
sense of community depended upon the fact of their associa-

tion and the security of their independence and individuality.

As has already been suggested, the institutions and associations for municipal reform which grew up throughout the Progressive era were not themselves clear and consistent representatives of Progressive thought. To the extent that Progressivism was a technological or scientific movement emphasizing the collection of data and the creation of organizations to facilitate not only its collection but also its useful dispersion, the various organizations for the study and improvement of state and local government did represent Progressive thought. But to the extent that Progressivism stopped at the threshold of constitutional form, adhering to the tradition of conservative, anticonstitutionalism in American political thought, the reform associations were not Progressive in their internal structure, although very much so in their relations with one another. This is only to say that while they organized themselves for most logical and efficient action, they looked upon their relation to the rest of society as governed only by loosest standards of free association. Just as the citizen-reformers of a previous era had emphasized their freedom from the dictates of politics and government, so the technician-reformers demanded their rights to study and observe as they saw fit. But the separation entailed certain problems. An organization like the National Municipal League could formulate charters of municipal and state government, systems which specified not only the workings of city government but the methods by which revolutions to such charters could be achieved by local citizenry. But such groups disassociated themselves from the federal government and its opposing traditions, refusing to argue that what was good for the operations of municipal government might also be applicable to the federal government. This was an effective schizophrenia, fully capable of coping with a reality it did not adequately describe but amply sensitive to a limited scope of needs.

One can say that, in effect, the post-World War I period found the associations for governmental reform withdrawing even more from any aspect of politics and concentrating even more upon the "scientifically" limited field before them. Effective as such concentration was for the increase of knowledge and understanding, it threatened the welfare of governmental research as a fundamental, community activity of self-examination. And yet the organizations were bound by their implied ordinances of self-denial. Progressivism had given a misleading sense of unity to the traditional chaos of American reform. Perhaps any effort to unify it beyond the shrewd generalities of Theodore Roosevelt would have led to failure; but certainly the extent to which Wilson moved to pursue a logic which, quite rightly, he saw in the reforms in society around him demonstrated that, where the logic of unified endeavor was concerned, public drive would shatter against the rocks which American traditions placed along the shores of American government as a safeguard against tyranny—the sense of revolutionary independence inherent in the spirit of federalism.

To those who observed from the vantage point of Progressivism, it was clear that the proper utilization of modern technology, science, and industry would require more rational structures of government. But to the professional associations, themselves already imbued with technology and its rationale, an equally rational relation to one another and to government was, by traditions more revered than machines, a threat if not an impossibility. From the point of view of Merriam and those who first thought through the idea which became 1313, the hostility to association would have to be surmounted. But there was no way of knowing how.

Progressivism in a strict sense had by-passed Brownlow, although Populism had not. The circumstances of this have already been suggested, but the reasons are difficult to define. Certainly "temperament" or "personality" are relevant factors. Brownlow shared with Progressivism its appreciation of detail, of science and technology; but he was willing to watch logic die, painfully, if necessary, in order to achieve important ends. Thus, 1313 was to him no more or less an inherently logical community than Buffalo, Missouri, or Petersburg, Virginia, or Knoxville, Tennessee. But like them, it worked. While its form, like any form, would to some extent have to be governed by the functions it served, function was by no means the sole or at times the central factor. Form was determined, too, by the people who did the functioning, by the ends they wanted to achieve, by the means which at any given time they were willing and able to use.

Brownlow's lack of a logical commitment to Progressivism made him in principle an old-fashioned liberal closer to agrarian reform than industrial, but in practice a man of the age of technology. Merriam had chosen to reform Progressivism for his own use by bending its logic. Brownlow preferred to ignore it. Brownlow's almost total ignorance of Merriam's sciences of society left him free to follow whatever courses seemed best without feeling, as Merriam often did, the need for apology or justification. He could pursue the logic of detail and assume, with a faith considerably more unquestioning than Merriam's, that the whole would look after itself. Even more important was the belief that inherent in the ways people evolved for living their lives and handling their affairs was the best way of doing those things, that salvation, whatever it was, was no secret. Efficiency lay in the reorganization of what people in any case were doing, not in the imposition upon them of stand-ards derived from any external analysis.[22]

When it came to the presidency of the United States, these beliefs seemed to some of the members of his calling, fantastic. Much of Brownlow's image of the presidency came from his observation of presidents. He saw no need to reorganize it along the lines of any other form—cabinet, for example—or to predict any new directions. Of the men who, in 1936, worked on the reorganization of the office, Brownlow alone reflected his own emphasis upon the men who held it as the source of the knowledge of what it ought to be. Herein lay his faith in the operations of American government, a faith which placed upon the people a future responsibility and credited them with past successes. The public knew best whom it wanted as President. The Presidents knew best what they wanted the office to be. Administrative knowledge functioned to implement and routinize, but to invent only in the context of needs which would have to be prescribed elsewhere. This was Brownlow's image of PACH and its fellow organizations. It was his image of his committee's relation to the President. It was also his image of the President's relation to the people.[23]

The implications of such attitudes for developing concerns over executive leadership in democratic government were profound. If his involvement in the city manager movement and his experience in Knoxville had taught one thing, it would undoubtedly have been the necessity of separating technical knowledge from democratic leadership. Democratic leadership was, and properly so, political leadership, and while it should and must depend upon technical knowledge, in a democratic society it would have to follow public knowledge. While one could hope that the two would never be too far apart, hope in itself would not be enough. The maintenance of the relationship would depend ultimately upon those whose public responsibility was the education of the people to an understanding of their needs. This was a function of politics, not administration. Administration could supply politics with its tools, but only by respecting the use to which they would be put could a continuing supply be maintained. In addition the tools would have to be machined to the specifications determined by politics. However ideal the reverse might seem to the student of administrative affairs, sure destruction lay in the course of anyone who persisted in inventing tools for which there was no need. This is what had ended nineteenth-century reform. But the preservation of the spirit of that reform was the work of men like Brownlow who found in science and technology not a frightening revolution but another opportunity for infinite improvement.

LUTHER HALSEY GULICK

*Administration and the
Mission of Economy*

BROWNLOW AND MERRIAM both had approached administration
as a new concept. For Brownlow it had been a culminating
idea, formed to give shape and direction to practical experiences which had gone by other names from other traditions,
most of all from nineteenth-century politics. For Merriam it
had been a peripheral idea, part of a congeries of subjects relating importantly to politics, though no less important for
being one among several. Both men had to arrive at administration from practical and intellectual positions which, in the histories of their lives and times, were older and more established
in American society. To Luther Gulick, however, the third
member of the President's Committee on Administrative Management, the study of administration provided a career with
which one could begin, a study which could be considered in
and of itself as a valid and original field of inquiry. This was
partly the product of a difference in age—Gulick was thirteen
years Brownlow's junior and eighteen years younger than
Merriam—and partly the product of academic training in an
atmosphere which included both administration and politics
as areas of study attractive to younger intellectuals. The effects
of the difference in age indicate, perhaps, the speed with which
the study of public administration developed after the turn of
the century. The difference in place was another matter entirely. Brownlow and Merriam had grown up in Missouri and

Iowa, respectively. Their training as younger men—Merriam's in college years and Brownlow's in newspaper work—had been midwestern or southern. Gulick's background had been considerably more cosmopolitan and international. Born of missionary parents in Japan, sent to school at Hotchkiss and Oberlin College, he had in fact been a product of the eastern intellectual and urban environment which produced Republican progressivism, a movement which touched him profoundly during his college days. But of the educational influences which moved Gulick most, the crucial one was Charles A. Beard.[1]

On commencement day of 1914, Charles Beard told the graduating class of Oberlin College that America stood in great need of a social ethic, and that it would be their responsibility to provide it. To Luther Gulick, one of the graduating seniors and a member of the committee which had invited Beard, the call carried meaning he would not forget. It offered a concrete possibility of a way toward the solution of problems which he had been working out in his own mind for at least the previous two years.

Gulick had taken his Bachelor's degree in political science. Toward the end of his senior year he had been persuaded by his family to go to St. Louis to hear John R. Mott, the prominent evangelist. The experience had not convinced him that the ministry could best provide him with the career he sought; but the alternatives were not clear. He agreed to enter the seminary at Oberlin to study for a Master's degree. Part of the graduate year was spent on a study of the political concepts of Jesus Christ; but there would remain some question of whether this combination of politics and theology relieved or aggravated indecision.

For a previous generation, and indeed for many of his own, the alternatives were clearer because they were more limited. Those who wished to spend their lives working for the improvement of society entered the ministry, particularly if the lack of sufficient private means closed other routes of professional activity. In addition, Americans at the beginning of the nineteenth century studied society under the guidance of, or in rebellion against, the ministers who governed their country's higher education. By the end of the century the revolution in American higher education, led by a German-trained cadre like Herbert Baxter Adams and Richard Ely, had opened up new areas of possibility to students with Gulick's social interests, but not necessarily to anyone with Gulick's name. The interest was a Gulick family tradition which reached back at least to the 1820's; and the method—the ministry and its mission—was equally fixed by the generations which had preceded him. The Gulicks were part of a great evangelical movement in the Congregational church in the early 1800's, a movement historically overshadowed by the more popular Unitarian liberalism to which it was a response. They had joined an eager group of New Englanders who followed the Clipper routes to the lands of the Far East and the South Pacific to bring Christianity to the heathen.

In 1810 four young men of the Andover Theological Seminary petitioned the General Association of Massachusetts Proper, a recently organized conservative Congregational group, that they be allowed to undertake missionary work in some foreign land. It was as a result of their petition that the American Board of Commissioners for Foreign Missions was formed, and in February of 1812 the first American missionaries set out from Philadelphia bound for Calcutta.[2] The first of the missionary Gulicks joined the trek in 1827, continuing a search for new worlds which had been begun, apparently, by a Hendrick Gulick who had arrived in America in 1653. Peter Johnson Gulick graduated from Princeton in 1825 and sailed for Honolulu from Boston two years later. It would be almost a century before any of the numerous members of that branch of the family would be born within the continental limits of the United States; but they would continue to cite Princeton as their home. It was a small but vital security in a rapidly expanding world.[3]

All of the seven children of the Peter Johnson Gulicks

entered the mission. In keeping with practices which came to be more and more consonant with their image of their roles in the mission field, the Gulicks devoted much of their time and interest to investigations of the environments in which they found themselves. Orramel Hinckley and his wife published studies of the social history and habits of the southern Pacific islands.[4] John, a friend of Darwin and Romanes, was better known in America and in Europe for his contributions to the theory of evolution than for his labors as a missionary in China where he spent more than twenty years.[5] The eldest of Peter Gulick's children, the first Luther Halsey Gulick, was born at Honolulu in June of 1828. Sent to America for his education, as was the general practice among the missionaries, he received his M.D. from New York University in March of 1850, was ordained a Congregational minister in 1851 and sailed shortly thereafter for the Micronesian Islands, for the American Board. Alternating religious work with medical practice and research, he published in 1855 *Climate Diseases and Materia Medica of the Hawaiian Islands.*[6]

Sidney Lewis Gulick, son of Luther Halsey, was born at Ebon in the Marshalls on April 10, 1860. He was educated at Dartmouth and Union Theological Seminary, spent a year preaching in Brooklyn, and sailed for Japan in 1887, under the auspices, of course, of the American Board. Mission work had not been his first choice; but his interest in astronomy, philosophy, and the sciences in general gave way before family pressures and, more important perhaps, the insistence of his fiancée. Japan and the people of the Pacific world captured not only his imagination but his practical interest as well. Under the influence probably of his Uncle Orramel he studied social and political habits, not with a view toward changing them—he considered this a most dangerous predilection of the westerner in the Far East—but with an appreciation of the civilizations they represented. In 1914 a serious and presumably fatal illness necessitated his return to the United States; and he decided to turn whatever time might be left to him to furthering greater international understanding, particularly of the peoples of the Far East.[7] He took the post of Secretary of the Commission on International Justice and Goodwill and of the Commission on Relations with the Orient of the Federal Council of Churches of Christ in America. His lay assistant was John Foster Dulles. In 1919 Gulick became Secretary of the National Committee for Constructive Immigration Legislation, a group which sought to apply rational principles to the growing racial hostility among legislators. These activities and the books and pamphlets he published in connection with them were part of an effort to bring Americans to a new understanding not only of the Orient but of their misguided racial theories about that part of the world. While Sidney Gulick did not argue such questions as marriage among the races, he went so far as to suggest that racial mixtures could well produce a better stock than any which had existed theretofore. He warned again and again that westerners and their oppressive attitudes toward easterners were fomenting difficulties which were both unnecessary and potentially of great political danger.[8]

Essentially a practical man and of political mind by nature, he prepared for Congressional committees tables and statistics which would, he felt, achieve the ends Congress sought with respect to immigration, while preserving traditional American justice.[9] Congress accepted his statistics and his percentages in its preparation of the Act of 1921—with the exception of those for Orientals, which they excluded. Sidney Gulick continued his fight. Like many American missionaries, his voyages had been important discoveries for him. In a period of isolation and exclusion, he sought to preach a gospel of internationalism based upon Christian love, common sense, and a realistic, scientific, social ethic, combined in parts perhaps more equal than those compounded by his family predecessors. But they were essentially the same parts.

His son, Luther Halsey Gulick, was born in Japan in 1892, and named for his paternal grandfather, the doctor-missionary, who died the year before the birth of his namesake. Sidney

Gulick followed the family custom and listed his new son's "home" as Princeton, New Jersey. When the appropriate time and age came, the gift of a scholarship enabled young Luther to embark on an education at Hotchkiss School in preparation for entrance into an American college.

The Hotchkiss years could undoubtedly have been unhappy years for any missionary child, regardless of his personality. The first decade of the new century was an active, opulent era, especially for those who enrolled their sons in such schools. Under these circumstances the scholarship student faced financial differences which went further and deeper than tuition, room and board. Caught by upperclassmen in an innocent violation of a rule against the wearing of trouser cuffs by newcomers, Gulick had his two new suits, the treasure if not the entirety of his wardrobe, gleefully mutilated by the eager hazers, an incident which marked from the outset the rather remarkable material differences between the young men of Hotchkiss and the child of a missionary family.

Eight thousand miles from parental surveillance and advice, attached to home only by the slender thread of mail service requiring something in the neighborhood of two months for a rapid exchange of correspondence, young Gulick pursued his new American career in an atmosphere of enforced self-sufficiency, spartan financial circumstances, and a growing resentment of the restrictions which the traditions of Hotchkiss could place on his own interest in experiment and adventure. With a persistence which was built as much of defence as of attack, he pressed all limitations to their outermost extremes. In order to take physics, he concocted a plan to enter Harvard —Hotchkiss deliberately and proudly prepared for Yale—thus making sure that he would be subjected to Harvard's science requirement, which Yale did not have. He enlisted his father's aid, by the somewhat cumbersome means of correspondence— a ruse which fooled no one, including his father, but which accomplished its purpose. A member of the debating society, he upturned a planned debate on the question: Should Taft be renominated by the Republican party. The debating coach had requested Gulick, who had the negative position to argue, to base his presentation on the preferability of Roosevelt rather than upon an attack on Taft. Assuming the young student's agreement, the coach had prepared rebuttals to the Roosevelt argument for the other team. His assumption, however, was incorrect; and the affirmative side found itself arguing against a viewpoint which had not been presented, while ignoring the one which had. The judges, themselves Taft Republicans, awarded the victory to the negative team. The school authorities questioned Gulick's school spirit, and ultimately, a year short of his graduation, withdrew his scholarship. In practical terms the action was tantamount to expulsion.

The news reached the Gulick family in Europe where they had managed to combine a brief tour with a welcome reunion. It was difficult at that distance to make alternate plans; but it was assumed that the boy could be placed in some appropriate school for his final year. He had, at Hotchkiss, taken college entrance exams as a practice testing. An aunt and uncle, as well as a sister, at Oberlin had suggested that he finish his preparatory work near Oberlin and in the following year enter the college. Oberlin, however, on the basis of his practice scores, was willing to admit him immediately, so in September of 1910 he joined the freshman class.

The Oberlin years were full of a kind of excitement which was new. The rebellion of the previous three years was somehow organized, liberalized, perhaps, but in any case encouraged. There was more family about, and the general environment of the Congregationalist college breathed a kind of familiarity which was, after the initiation into strangeness, pleasant. Robert Cushman, a senior during Gulick's first year, influenced him not only in his awe-inspiring capacity as Oberlin's great debater but in his interest in and respect for Karl Geiser, Oberlin's professor of political science and a disciple of Francis Lieber. There was, in addition, a brief romance with psychology—the "laboratory method"—as well as the new sociology and doctrinaire economics.

The financing of his education was not altogether a simple

matter, but it challenged a youngster newly enthralled with ideas current to an atmosphere so foreign to his earlier upbringing and family background. Business enterprise was exciting, and the organization of work a challenge. From odd jobs during his first year he moved rapidly into the organization of various student services, lawn mowing and snow shoveling, culminating in the management of the Northern Ohio franchise for the Curtis Publishing Co. After the first year his Oberlin experience came to be a relatively luxurious one from every point of view.

Beyond an apparent wish that he look upon religious study as an important part of his education, his parents maintained a quiet and even distant position with respect to his career. The opportunities for influence were, of course, limited by distance. Mission families, accustomed to maintaining ties by correspondence, by relatives who entertained at holidays, and by the innumerable mission "aunts" and "uncles" who returned home on "furlough" and brought news, grew accustomed as well to a certain reserve which the written word and the kind intermediary seemed to demand. Although the Gulicks returned from Japan in 1914, their active influencing of their son extended only to their request that he hear Mott in St. Louis and that, above all, he make his decisions in accordance with his conscience.

The year in the seminary increased the puzzle, but it was not unpleasant. The contrast between the theological training and his previous political science course was nowhere near as great as it might seem. The seminary had its coterie of adherents to the Social Gospel movement,[10] although it seemed clear enough to anyone newly come from a degree in political science that the movement no longer offered the chief, if not the only, alternative. Social science promised techniques of understanding which were, at least in practical terms, vastly superior to the promise once held forth by Social Gospel. Now many voices called to work in social welfare.

Part of the problem of decision lay ultimately in questions

of creed. As the mission was representative originally of conservative Congregationalism, the American Board was committed to doctrines of a kind which seemed to place interesting restrictions on social reform. Despite the fact that those doctrines had, since the enunciation of the creed in 1863, attempted to avoid the internal dispute between the orthodox Calvinists and the Arminians, the basis of belief was a fundamental, evangelical Protestantism which held that regeneration, salvation, and ultimate unity with Christ lay in faith, not in works.[11] While Congregational theorists continued to criticize the Socinianism of the Unitarians, they were, after 1863, willing at least to be silent on the subject of Calvinist orthodoxy. The emphasis upon governmental liberalism within the church—its essential "congregationalism"—provided an increasingly convenient screen for the doctrinal dispute; but education for the ministry penetrated the screen and left the most pious student face to face with doctrines which questioned the validity of the very endeavor in which he sought to engage. Doubts which had seared the conscience of Puritanism could be soothed by Progressivism, in part, at least.

Within the context of its evangelical faith, Congregational missionary activity at home and abroad consisted in the continuation and expansion of the traditional method of conversion as well as maintenance of the faith: education. Well before and long after Harvard College fell to the heretical forces of Unitarianism, Congregationalists continued to found colleges for the education of the ministry—Williams, Mt. Holyoke, Middlebury, Bowdoin, and, in 1833, Oberlin, among many others.[12] In every place where the American Board planted missionaries, colleges grew up to educate the young of the new lands in the new faith.

The environmental nature of evangelical missionary activity held as a tenet that conversion would, it would seem, be made possible only by adequate preparation of that which surrounded the individual rather than by exhortation or influence actively working on the state of his soul. Such a tenet clearly supported the idea of social work, not to improve men but to improve their environment so as to enable them to better themselves. But to base a career in theological doctrine or, indeed, to allow doctrine to limit either one's actions or one's beliefs was no longer as necessary as it had been to previous generations. By 1912, certainly, a new faith was being formulated as a base for social justice. While it was possible to choose different leaders as representative of that faith, the name "progressive" could ultimately be applied to all of them.

Gulick's decision to go to Columbia for graduate study in political science rather than into the ministry and the mission was a great disappointment to his family, but it would be years before he would be aware of this. Beard's Oberlin address had made too deep an impression to be ignored; and Columbia's award of a fellowship in 1915 brought the practical reality which was needed for a decision. As part of his application, Gulick had submitted his essay on the politics of Jesus Christ.

The Columbia faculty in 1915, or that portion with which a graduate student in political science would have made contact, included a wide variety representative of fifty years of the development of social science in America. For students with Gulick's practical interests, the existence of the Training School for Public Service and the Bureau of Municipal Research tended to divide the social science faculty into two groups. There were men like William A. Dunning and Howard Lee McBain who concerned themselves with the theory and structure of government. Influenced by an older school which held that biological classification was the route to knowledge, they ordered politics for themselves and their students. McBain was known as a man who had never been in a city hall, a description which, to the new generation of students, was more often a term of opprobrium than reward, but one which could be used, in his case, with a certain affection. E. R. A. Seligman, who taught courses in public finance, and Henry R. Seager, whose exciting approach to labor economics drew interested students, provided an opposite point of view, urging their students to observe government at the source and directing them to the Bureau of Municipal Research. At the Training School they could take courses in the operations and practices of government and hear the historical method of Charles Beard.

Seager argued against the exclusion of economic history from the study of political and social history and its isolation as a separate endeavor. He disputed as well the emphasis of much economic history of his day on economic theory, outmoded or otherwise.[13] Beard, as a historian, had argued similar points. Both saw economic history less as a body of theory than as a description of practices which lay somewhere between economic theory, on the one hand, and "pure history" on the other. Seager, trained at The Johns Hopkins under Herbert B. Adams and Richard T. Ely, both of whom had imported the German historical method to the American classroom, rebelled against the institutionalism of his teachers but espoused the interest in "laboratory method." In a sense, the Bureau made a laboratory of the city by providing the "practical reason" which the study of government required.

The search for practical reason, for a kind of knowledge which would not be uselessly a priori, directed Americans concerned with the science of government to institutions like the Bureau because they provided an intermediate step between the confines of the academic closet, rigidly classificatory in its logic, and the raw, disorganized "data" of the city. Despite the use to which the academy could put the Bureau in its search for a revitalization of the knowledge it already felt it had, the Bureau had and maintained a life of its own—and a mind of its own, a mind conditioned by the history of reform which it had articulated. The conclusion of that history and its experience had come more and more to depend upon budgets and accounting—not human morality and conscience—as the basis for adequate, effective reform. This was a conclusion born, to some extent, out of disillusion; it dovetailed neatly, if accidentally, with the view of academics like Beard, Seager, and Seligman when they argued that the basic data of human life would inevitably be economic. To say "accidentally" is not to deny the preoccupations natural to the first generation of social scientists to inherit Marx and Engels. The emphasis upon the economic base was part of a whole milieu. But one must distinguish the experienced social reformer who turned to economics after his failure to rejuvenate individual morality from the academic whose discovery of economics was a fresh adventure in a great new world. While they agreed on their new starting point, they had reached it from parts so different as to color not only what use they could make of it but also their attitudes toward one another.

Centering the economic argument in one political institution, the budget, did not solve the problem of basic differences, but it did obscure it sufficiently to translate disagreement into compatible practical ends. Budget reform and budget reformers could often be found in two separate camps, arguing not primarily with any sizable opposition to budgets as such, but, more often with one another.

Thus, the budget could be the means whereby a legislature could control an unruly, immoral executive; or it could be the means of freeing a purposeful executive from the confusions of legislative indecision. The distinction led to completely different approaches to budget reform. Those who argued legislative control also argued for economy, for less government, for popular decentralized sovereignty, by which they meant legislative sovereignty. They saw budget reform as an added step in a tradition of reform by legislative enactment. Those who argued fundamental executive control tended also to argue for efficiency, for clear responsibility through more centralized authority. They saw budget reform as a constitutional problem in a changed relation between the executive and the legislature. Among the first group were the old reformers who saw the budget as a new device for the enforcement of an old morality. Among the second were the new reformers, the progressives and the economists, who saw the budget as a means of making moral questions appropriately irrelevant.

The New York Bureau of Municipal Research was the center of an essentially new preoccupation of reform. Its history, particularly the years in which it provided those first exciting links between philanthropically oriented reform and academically inspired research, provides one of the most important chapters in the detailing of new attitudes toward and methods of coping with problems of American urban society.

II

Mrs. E. H. Harriman was vitally interested in her family, her charities, and the government of the city of New York. She gave much of her time to the many activities underway in the Broadway offices of the Bureau of Municipal Research. On her various trips to Europe she observed as much as she could of the operations of the civil service in countries like Great Britain and Germany. Sometime between 1906 and 1910 she proposed to several of America's major universities that she endow a school of public service to train what she thought of as a class of governmental experts. She was refused; but in 1911, largely through her continued efforts, a school was founded by and attached to the New York Bureau of Municipal Research.[14]

The New York Bureau of Municipal Research had been founded in 1906, the first organization designated as a bureau of research, yet part of a continuing stream of older organizations, all dedicated to reform. The transition from reform to research was clearer in this instance, perhaps, than in any other. The founder of the Bureau was Robert Fulton Cutting, who, as president of the board of the Association for Improving the Condition of the Poor and president of the Citizen's Union, had for mnay years been active in municipal reform groups of New York. Mr. Cutting, a man of wealth and family, prevailed upon his acquaintances, John D. Rockefeller and Andrew Carnegie, to join him in providing funds for the continuation of the Bureau which he had begun as an experiment in the Citizen's Union. He took William H. Allen and Frank Tucker from his Association for Improving the Condition of the Poor, and with Henry Bruère and Frederick A. Cleveland set up a staff. Bruère had been in charge of welfare work for the Mc-Cormicks of Chicago. Cleveland was then a professor of finance at New York University.[15]

The Bureau of Municipal Research was established as a "fact-finding agency," a "mechanism for learning and publishing the facts of municipal life and administration." The purpose of the "facts" was to "base judgment" for the public to enable it to "intelligently direct and control the administration of the city. Without control by the public, efficient and progressive municipal administration is not possible." The emphasis upon "facts," and the reasoning process "from facts to policy" points to a definition of research as well as to the distinctions which Cutting and his friends wished to make. Politics, for example, "subordinates fact to expediency." But "expedient" and "efficient" were by no means to be confused, despite the fact that the difference between them was never explained. The distinction spelled the difference between "research" and "reform." [16]

"In private affairs," Cutting's staff wrote, "it is already realized that good service means efficient service, and that an honest man who is inefficient can do more to defeat the purpose for which he is employed than a dishonest man compelled by intelligent supervision to render efficient service." [17] Honesty and the moral character it presumed, the old aims of reform, were being replaced by facts and the presumably objective research which would reveal them. Expediency as a standard by which action could be judged was honest and dishonest by turns; efficiency, one could presume, was another matter. Research obviated the necessity for individual moral reform by circumventing both individual character and the qualities of moral leadership demanded by more traditional reformers, seeking to replace such qualities with techniques of observation whose inherent morality would make all who acted in accordance with them moral, even if in spite of themselves. "Mere goodness" was derided as useless and imprecise, subverted by a lack of facts and, above all, as a poor standard by which to judge objective reality.

"The average citizen earnestly in favor of 'good government' does not yet understand that there is a technique of intelligence and a technique of efficiency as far beyond the reach of mere goodness as is business efficiency beyond the reach of mere good intention." [18] The road to reform was paved with facts. Facts were produced by research. Research was the objective examination of reality. Neither goodness nor politics had anything to do with it.

It was abundantly clear to Cutting that the voluntary association dispensing charity and unheeded advice had been swallowed up by the complexity of modern city life. But however clear the need for a new approach may have been to him and his associates, the techniques of that approach would, along with the treasured facts, have to be a product of research. The beginning point was not easy to find. For one thing, intentions, whatever they were worth, were not precisely the same for each of those actively engaged in the enterprise. Cutting was a reformed reformer, Bruère a guide of the wealthy, emerging as a professional in the administration of social work. Cleveland, a professor of finance, was concerned with the purest form of practical efficiency, the rationalization of accounting systems for cities as well as for businesses. [19] What they shared, perhaps in different ways and for different reasons, was a belief that wherever lay the methods for the improvement of government, politics and the personality of leadership had proved themselves less capable of showing the way than some of their predecessors and contemporaries imagined. Techniques of organization and finance, "administration" in their view, would be the heart of the new reform.

Important as business and industrial concepts of efficiency were to such notions of reform—and the influence of men like Frederick Taylor cannot be overestimated, whether or not it was original—it would be a mistake to see financial reorganization of government as a product solely of the industrial revolution in America. Wealthier city dwellers had always shared with rural landholders an objection to taxation for purposes of the administration of government. Robert B. Roosevelt had, as early as 1866, headed a group entitled "The Citizens' Association of New York" which led a campaign to secure, among other things, "A large Reduction in Taxation through a reorganization of the Departments of the City Government." His group argued that the organization of city government encouraged corruption and cost money, that they had discovered this "by careful investigation," that this "Foul and Monstrous Conspiracy" could be corrected only by consolidating departments and bureaus.[20]

In the seventies, in the days of the Tweed Ring when municipal reform was one of the city's major public preoccupations, a Bureau of Municipal Correction busied itself with the publication of "facts" concerning the "trading politicians" who "discovered that the city of New York might be made the Galconda of fraudulent cupidity." The New York City Council of Political Reform fought for reorganization of the city charter and claimed victory in 1873. They pushed successfully an Act to Consolidate the Government of the City and County of New York, arguing that "this measure saves not less than half a million to the taxpayers of this city, and cuts off the opportunities to a much greater amount of corrupt and corrupting jobbery." Such reorganization led, of course, to temporary reductions in taxes.[21]

Insofar as waste was in itself a moral evil, whether or not it was motivated by corruption, savings in taxes represented moral victories. The crusades which eventuated in such victories marched arm in arm with those which sought to improve the condition of the poor, to correct evil practices in penal institutions and hospitals, and to prohibit the consumption of alcohol.

As important as the morality of economy in the American tradition was the belief in the essential democracy of the frugal-

ly operated government. Early debates over the salary of the
American President raised the question of the appropriate
standard of official living and its expense.[22] The governors of
America were exhorted not to model themselves after the
profligate monarchs of Europe; but when it got down to such
questions as the kind and the nature of official entertaining or
the size and title of the President's residence, comparisons not
only became less odious, they became, after a time, irrelevant.
To a nation which had glorified its refusal to submit to
taxation, thereby entangling the cost of government among the
most treasured of its national mythologies, principles of democracy and principles of public finance would be bound, at times,
to look to one another for such definition as a busy people
would demand.

Thus, the introduction of talk about the "business" of government was not necessarily or solely the product of America's
chaotic stumbling into the world of trade and industrial technology. Americans were conditioned to suspect the bills they
paid for the nuisance of having a government to look out for
the things they had no time to handle themselves. Like the
Victorian husband checking his wife's household accounts,
the American taxpayer expected to examine at intervals the
cost of his government, to find it excessive, to exhort his representatives to virtue, even to reform them; but he also expected
to insist that he had other more important concerns, that his
own behavior, if only government were virtuous enough to
imitate it, would provide the proper model, that he expected
constant improvement, nonetheless, and that the simplicity
and clarity of the task he had assigned was such that failure
was obviously the result of ignorance or cupidity.

After the Civil War, corruption in municipal government
and corruption in business came to parallel one another ever
more closely, if not in method, then occasionally in personnel.
By the latter part of the century the muckrakers could plunge
their rakes into either area and find plenty with which to
arouse public response. A certain confusion in public images

of the two may well have been clear to a man like Cutting who criticized his wealthier friends for their unwillingness to assume public responsibilities while he knew that the public was reading about some of those same friends as manipulators of legislatures and corruptors of democratic politics. John D. Rockefeller gave money for the founding of the Bureau of Municipal Research, as did Carnegie, but it was some years before either name would appear on the Bureau's literature or either man could officially sit on its board of trustees. The Rockefellers would, for the next fifty years, be the mainstay of research and reform through public administration, but the Rockefeller name would be carefully concealed where anything remotely related to politics was concerned, lest its mention raise the specter of Standard Oil and activate the pen of a new Tarbell.

Men of business were attacked by some for the influences they sought to exert in politics and by others for the responsibilities they refused to assume. The conflict, the contradiction, was compromised in many ways by the Bureau of Municipal Research. The Bureau was a citizens' organization, from Cutting's point of view, which had nothing to do either with politics or with the old-fashioned voluntary reform associations arousing specific angers over specific abuses. In its early years it became involved in politics to the extent of aiding in the election of a reform mayor, John Purroy Mitchel, and earned from its enemies the name "Bureau of Municipal Besmirch." [23] It carried on for many years one of the older reform notions modernized—a weekly newsletter informing the citizenry of the abuses it uncovered. Entitled "Efficient Citizenship" the postcard-sized notes were compact treatises on reform.[24]

Gradually, however, the professionalization which Cutting and Mrs. Harriman had sought as an element in the whole picture, came more and more to dominate. The Bureau became more clearly and in fact an organization of professionals whose chief concern was accounting and the machinery of public finance. From the professional point of view, good government and corruption could ultimately be read from the same text—the ledgers of public expenditure. By providing government with proper systems of accounting and opening these accounts to public scrutiny, the new reformers could encourage and maintain just government. Efficient procedures of accounting would lead to economies and enforce honesty. When Cutting spoke of a "technique of intelligence and a technique of efficiency" which were beyond "mere goodness," he was speaking largely of the accounting of public finance. Just as in a well-run business organization, the keeper of accounts was the watchdog guarding against dishonesty as well as error.

Mrs. Harriman's Training School for Public Service attracted the attention of many on the faculty at Columbia. It would be some time before Columbia, one of the schools which presumably had refused Mrs. Harriman's original suggestion, would consider the Training School an accredited institution. But E. R. A. Seligman and Charles Beard would find the new venture an interesting one. Seligman, in fact, sat on the initial Board of Trustees for the school. Beard sent his students down to the Bureau and to the school to observe their operation. They were, to him, the heart of the city as a laboratory, utilizing the "laboratory method" as a means of coming to understand municipal problems. While the Bureau's accountants tended to look upon such descriptions as purest poppycock and to resent the academics over whom they stumbled periodically, it would not be long before such influences would play an important role in further change within the Bureau itself.

Of all of the academics, Beard seemed most to sympathize with such principles as the Bureau was willing to profess. Beard extolled the "laboratory method," but he brought his sense of economics down to the level which the accountants were willing to accept as concrete or, an even more interesting hypothesis, his sense of economics had never strayed too far beyond their businesslike demands for efficient, economical techniques of government. In this respect, Beard's "economic interpretation" of American history was completely American in its context as well as in its origins. He shared with both Frederick A. Cleveland and Cleveland's friend, F. W. Taylor, a belief that the techniques for achieving moral ends were not themselves moral, but that the achievement of moral ends was essentially the aim of man in society. From their point of view the understanding of amoral techniques was the only road to reform. The economic interpretation in 1913 of the Constitution of 1787 was as much a thesis in reform as any of the documents produced by any of the reformers of the previous hundred years. Many of America's major historians have been reformers eager to appear as scholars, sharing with the new reformers a faith in the objectivity of facts. Perhaps Beard's most exceptional quality was the extent of his success.

In some important respects the New York Bureau of Municipal Research represented the successive stages in America's economic interpretation of itself. It was founded out of a recognition of the inutility of moral means as the key to reform. Corrupt men stole money; moral men, in innocence and ignorance, wasted it. The difference could come to be negligible.

The economic basis of reform could be defined only in fiscal machinery realistically representing the balance of interests in the community. In a day when the Constitution was being used by the Supreme Court to thwart economic and social reforms, Beard could demonstrate the presumed historical fiction of its economic base, and find the proper balance not in any futuristic ideal culled from the sciences he revered but in the America which preceded the Constitution of 1787.[25] The Bureau in its increasing espousal of fiscal reform as the real reform had started with principles of finance drawn, so most of its research staff seemed to feel, from America's business success. Beard gave the Bureau its ideology, drawing upon history and economics for imagery and inspiration.[26] If constitutions as forms were fantasies, budgets as forms were not.

The ideals of a democratic society could receive their most realistic statement through fiscal controls which made government work. Municipal government could be good government not because it eschewed form, but because its forms faithfully represented the true economic base of the society.

Beard's search for realism ran headlong into the hysterical nationalism which blended imperceptibly with the patriotism of World War I. But even in addition to the public matters which presumably brought about his resignation from Columbia, Beard's analysis posed problems for his fellow social scientists as well as for his fellow reformers, problems which paralleled those which such colleagues were coming to face in their own work. For men like Brownlow and Merriam, the term "economic determinism" came to mean Beard first and Marx only secondarily, if at all. And in the efforts of such men to relate "theory" and "practice," as they like to put it, the relation between the economist and the accountant presented particularly difficult problems.

Part of the difficulty could be found in the development of important ideas in the translation of American traditions into the vocabulary of industrialism and technology. Henry R. Towne, friend and mentor of Taylor, had touched upon the problem in 1886 when he advised his fellow engineers to become economists, by which he meant, largely, that they should learn cost accounting.[27] Economics and theories of economics were new, and indeed foreign, to American professionals trained in specific, practical pursuits. To Towne an economist was a man who kept books, and who differed from the traditional bookkeeper only in the nature and degree of his training.

Taylor's theories of work were related to the pragmatic image of the economist, but with a rather important difference. For Taylor efficient organization of action meant economical action. For Towne the economical organization of action meant efficient action. The shift in wording is not just an exercise in verbal maneuvering. The relation between economy and efficiency was a necessary one. The two were totally and irrevocably dependent upon one another for the creation of that moral atmosphere in which the natural honesty of man could flourish. But emphasis could, in the long run, become strikingly important. With respect to the operations of government, economy and efficiency and their related pairs of terms—business and engineering, economics and accounting—provided two arguments for the reformation of government, arguments which sometimes reinforced one another and sometimes clashed in angry, ineffective confusion.

The Taylor definition of efficiency involved a rationalization of motion, carrying with it the stated assumption that such rationalization was an improvement. That this involved an "economy" of motion was obvious, but economy only in a metaphoric sense of the term. Economy in terms of money or profit was, if anything, a by-product of improvement, and the meaning of economy became so intimately involved with efficiency that it took on much wider meaning: the good of society as a whole, national wealth and well-being, and the like. The governmental counterpart of Taylor's work-efficiency was reorganization of offices and rationalization of work flow. Its purpose was not primarily to save money; it was not to waste that which was to be spent. It was economical in the sense that it was appropriate, not necessarily in the sense that it involved a smaller outlay of funds.

While the Taylor system stressed, by implication at least, the simplification of action, it could be interpreted as a move toward the obliteration of many of the kinds and varieties of action in which government was involved, an economy in the sense which Taylor himself seemed to disavow. Taylor saw industrial efficiency as a key to expansion. The application, or misapplication, of it to government could produce the opposite result. But such results had been the purpose of those who, ever since the period of governmental expansion which followed the Civil War, viewed with considerable alarm and much inherent justification the rapid and chaotically irrational proliferation of functions and offices which marked the federal government.

Debates over reorganization were fundamentally involved with two alternatives: the halting of "duplication" and "overlapping," which tended to presume a basic necessity for the functions being performed and hence sought only a rationalization of the operation of offices; or the cutting out of federal functions properly belonging to the states or to individuals. Although both points of view argued economy and efficiency as their basic aim, the first presumed that economy would come through increased efficiency, the second that efficiency would result from the institution of increased economy. Again, the direction in which one argued was, as it continues to be, a crucial evidence of the existence of conflicting theories of the function of government.

The two points of view were indicative of two approaches to reform, approaches as old as the Jefferson-Hamilton dispute in American government and as recent as the misunderstandings within the Bureau of Municipal Research between Beard and his associates. Philosophically speaking, the difference was this: either economy was a virtue which "caused" efficiency, or efficiency was a kind of knowledge which produced economy; either economy or efficiency was an objective technique which could be learned and applied. Economy as an objective technique meant that bookkeeping properly handled could produce efficient, honest government, and the accountants could argue this point. Efficiency as an objective technique meant that the structure and organization of offices, responsibly arranged, would produce economical, honest government. The chief instrument of the first group was systematic accounting and control. The chief instrument of the second group came to be the executive budget. The second had developed out of the first; but, as we shall see, its aims came to be so distinctive as to constitute an opposition to that which had originated it.

What the two groups agreed upon was of fundamental importance: economy and efficiency were objective factors superior to and productive of honesty, not subject to it and not necessarily produced by it. Objectively speaking, morality was produced by the proper machinery of government, not by the insistence upon selecting or reforming the characters of men. To this extent, the reformers of the economy and efficiency schools rejected both politics and the political, centering their attention upon economic and organizational machinery. This was the basis of a dispute between Beard, on the one hand, and Brownlow and Merriam on the other. It was a dispute which continued well into the 1930's at least, and had a major influence in the struggle over reorganization in 1937.

This is not to say, however, that Beard held quiet court in his own realm. His appointment in 1915 as supervisor of the Training School for Public Service, and his subsequent assumption in 1918 of the directorship of the Bureau of Municipal Research indicated transitions which had not come easily to the shifting and often amorphous battleground of municipal reform. The Training School had begun as an enterprise devoted to field work, deliberately disavowing the closet approach of the lecture and the classroom, "learning by doing" at an adult level. Beard introduced both the lecture and the classroom discussion in his reorganization of the school in 1915. By 1918 Columbia, New York University, and the University of Chicago were willing to recognize the school as one having a program contributing to higher degrees, and they all authorized exchanges of students.

The character of the Bureau was changing, and the character of reform and of reformers was changing with it. Men like Cutting had builded better than they knew. Their effort to by-pass the dangerous zeal of the old reform had succeeded. But they were not being joined by a younger generation like themselves to perpetuate the inner motives for social improvement. They were gradually less able to stir their contemporaries with the promise of a better world combined with a lower tax rate. The Training School was turning out specialists, not philanthropists.

The Bureau was deeply involved in budget reform and in the reorganization of government for cities and states requesting its advice. Its activities had become increasingly national in scope and in 1921 it was reorganized as the National Institute of Public Administration. Beard chose as his successor and as head of the new organization Luther Gulick, who had been a student of his at the Training School and at Columbia. Cutting remained chairman of the board. The Carnegie Corporation and John D. Rockefeller Jr. pledged financial support, and on April 13, 1921, the Bureau of Municipal Research was happily joined by the National Institute of Public Administration, just as, fourteen years earlier, the older reform groups had produced the Bureau of Municipal Research. Then, reform had become research. Both now were public administration. Equally important, Beard and Cutting in their choice of young Gulick gave what was perhaps an unexpected continuity and combination to the interests and motives which had so meaningfully moved them both.

The atmosphere of the Bureau of Municipal Research combined all arguments, and in doing so provided a thorough education to students like Gulick who moved between the classrooms of Columbia and the offices of the Bureau with an ease which older members of either camp could not always enjoy. The economist and the accountant, the scientist and the technician debated and disputed within the confines of both arenas, and the canopy which was ultimately raised to cover the two hid their disagreement without solving it. The new title was "public administration," and Luther Gulick was chosen as the personification of the compromise.

The sense in which this was a successful choice is apparent in the dissertation with which he obtained his degree. In 1917 the state of Massachusetts appealed to the Bureau, as had others before it, for help in preparing the introduction of the new budget idea. Gulick was sent to serve as staff agent to the legislative committee preparing the report. His history of that experience combines in neatly modern terms the past history of debate while it forecasts, perhaps unintentionally, the future of the endeavor it represents.

III

Gulick called his book *Evolution of the Budget in Massachu-setts*,[28] a title which was itself an interesting recognition of several important factors. First, Gulick chose to deal with the budget idea as evolutionary rather than revolutionary. While this was not original with him by any means, Gulick's tracing of budget ideas back to early Massachusetts charters distinguished him sharply from those who looked upon budgeting as a product of contemporary thought, indeed, of the previous decade. Secondly, the use of historical method as the basis for the evolutionary approach was, in part at least, an acknowledgment of the influence of Beard, as well as a recognition of his own belief in the values of government as a habit and of the security which lay in habituation to forms and methods. Thirdly, there is the indication of a choice to be made between the methods of reform, which are revolutionary, and the methods of administration, which are yet to be defined. Gulick summed up these concerns with characteristic precision in his Preface:

> It is not the purpose of this discussion to prove or disprove any of the current budget dogmas, but solely to record in orderly fashion the long series of events that have led up to the present budget system of Massachusetts. The reformer who looks for immediate and revolutionary changes in the financial methods will find little consolation in the history of Massachusetts. For this very reason, the student of government who believes that there is some value in the gradual growth of the habits and forms of government, will see, it is hoped, a justification for this presentation of the evolution of the budget in Massachusetts.[29]

Beard's "Prefatory Note" repeats part of Gulick's warning as well as his plea for justification; but it analyzes Gulick in terms somewhat different from those in which Gulick analyzed himself: "Although Mr. Gulick's treatment is for the most part historical, the writing of history has not been his purpose. On the contrary, it is his intention to present for the practical administrator dealing with state budgets an account of actual appropriation methods and the practice prevailing under an important piece of budget legislation." [30]

As Beard continues his introductory statement, it becomes clearer that, while he, too, denies the effectiveness of the revolutionary approach, the revision of budget systems is, somehow or other, superrevisionary, being more than revision, less than revolution. Just what this means is difficult to discover in the seeming conflicts of his description. It is not "the relatively easy task of adding a wing to an old structure or of devising a new bureau or office of government." [31] Quite the contrary, we are touching the very nature of the complexity of modern government and dealing "with processes which go to the very root of our constitutional law and political system." [32] Change is going to involve abandonment by the public of some of its traditional attitudes and necessitate "a long campaign of public education."

In the two prefaces one can catch a glimpse of the differences which made Gulick something less of a student than the teacher might have wished. "Historical method" appeared to be for Gulick a force for continuity and conservation which revealed in the past the logical and rational basis of present rational designs and future logical directions. Continuities which could be traced from 1631 to 1917 seemed to show that, properly educated and reasonably directed, man's intelligence brought him to the most appropriate solutions to his economic and political problems. While Beard seemed to argue a similar "natural" continuity revealing the rational, objective basis of man's search for economic and political satisfaction, Beard looked to a certain discontinuity in the course of at least recent history which had, on the grounds of obsolete or unrealistic theory, seen the usurpation or, if you will, appropriation of economic common sense by a kind of political fantasy. In short, Gulick did not choose to trace the history of public finance in Massachusetts in order to show that a "budget" which had existed in 1631 had been taken away, and that budget reform involved its restoration. While Beard undoubtedly would not have held to such an argument in this instance either, the element of "restoration" which characterized his reform view of American history made him appear strangely equivocal with respect to "change" and "revolution" in his historical method.

Fundamentally, historical method for American reformers consisted in the use of history for purposes of substantiating whatever action seemed wisest and most appropriate. Revolution was a tainted notion, despite its inevitable and perpetual embodiment in the continuity of western liberalism. Reform carried the stigma only to the extent that it awakened older threats of social disruption; but it was difficult to draw the line, impossible to know when the illumination of present realities would touch on older recollections fearful to encounter. Historical method and evolutionary science alike could justify change, the new, even the revolutionary, by showing their natural and organic contact with the old. But while the new, in this case budgetary reform, helped determine in a general sense what of the old would be relevant, the scientific disposition of the times placed certain limitations on the uses of history as the vehicle for advance in social justice. Thus, for anyone addicted to accuracy and evidence, the examination of history would have to influence reform, if necessary, as much as the choice of reform would have to limit the approach to history. Left to themselves and the arid objectivity of the ideal laboratory, history and reform could well have stifled one another. The human impossibility of the ideal avoided the catastrophe; but it made the history look a little strange—witness Beard's "discovery" of the Constitution—even though it gave a scientifically modish dignity to reform.

If Beard and Gulick did not see history through completely companionate eyes, they were also inclined to look differently upon those they chose as their common enemy: the reformers. Here, perhaps, was a difference even more marked but even more difficult to define. It lay in part in the difference in experience produced by the distinction in generation. Beard knew muckraking and its causes more intimately than did Gulick. More important, the failure of the reformers was to Beard part of the disillusionment of his own generation, while to the much younger Gulick it was only a lesson to be learned as objectively as possible so that the errors could be avoided. His commitment was to the future; and past failures which could teach him lessons were triumphs.

Beard scarcely defined what he meant by "reformers." One can see only in scattered pieces of his work how he might have chosen to characterize social change and its appropriate methods: budget and accounting reform, city, state, and county reorganization through charters, the pieces of a whole which is never looked at from the point of view of its completeness but is nonetheless dimly outlined. He criticizes the superficial attempt, attacking the notion that either through legislation alone or the addition of a "bureau" will one accomplish the needed revision. But what is the necessary way? Science and education are, to be sure, adequate generalities, and he uses them. But even in his approval of specific, particular devices he gives the impression of working with some larger, general structure which is not, somehow, within the realm of description.

In many respects Beard's basic argument concerning the structure of American government was based upon two points which were, in one sense at least, within the realm of contradiction. First, efficient modern government would have to be based upon a strong executive responsible to the people. Second, the preservation of the Constitution in its "original" form was essential to the health and well-being of American government. Thus, when he appeared before a Congressional committee to discuss the possibility of a national budget, he disagreed with the notion that a budget officer would have to be a "new" officer in American government.[33] He suggested that all the necessary functions could be placed in the hands of the Secretary of the Treasury whose responsibility to the President would insure ultimate executive responsibility. For historic precedent, he referred the committee to Alexander Hamilton and George Washington. That the cabinet was extraconstitutional and the strong executive questionably constitutional at best, not to mention the administrative and historically muddy relationship between the first President and his cabinet, raises questions of evidence which go unanswered. Beard's Constitution was an idea as well as a document, and the plea seems at times to have been a private one.

The potential contradiction was clear by the 1930's when Beard began to criticize Franklin Roosevelt for wielding strong executive power which was, he argued, opposed to the Constitution.[34] Essentially Beard's image of executive power was dependent upon his image of the Constitution, but he tended to define the two in terms which were separate and distinct rather than in terms of one another, attempting to separate the Constitution as a worth-while ideal from the facts of executive functioning. This avoided the possibility that his concepts of the two might not really be consistent with one another; but to Beard's critics as well as to his followers it gave the appearance of a *volte face* of major and disturbing proportions. One could perhaps reconcile a theory which combined strong leadership with fundamental economic causation only by having a strong leader who believed in economic causation. Beard's assumption that all truly rational men were economic determinists excluded many of his generation from the counsels of reason, Franklin Roosevelt among them.

Gulick's translation of Beard's dilemma into terms which were not only more acceptable but more successful as well made him perhaps the most understanding of the generation which succeeded Beard. Gulick gave life and continuing reality to that aspect of Beard which revelations of Beard's techniques of historical scholarship could not quite touch—Beard the reformer. But it is possible that here again the translation was as much a process of incorporation as that of "historical method" had been. It brought traditions of the older Gulicks into a relationship with modernity, perhaps, but it demonstrated again the difficulty of drawing a clear line between economic causation and original sin. Writing retrospectively of Beard in 1954 Gulick said, ". . . most publicists, many reformers, and even some historians have missed the central distinction between action based on knowledge and action based on human desires, human beliefs, and human interests. The first we are reducing to technology; the second is still the major realm of politics. The first rests on science; the second on human nature, man's aspirations, and individual and social drives. Human nature is not changing perceptibly, but human knowledge is going forward by leaps and bounds." [35] The puzzling relationship between human nature and human knowledge was not going to be solved by the creation of new, or the refurbishing of old, dichotomies; but the temptation was irresistible.

The multiplicity of approach and the fundamental differences which underlay the whole movement for budget reform in America were clear both in Gulick's study of Massachusetts and in the arguments within and around the New York Bureau of Municipal Research. The agreement on budget as an executive function tended to obscure disagreements on methods of achieving and institutionalizing budgeting in American government. Gulick's opening disclaimer of the intention of dealing with the variety of "budget dogmas" which existed by 1917–1918 left him free to illustrate those dogmas through descriptive history without clearly identifying the traditions of debate which had already grown up around them.

In 1915 Frederick A. Cleveland, then director of the New York Bureau of Municipal Research, published an article entitled "Evolution of the Budget Idea in the United States." [36] Unlike Gulick, who later would argue that the "budget idea" had an old American history, Cleveland began his "evolution" in 1910.[37] In keeping with his intention of achieving scientific precision, Cleveland proposed a definition of budget. It is, he wrote, "a plan for financing an enterprise or government during a definite period, which is prepared and submitted by a responsible executive to a representative body (or other duly constituted agent) whose approval and authorization are necessary before the plan may be executed." [38]

Certainly most, if not all, of those advocating budget reform would have subscribed to Cleveland's definition. But agreement did not necessarily imply the kind of total agreement which Cleveland's drive for precision had as its goal. In the first place, the elements of the definition were themselves subject to debate. Secondly, the relation the elements bore to one another could constitute rather serious disagreement. Thirdly, the relation of the elements to the constitution of government, wherever it happened to be, could generate heated dispute.

As far as the elements of the definition were concerned, among the key terms were "plan" and "responsible." Cleveland had specific, technical meanings for these two terms, and they bore a precise relation to one another. For example, plan meant plan of action, which Cleveland chose to distinguish carefully from a diagram, document, or statement. It was not, then, a kind of financial sheet drawn up in advance, but a proposal to act financially in a given fashion. It was a statement of policy couched not in political but in basic, dollars-and-cents terms. As such, it had to be drawn up by those whose responsibility it was to engage in the actions involved—thus, the *executive* budget. But, apparently, "responsible" does not define "executive," or vice versa, there being executives who are "irresponsible," not ultimate, active agents. This term and its precise or imprecise use were part of an argument which would develop importantly through the next two decades. "Responsible" is not used in a moral sense but in a technical, legal sense, to describe an individual designated by law as the actor or executor of fiscal plans. The use of the term in its specialized sense involved not only a definitional and grammatical confusion but a historical one as well. "Responsible" without an indirect object had tended to signify a moral quality. "Responsible" with an indirect object, i.e., "responsible to someone or something" had been used as a basic term in such descriptions of democratic politics as "responsible to the people," "to the legislature," etc. What Cleveland seemed to be seeking was a use of the term which would retain the "quality" of the moral use, without its morality, and the legality of the second, but without specifying the indirect object. Establishing responsibility to the legislature could remove the executive independence which budgeting required. To be responsible to the people, except under certain circumstances, was, in the traditions of recent American government, too ephemeral to be useful.

Relation of the elements of the definition, particularly the legislature and the executive, could produce different senses of the definition for different groups. The ambiguity of "responsible" served to give the illusion of agreement about the relation between the two. Being responsible to the law but not to the legislature gave the executive budgetary independence with respect to the formulation of plans, but did not satisfy those of more traditional stripe who saw the legislature as the true representative of the people and hence the great wielder of economic power. They, however, could also define "responsible" for themselves in such a way as to produce the relationship which was more pleasing to them. But such juggling could, when the cards and the terms were down, produce endless debates among puzzled people who thought that they agreed.

Both the definition of terms and their relation to one another rested on an even larger question, however, which concerned the very constitution of government itself. If the formulation of government in America already, or originally, included the elements as defined and arranged, then reform could come through legislation which tightened or corrected an existing system. If, on the other hand, budgeting was so new an element that previous and existing formulations of government did not and could not include it, then reform would necessitate constitutional amendment. Those who argued the former view (Beard was one) looked to the addition of machinery as the basic necessity and eschewed notions of fundamental governmental and political change. Those who argued the latter view tended to see British cabinet government as the model toward which formal change could move. They included among them, in addition to Cleveland, W. W. and W. F. Willoughby, whose studies for the Bureau of Municipal Research were of exceeding importance.[39]

The difference between the two groups tended to center upon the question of effective legislative government as a base for effective executive government, or the necessity of an independent, strong executive to counter, control, or supplement (depending upon how you looked at it) the existing systems of legislative operation. For a period of time Woodrow Wilson's *Congressional Government* served as a guide for the first group, while the second added their interest to the various aspects of progressivism. The switch in Wilson's own thinking, which might have been predicted, perhaps, served as a convenient means of bringing Progressives disenchanted with the Republican party into Democratic ranks during World War I. In any case, those who emphasized executive leadership included A. Lawrence Lowell, Beard, and Gulick. From their point of view, traditional institutions of government were a necessary historical base to any evolution of reform, and such institutions evolved under the impetus of intelligent leadership.

Gulick came to understand from his experience in Massachusetts during 1917 and 1918 that the arguments there presented in their most concise form all of the major "dogmas" in active conflict with one another. In that sense, Gulick's opening disclaimer about not dealing with budget dogma was indeed a clever irrelevance. The arguing participants did the work for him. Massachusetts had moved from an attempt to institute a budget system by legislation to a constitutional convention called to take care of those elements which legislation could not insure, i.e., the ultimate permanency of whatever system was introduced, and the very touchy point of item veto.

Cleveland introduced a proposed amendment which left no doubt as to the origins of his faith. Despite the fact that the work of the convention was, in view of the legislation already passed, quite simple, Cleveland launched into proposals which would have the governor and his staff appear before the legislature at stated intervals to debate the budget. More important, a failure to approve the proposed budget would result in "an election, [in which] both the general court and the governor shall stand for reelection, and in any event [in which] new nominations may be made in the same and under the same conditions as for other elections." [40]

Cleveland testified before the convention in defense of his proposals, arguing that it was the only way in which "truly responsible" government would be achieved." [41] The rebuttal was undertaken by A. Lawrence Lowell who argued that, historically, American financial administration was itself a fundamental reform of its British origins by the establishment of a popularly elected governor. "The English system and ours are not the same and cannot be run in the same way. We cannot put into practice the same initiative of legislation which the English have." Lowell felt strongly that a budget system in harmony with American institutions could be adopted without damaging the basic essence of budget reform. [42]

The extreme amendment proposals were voted down. Interestingly enough, those who argued against them divided up in curiously confused fashion, some opposing the fact that the proposals would destroy party government, others that they would create party government. The British model, however revered or condemned, was rarely understood. [43]

Emerging from his historical description to comment finally on the Massachusetts battle, Gulick took the position, by implication at least, that budget reform needed to be flexible. He arranged types of budget. Instead of defining budget as Cleveland had done, he listed elements of budget reform, a kind of "creed." But the dogma was gone, dissolved in history, the universally objective solvent. It would, however, be some time before Gulick's view would dominate; and even when it did, some of the elements would refuse to melt into history. They would continue to be viewed as revolutionary, not evolutionary. They would continue to raise cries of usurpation of legislative right, and, later, of "dictator." For the spending power, traditionally a legislative prerogative in defense against tyranny, was to be preserved, however inefficiently, however irrationally.

Gulick's immersion in the short history of budget reform gave indications not only of the future course which "the budget idea" would take, but of a kind of thinking which would characterize his whole attitude toward politics and administration. For the chief features of budget reform, stripped of Cleveland's emphasis upon the need for constitutional change, made the budget a factor in the evolutionary process of the adaptation of governmental institutions to political requirements. It became a method in a natural evolutionary development, not a center of revolution. The facts of government were budgetary by description, if not by nature. This did not imply economic determinism for Gulick any more than it had for Beard. It simply pointed to the obvious fact that the collection and distribution of community income provided the one genuinely tangible center of information about community life, its health or lack of health. All values ultimately had to be translated into something like budgetary categories before their reality could be assessed and their continuity assured. It was a practical point of view and, above all, good business.

That there were limits to such a point of view was clear to Gulick as well as to his critics, and the limit most often encountered was politics. Gulick was fond of recalling an experience with Franklin Roosevelt which had called the problem quite sharply to his attention. Gulick had recommended that the original individual accounting system set up for Social Security be scrapped and that some type of central fund be established. It would be far more efficient and cost a good bit less to operate. The President rejected the proposal immediately. There would always be Congressional criticism of Social Security, the President told Gulick; and future Congresses might want to take a second look. They could look all they wanted; but no voter would ever permit the disestablishment of the personal account which bore his name and number. Expensive though its maintenance might be, it was his own, his individual source of security in his government. Politics could point to the limits reached by the intentions of economy and efficiency.

In 1948 when Gulick published a series of lectures which he called *Administrative Reflections from World War II* it was clear by the central metaphoric structure of his argument that, while the old schools of budget reform were no longer the center of his thinking, the symbol remained. For he continued to speak of "balance sheets" of government as devices for evaluating the successes of America in the war. His discussions were frequently set up as profit and loss statements in which successes were to be measured against failures and a sum, presumably in the black, reached. He was seeking precision, a genuine sense of direction which could be achieved only through machinery which would enable administrators to know both where they were and where they were going. And he continued to hold as the major premise of effective administration "a clear statement of purpose universally understood." With reference, perhaps, to the earliest influences on his thought, he went on to say that "in administration, God helps those administrators who have a clearly defined mission, and thus the beginnings of authority commensurate with their responsibility." [44]

Gulick's early work in Massachusetts was thus part of the culmination of a movement which he himself would help set on a new course. But the first real peak was reached in 1921 when the Congress of the United States passed a Budget and Accounting Act, giving to the federal executive its first modern budget. Congress garnered advice from Frederick A. Cleveland, A. Lawrence Lowell, R. Fulton Cutting, Charles A. Beard, and Assistant Secretary of the Navy, Franklin D. Roosevelt. The Bureau of Municipal Research sent a team to Great Britain to study the British Treasury system so that a model, if one was needed, could be formed.[45] Of that team, one member, W. W. Willoughby, worked directly with the group which drafted the bill.[46] In many respects, the bill reflected two chief problems of the history which had produced it: first, that an executive budget was a public necessity; and secondly, that an executive with a budget was a public danger. In its compromise with evil, Congress created an executive budget, but refused the President several crucial elements of control over that budget, including the item veto. Equally important, in an apparent last-ditch stand to preserve a Congressional fantasy of dispassionate, nonpolitical honesty, it created the General Accounting Office, placing over it a Comptroller General appointed to a fifteen-year term by the President but not subject to removal by him. Reporting neither to the President nor the Congress, the Comptroller General became the first truly independent executive in American government, the institutional embodiment of fifty years of disagreement over the definition of efficiency and economy and the distinction between the economist and the accountant. Giving the executive his budget required that a watchdog be placed over his activities; but no one could decide who should hold the leash. Confused, perhaps, over conflicting images of the conflicting attitudes toward British government, Congress attempted to compromise again. If it could not hold the leash itself, and apparently it felt it could not, and if it could not trust the leash in the hands of the President, then the answer was obvious. Congress gave it to the dog. The Comptroller General thereafter governed disbursement of funds, settlement of accounts and the auditing of those accounts without the responsibility of explaining his actions to any branch of the government except the various judges of the various courts of claims to whom those who had the time and the necessity came more and more to appeal.

In 1936 when the President appointed his Committee on Administrative Management, the Comptroller General, following a habit which had by then made him notorious, refused to acknowledge the request, delaying disbursement of committee funds for several weeks. This office was one of the objects of correction by the committee, and Gulick's presence on the committee indicated certainly the line that correction would take. But when placed before the Congress, suggestions for change would again become a source of major dispute. If, as Gulick and his teachers had pointed out, economics was a traditional source of heated controversy in American history, the raising of the issue, however logical its defense and however rational the view, would bring out a host of enemies who scarcely knew what it was they were opposing but who knew full well that they opposed it to the death. The fact that members of the committee were apparently unprepared to face this as a crucial issue reveals some elements of the history which are worth discussion in future chapters. But in the final analysis, it would be an awakened dispute among the reformers themselves which would aid Congress in its articulation of its concerns. The disagreements which a common cause for years had concealed would be sharpened not only by the man who was President but by the focus which time itself had given to traditional irresolutions.

# THE PRESIDENCY
## *Reorganization and the Habits of Reform*

I

WITH RESPECT to the need for executive reorganization, the New Deal could be called a cause only in the sense in which the famous last straw "caused" the camel's broken back. Ever since the end of the Civil War the Congress had piled one agency upon another, adding commissions to the executive branch, and committees to itself in the hope of providing for the obvious needs of industrialization without relinquishing any of the powers which the aftermath of the Jacksonian revolution had given to the legislative branch. Awareness of the fact that the trend of governmental growth constituted a problem was almost as old as the problem itself. The heat generated by Andrew Johnson's battle with the Congress has obscured the fact that Congress' efforts to conduct reconstruction single-handedly was not only the product of its disapproval of the President's point of view, it was also an effort to assert control over vastly increased federal responsibilities which had not existed prior to the war. The debates between the President and Congress may have been part of an old practice; but the prize was new: the economic, social, and political power which would continue to attend America's rapid industrialization. The contest to distribute new power was not like the struggle to interpret old power. Traditional structures might well have to change. As a young man Woodrow Wilson had examined American government and had sought an answer to its sprawl-ing chaos in a reorganization of the legislative branch which would place more efficient executive power in the Congress. He was not then inclined to see the presidency as the center of proper executive power, although by the time he himself assumed the office the experience of his predecessors, most particularly Theodore Roosevelt one would assume, had combined with his own executive experience to produce a different point of view.

World War I established executive power beyond the force of personality which had carried it from Lincoln through Theodore Roosevelt. The complex organization which the war effort entailed had forced Congress to a reluctant understanding of its own limitations, but that same and traditional reluctance had also led Congress to make its delegations of power temporary. Presidents through the twenties struggled with an awkward and continuously growing executive branch, still without the authority to deal with it themselves and hampered even more by the postwar reaction to any governmental control, let alone executive control. The New Deal added emergency and urgency to the picture, but it could not radically change the trend or the direction. For many years observers of the Washington scene had pointed to the "monster" of executive government. Some saw him as a headless monster, others as a multiheaded one. But whatever the exact lineaments of the grotesque, he was a familiar monster, indeed a rather amiable one who ambled about the corridors of the succession of new buildings built to house the growing executive branch.

Thus, in reaching a decision to do something about the problems of executive organization Franklin Roosevelt was embarking on a course which, as we shall see, was well worn by the steps of his predecessors; but it was oddly worn in that it was an almost habitual path through the offices of government and up to the halls of Congress. There it split into visible but less familiar routes; and the changes which emerged bore the marks of a tour through Congress rather than through the executive branch itself. For the primary concern of Congress was efficiency and economy with the emphasis upon economy. This meant improved systems of bookkeeping, ultimately a budget, but above all a curtailment of offices and agencies where possible. This was not only the Congressional view of executive government in 1932, it was the opinion which Franklin Roosevelt brought with him to the presidency. It was also a view supported by several influential members of his early council of advisers, most particularly Lewis Douglas and Raymond Moley. But if it was the predominant view of the federal executive, it was by no means the dominant view of executive government elsewhere in the country. City government and state government in many parts of the nation, including the governorship of New York, had undergone reorganizations which sought to strengthen the role of the executive, to reduce the constant muddle of overgrown legislative supervision, and to rationalize the relations of executive offices to one another. As we have tried to show in previous chapters, the three men whom Roosevelt appointed to his Committee on Administrative Management were experienced in the problems of local executive government. Their points of view were no longer dependent upon the Congressional traditions of reorganization. Roosevelt's selection of them could scarcely help but give new emphasis to the problems he was attempting to face. Each in his fashion had been trained by the governmental disputes and paradoxes of the post-Civil War period. Although by the time of the New Deal it may have appeared strange that Roosevelt would have chosen men whose governmental careers were involved predominantly with state and city government, it appeared so only in the light of a persistent misunderstanding. Cries of corruption and the inevitable smoke from the fires of reform had long hidden the fact that city governments were not only the first to face the realities of industrialization, they were also the first to do something about them. Their successes were never as dramatic or as satisfying as the movements for investigation and research which their problems encouraged. But there were successes; and experiences with them produced men educated in new methods of reform.

Brownlow's career had been in city government; and his intellectual endeavors had led him to formulate a definition of the modern profession of public service, a definition which moved away from doctrines which identified democracy solely with popular election. He sought a status for public service as a popular profession which retained its essential democracy by the continual interrelation of services and the maintenance of relations both among the professions themselves and with the public. His work as a city manager and as a manager of managers in PACH had distinguished him as a representative of the values of professionalism and the values of the public tradition of democratic process.

Gulick had worked in state and local government with the establishment of methods of organization which would make modern democratic society efficient with respect to its newer responsibilities, urban and industrial. Governmental budgeting and accounting was central to this endeavor, not simply with respect to the reform interests of the old New York Bureau of Municipal Research, but with respect now to the broader problems of public responsibility and the necessities of a newer society. He did not seek dispute over questions of politics and democracy, not because he doubted their importance or their relevance, but because he felt that the reality of the assumptions on which democracy rested was coming more and more to depend upon efficient means of coping with problems of social development and change.

Merriam had been initiated into city politics as a student in New York and in Germany. He had been extremely active in Chicago city politics; but his academic orientation had been toward relations between the practice of government and the development of governmental theory in social science. Merriam had concentrated upon the application of rationality and method to political problems; and by emphasizing the accumulation and organization of knowledge for public benefit, he had found himself enunciating a theory of planning which involved the organization of the academic and scientific communities for purposes of public good. There was virtually an unbroken continuity in the relation between the founding of the SSRC, the proposals of the Committee on Social Trends, the President's Committee on Administrative Management and the only partly realized dream of an agency for national planning.

In a very important sense the careers of the three men paralleled the three-part analysis which would serve as the basis for their report. For Brownlow's interest in professionalism and personnel, Gulick's concern with budget problems, and Merriam's philosophical preoccupations with planning certainly directed the formulation of the major categories of reorganization: planning, personnel, and budget.[1] These three terms had definite roots in the history of reform. That they seemed not, in any explicit form at least, to have reached the level of national consciousness was more a matter of terminology than of fact, for the Civil Service Act had given the President control, albeit limited, over federal personnel and the Budget and Accounting Act had given the President far greater fiscal authority than he had once had. Planning, the most controversial factor by reason of its implications of social and economic control, had never explicitly been incorporated into the organization of government; but even so no one would be willing to deny that Presidents had always had the power to propose long-range projects and to succeed in getting a degree of influence over their implementation.

The fact that the efficient and responsible functioning of the executive depended upon his capacity to propose policy, to choose sympathetic and useful advisers and assistants, and to manage the finances of his administration was known to and debated by the first administration of American government. While budgeting in its modern sense was not part of the early arguments, certainly the continuing quarrels over federal banking and currency placed upon the President a responsibility for economic management equal, relatively speaking, to latter-day concerns with budget management.

Nonetheless, the lines of division among the three factors have never been clear, since each can serve as the key device for the administration of a given President and by its key position relegate the others to a secondary and dependent status. If policy planning proves central to immediate circumstances, the economic considerations are forced to conform while chief advisers serve as implementers of that policy, gathering and analyzing information necessary to its execution. All wars tend to throw the nation into such a situation. As an end, victory subsumes all other considerations.

While war is a unique and terrifying example of the control by plan, in normal circumstances any national end or goal can serve a similar purpose. Jefferson's purchase of Louisiana and Seward's purchase of Alaska were both attacked as economically unsound and unnecessary. Public works during the Franklin Roosevelt administration came to serve purposes which many could claim were economically unsound and which did indeed go beyond the inducement of economic recovery, entering the realm of project planning for general public improvement. The "bold strokes" of administrative history, whether in wartime or peacetime, have often been taken against the advice of economists or advisers intent upon other aims and purposes. The current debate over the proper line to draw between National Defense and a sound economy illustrates the difficulty in distinguishing planning for national purposes from economic planning.

Economic planning in its various forms from Hamiltonianism to Socialism places its emphasis upon the relation between present material resources and future possibilities for an expansion of their use. TVA was one of the more dramatic instances of such planning in the New Deal era; but it joined a tradition of debate which included canals and some earlier "public improvements," as well as the controversial relation between public lands and the early days of the railroad. For rationalization, such projects may depend upon a belief in some "system" which rests on a base in economic doctrine.

Intensely realistic in its view of such resources, economic planning bases its arguments upon a current economic dogma, ignoring if necessary popular political advice and acting as a brake upon supposedly wild, imaginative, but impractical schemes. The objective and "mathematical" nature of economic doctrine gives to such planning arguments an impressively "nonpolitical," "natural," "scientific," or "realistic" cast, depending upon current sanctions being posed by students of economics. If the occasional lack of optimistic idealism and the limitations upon future dreams seem in some respects impressive, the security which can come from the dependence upon familiar behavior tends to make up for the absence of imagination during periods when the desire for such security runs high.

From the point of view of personnel, the idea of planning assumes a form quite different from those described above. Policy planning depends upon some concept of national purpose or goal beyond the objective calculation of material needs. Economic planning depends upon a theory of the structure of economics, either implicit or explicit, as the basic source of the good life, the ideal society. Planning controlled by a concept of personnel depends entirely upon individual minds and hence assumes different proportions as ideas of what might be called the governing individual change. There seem to have been, however, two basic types. Theories of democracy which prescribe the active participation of each individual as a fundamental requirement make government planning dependent upon a general, public will expressed in direct, individual action. Planning is thus immediately tied to whatever the people want. In representative democracy this approach can take forms varying from such ideas as initiative and referendum to publicly elected committees of citizens or radical doctrines of constant rotation of all public offices. Benthamite doctrines of participation, like Jacksonian arguments for broader public control through electoral reforms, share with modern movements to "get out the vote" and to encourage participation in local government a dependence upon individual action as a base for democratic government.

The same emphasis upon individual personnel can be found, at the other extreme, in elitist theories which direct themselves to the search for special talents. This can range from qualifications presumed either to be transmitted by birth or race or to be learned in the study of special fields or through experience in special occupations. In such theories planning is determined by particular knowledge or particular powers possessed by certain individuals whose access to public office in democratic society is expected to be by appointment, by merit examination, or such devices. This point of view was as familiar to men of John Adams' generation who looked to property qualification as assurance of public fitness as it is to the generation of modern scientists and technicians who seek similar assurance in academic degrees or other certification of specialized knowledge.

Either concern with personnel can in fact be closely tied to concepts of purpose or of economics, but arguments called to their support tend to center on the individuals or group of individuals involved. The great difficulty of planning centered on personnel is its lack of centralized direction as it shades toward radical democracy or its lack of public support when, in an effort to be more efficient, it shades toward elitism. There is no assurance that public will is being properly read by those to whom it has been delegated, and finding agreement among "expert" opinion as a means of reaching decision is no less difficult.

Such forms of planning are as characteristic of the spoils aspect of Jacksonian democracy as they are of the Civil Service reform groups which arose in answer to it. One can find them in the dependence upon public opinion polls, election statistics, and analysis of voting behavior or in the reliance upon committees, expressions of interest groups, cabinets, or professional representatives. Personnel planning, the hardest of the three types of planning to define, is at the heart of liberal democratic government because it is the definition of government as an occupation in which people are engaged for their own good, regardless of the inevitable generalities expressed in terms of national goals, public purposes, or the science of wealth and its distribution.

That all three forms of planning, policy, personnel, and economic, were functions of one another and essentially inseparable was obvious to anyone who found that, in his responsible involvement in one, he was in fact manipulating the others. Yet it is also clear that three separate points of view could be involved in choosing one of the three elements rather than another as a fundamental commitment in the formulation of a role as chief executive in American government. It has been from the standpoint of such attitudes and their reflection in the uses to which the traditional machinery of executive government has been put that each chief executive has reorganized his own presidency. His own attitude toward the office, toward his cabinet, toward the Congress, and toward the problems he faced has tended to govern the operation and control of his office. Today, despite the development of the Bureau of the Budget, the various councils dispensing economic advice, and the boards governing national economic practice in money and banking, the President of the United States can gather information and ideas for the formulation of economic policy from whatever sources he deems reliable and exercise his powers accordingly. He can listen to the Director of the Budget, the Secretary of the Treasury, or the Department of Economics at Harvard. He can ignore them all and give sole ear to the Pentagon, the Congress, or the pollsters. Whatever he does and whatever consequences it has for policies of government, his choices and the habits they reflect make his presidency what it is.

II

From his oval office in the low "business" wing of the White House the President of the United States can look out across the rose garden to the obelisk which memorializes the first man to hold the position from which his authority descends. That the monument to George Washington should continue to dominate the landscape of the city which also bears his name is in some ways much more than simply a matter of tribute. It is a constant reaffirmation of a historic fact. Having presided over the convention which created the executive of the new government and having sworn to uphold the Constitution which guaranteed it, Washington spent the next eight years carving a practical, workable federal office out of the amorphous instructions issued him by that Constitution and implied by the debates which had preceded it.

For Washington as for many of his contemporaries the success of the new government in its role as Exhibit A of the democratic experiment lay less in the principles it embodied, more in the fact that self-government could be made to work. To this end he sought practical compromises, broader standards by which to measure disagreement, and long-range solutions to immediate problems. The explosive debate between Jefferson and Hamilton could not obscure the fact that over and above the doctrines to which the two sought adherence stood the President, either unable or unwilling to see the sharpness of the opposition as clearly as they saw it, but nonetheless attempting to make use of good minds in open dispute in the practical execution of his office. From the beginning the presidency was a pragmatic position midway between the bright new drama of democratic liberalism and the older, harsher facts of political life.

It was not easy to define the functions of an executive to a nation for whom George III and his royal governors were among the most recent examples of executive authority. Despite the practical assumption that the office would have some kind of attendant organization, it would be a long time before presidential moves in that direction would cease raising cries of "monarchy." Washington, who had presumably listened to the convention's debates over the question of advisers to the executive—some wanting a council constitutionally defined, others wanting a committee of the Congress to function as an advisory board—took over the departments left by the Articles of Confederation and constituted their heads as his cabinet. But the convention had apparently left him somewhat confused on his own relation to the legislature.

The delegates had begun with a majority in agreement that the President be an appointee of the National Legislature. But their fervent desire that the executive be independent of the legislature had turned them ultimately to the scheme finally expounded in the Constitution itself. Yet the interdependence of the two parts of government, only vaguely defined, seemed also to have been an assumption by those who mistrusted executives as well as by those who were doubtful of the supreme authority of legislatures. Washington discovered relatively early in his career as President that Congress could guard its prerogatives as jealously from him as he would be forced to do from them. Whatever the intended nature of their interdependence, it was clear by the end of his two administrations that it was bounded by a mutual distrust.

Ambiguities in the location of the power to organize the executive departments were the result of what seems to have been a deliberate intent of the framers of the Constitution. The independence of the executive and the legislature from one another was accompanied by controls which gave to each an important hand in functions specifically assigned to the other. The President was authorized to propose legislation and to veto it, the legislature to approve executive appointments and provide funds for executive activities. The system of "checks and balances," so-called, was not constructed as a violation of independence but as a protection of it, as assurance that the activities of each branch of government would be independent not only of the other branches but of such other internal and external influence as might interfere with the proper functioning of government. In some ways the strength of the new government lay in the fears it sought to allay rather than in the positive benefits it strove to confer. These were men more experienced in the definitions of tyranny than in explanations of "the blessings of liberty." Executives could be tyrants; legislatures could become mobs. Either way, protection was requisite.

The difference in point of view, however, would have profound and lasting effect on the question of the organization of the executive branch of the government. From the executive point of view, efficiency and responsibility were individual, indivisible, and undelegable. The convention had settled on the unitary executive for precisely that reason. While Congress tended for the most part to agree, it sought to define efficiency and responsibility by its power of concurrence in appointments and its distribution of funds. The first, appointments, would provide the earliest and the most constant battleground for the presidency. Presidents from Washington on failed to see why they should be forced to include in their governments men with whose opinions they did not agree or whom they knew to be in disagreement with announced administration policy. From time to time Congress, through its belief in the inviolability of its concurring powers, saw otherwise. The development of parties, the problems of political patronage, the zeal for Civil Service reform, and latter-day concerns with party responsibility would all stem from disagreements over the relation between executive personnel and executive policy.

Financial disputes during the early history of the government were moderated, and at times obscured, by Alexander Hamilton's habits of politics as Secretary of the Treasury. His close relationships with Congress established his office as a particularly troublesome one where problems of executive independence were concerned; but the practice did smooth paths of compromise over questions of banking and tariff policy by assuring the legislature that it did indeed have control over the purse. Andrew Jackson's refusal to allow such practices to be carried on during his administration brought him a vote of censure but established the point about which the Constitution had been unclear: that even where financial matters were concerned, the executive branch had to be independent of the legislative. Members of the constitutional convention, sensitive anyway to problems of taxation, had not been able to clarify their various opinions concerning the appropriate cost of government. The salaries of those who governed had been a traditional leash by which the legislature could control its governors; but to couple such a method with the belief in the necessity of an independent executive was no easy matter. Ben Franklin, in typically unconscious self-caricature, had argued in the convention that there should be no salaries at all in the national government. To prevent dishonesty and greed, one could root out the absolute source absolutely. From such a beginning the argument over the cost of government and legislative control over it could move any distance in any direction.

The Congressional view of executive organization centered frequently around the question of its cost, and the executive tended for the most part to agree, differing only, but importantly, on what constituted a necessary service and a justifiable expenditure. More fundamental disagreement, however, lay in the Congressional view of the executive as the responsible executor of Congressional policy. In the theories of some, if Congress represented the public will and the presidency reflected it, then disagreements between them would have to indicate a misconception by one of them of the public will. In times of crisis each could point accusingly at the other.

Constant argument of a less arousing, ultimately routine variety hung on the Constitutional injunction to the President that he provide the Congress with information and recommendations concerning legislation. That Congress enunciated its intention of formulating its own policies independent of President Washington and his advisers, and that the executive continued to look upon itself as a policy-making branch regardless of Congress's prerogatives left much room for disagreement, even before the more clearly cut oppositions of political parties had developed.

From the beginning, then, there existed a basic difference of point of view, executive and legislative, on the three major areas of governmental administration. Two of them, policy and personnel, had been obviously left open to interpretation by the constitutional convention. The executive and the legislature shared the burdens involved in the formulation of policy and the appointment of responsible officials for executing it, but the practical expression of their joint custody of these two functions left much room for dispute. The third area of administration, fiscal management, was placed squarely in the hands of the House of Representatives. It became clearer and clearer as time went on that the legislature could hold the strings of the purse, but the purse itself was an executive property in practice and might have to become more so, ultimately, in law. To have drawn the lines more sharply at the beginning would have been difficult and unrealistic.

Given the unresolved questions with which it began, George Washington's administration seems part genius, very lucky, and often miraculous. Surrounded by doctrines and disputes both within and without his official family, with little in the way of positive direction and much in the way of suspicion and incipient opposition, Washington dedicated himself to making the new machine work. He watched many of his assumptions about the meaning of the Constitution overturned by his experiences in office; but he accepted such disagreements in practical terms, not as threats to his image of government but as indications of his responsibility for providing other routes of necessary action. The government was new. Its only models existed in the complex blueprints of theorists and philosophers. Its continuing existence was its greatest test, not its capacity for strict adherence to the patterns out of which it had been constructed.

Eight years of the country's first administration could not resolve conflicts in point of view so central to political disagreements already established in the country's colonial history. But during these new years habits of dealing with traditional disputes in new forms were justified within the framework of the Constitution, backed by the prestige and authority of the first President. Thereafter it would be the interpretation of the office rather than its proper and ideal constitutional structure which would raise argument. Washington established the office beyond the need for further constitutional revolution, but in so doing he embodied a kind of revolution within the nature of the office itself. Presidents of the United States would continue to seek advice from sources which would continue to be extraconstitutional and issue commands in ways partly statutory as an execution of legislation and partly purely executive. Yet each executive would have to define his own use of the administrative tools available to him by law and by tradition and each executive would after his own fashion and in accordance with his own needs and the needs of his time reorganize the executive branch of the government. In a broad sense, the organization of executive government would become the basis of the issues developed every four years, for the functions appropriate to the executive would continue under a variety of names to be variable, debatable to say the least, and at times the signal of another of America's peculiarly systematic revolutions.

In the light of the foregoing discussion the history of the organization and reorganization of the American presidency can be seen to have assumed a dual nature: first, there is the image of himself as President which every man takes with him to the office. Carved out of political debate, out of his own personal executive experience, out of his belief that he was elected by the people to *do* something or to prevent something from being done, the image is essentially executive, directly responsible to the public which elected him, and framed in some variation of the traditional picture of the American president as the leader of his country. Definitions of that leadership can vary widely. They can depend upon different forms of what we have been calling "planning," either in its general or in one of its most specific senses. But the weakest of American presidents, by whatever standard one uses to qualify the term, has still had to run the executive branch of the government and accept responsibility for its operation.

Secondly, however, there is the relationship of the executive to other branches of the government, most notably the Congress, but occasionally the Supreme Court. The ambiguity of the dependence of Congress and the executive upon one another has contributed to a comparatively gentle but always important vacillation between a purely presidential and executive image of the office and the Congressional view of it as executive of public will expressed through and by the Congress. Few Congresses have ever completely or for long enforced their will on the President, the years between Johnson and Cleveland offering some of the best examples. And by the same token Presidents have rarely approached anything like freedom from the irritations of a questioning, probing Congress. War periods, of course, have been temporary if cautious examples, while the first hundred days of the New Deal are virtually unique. Thus the extremes between which presidential independence and Congressional control have moved are relatively narrow, given the length of time the institutions have existed and the trials they have faced. The existence of an independent executive and an independent Congress responsible to one another for the formulation and carrying out of national policy is a pragmatic institutionalization of the American desire both to preserve a faith in some kind of general will and to protect a classically liberal individualism and its imprescriptible rights of dissent.

Congress and the President shared a concern with the organization of the executive branch prior to the Civil War, with most of whatever steps were taken to reorganize shared between them. The Jacksonian intention of returning government to the people created some disturbances in organization which, by the 1830's, were studied by Congress in an equally

Jacksonian effort to simplify and make more economical the operations of government.[2] By the eve of the Civil War executive functioning had been narrowed sufficiently to place effective control in Congress of functions which, in later day analyses, would be considered primarily executive. The advent of the War brought the abrupt change which could be expected from such an emergency, with the President assuming powers considerably broader than ever before, in some respects broader than any President has since possessed; but in addition to the power of the President himself the War increased immensely the functions of executive government as a whole. The conduct of the War had necessitated a greater military establishment, to be sure; but the work of Reconstruction and the continuing problems of veterans' interests focused attention on the national capital at Washington as a growing center of executive authority.

In part the increase in executive authority was a natural outgrowth of the developing industrial nationalism, the existence of which had been painfully and ruthlessly revealed by the War. Thereafter the demands of a rapidly growing national industrial complex would work with ever-increasing energy to crush interference from outdated regional, localized interests. In the process both industry and local interest would look to Washington for encouragement and protection, recognizing in fact if not in principle that there lay the center of just, or at least uniform, solutions to the new problems brought about by the transition from an agricultural society to an industrial, urban community with complex forms of interdependence. With the idea of uniformity and generalization came the idea of management, now to be as applicable to problems of governing as it had begun to be to problems of industrial efficiency.

Management was in many respects a consequence of both industrialism and nationalism. The chief value of centralization rested on the increase in efficiency which it invariably seemed to bring to the growing urban and industrial chaos. But efficiency could also become identified with national purpose. The idea that human effort could be wasted when undirected and uncontrolled, while a direct violation of the liberalism which had rebelled against the public control of human effort, was central to the growing concern with efficiency, leadership, and planning. But fitting these concerns into the context of traditional liberalism was not an easy matter. Traditional liberalism depended upon a faith in the natural efficiency and ultimate utility of representative processes of government expressing public will. Public will was automatically efficient because it was public. Hence leadership resided with the people as a whole, not with heroes or specialists; and planning depended upon some generalized expression of public desire. The times which had justified such faiths were, by the end of the nineteenth century, history. But on these faiths and the values they bespoke depended the security of knowing that the future could be both "good" and efficient. Without these values, transmuted or transferred in some reliably acceptable form, American democracy, as distinguished from the already mutated European varieties, might be seriously endangered.

The European response to the problems raised by industrialization and urbanization had long been to toy with the propositions suggested by collectivized versions of democracy posed by various forms of social doctrine. Most such doctrines tended, from America's point of view, to be singular violations of the fundamentals of democracy; but the increasing recognition in America of the need for greater efficiency of government and of the uses of human and material resources led to the borrowing of elements from technical solutions to common problems as well as to an enormous amount of inventiveness of a purely indigenous sort. The purity of the original doctrines of American liberalism was preserved by the disavowal of any relation between new elements and new, alien doctrines. American technical mastery, its "know-how," came to be vociferously anti-doctrine and pragmatic, and woe to the technique which inadvertently became associated with any political doctrines save those directly or presumably traceable to the beliefs of a century past.

Men imbued with new doctrines looked with scorn on this

fundamentalism. Trained as many of them were in the schools and traditions of European higher education, they watched the fumblings of what seemed to them to be an intellectually backward society foolishly praying to plaster and tinsel gods whose powerlessness was amply proved by the poverty of the slums of the growing cities of the land. That the jeremiads of men like Veblen would serve as guides even to their own most bitter critics may well have seemed small reward for a lifetime of nourishment by little more than inner satisfaction.

Put in its simplest form, the public paradox was this: America's social inefficiency was rendering the country undemocratic by making possible the usurpation of public authority by unscrupulous individuals. But the cure broadly proposed, an increase in the effective power of government, was itself a violation of what was presumed to be an earlier, more fundamental democratic creed, the freedom of the individual from the coercion of government.

The fact that governmental power had been on the steady increase since the Civil War made the arguments somewhat academic and obscured for a time the real issue: that the question was not the presence of governmental power but its location and distribution.

Congress's first entry into the field of executive organization after the Civil War was much like its excursions in the 1840's. From 1869 to 1871 a Committee on Retrenchment under the chairmanship of Senator James W. Patterson looked to the abolishment of offices, the reduction of salaries and staff, and other matters similarly in justification of its name. In its investigations it was impressed by the scandals and frauds which inquiry into federal operations revealed. Its answer, in keeping perhaps with old Franklin's earlier advice, was to root out evil by depriving fraud of its nourishment—excess funds. Patterson's own involvement in Credit Mobilier ultimately brought him even closer to the troubles he was investigating.[3]

Senator George S. Boutwell's committee of 1875-1876 took the moneysaving approach, but became bogged down by details which, without the obvious heat generated by direct revelations of corruption, made any conclusive investigation meaningless.[4] A Senate resolution in 1880 brought another round of inconclusive and unanalyzable data to the Senate, resulting in again another useless, nit-picking report which momentarily relieved Congressional pressure but offered little in the way of help to the sprawling administration.[5]

Both the Patterson and Boutwell committees followed patterns familiar from their counterparts in municipal reform. The inextricability from one another of organization, expense, and corruption predetermined both the problems to be investigated and their insolubility. It was assumed throughout that there was an evil, moral and probably individual, to be searched out, identified by name, and destroyed. That the difficulty could possibly be more objective—at least in the sense of being unintended—and that it could be described as a continuing problem inherent in modern government was an idea which was forced to wait for later, almost belated revelation.

From 1887 to 1889 a Senate committee headed by Francis M. Cockrell investigated government operations using an interesting variation on the old techniques of collecting information presumed to be incriminating. The committee asked the departments for details of business methods rather than simply for random data or individual recommendations. With no staff to analyze the information the effort was in part a waste. But the committee did suggest that committees on reorganization be set up within the Treasury and War Departments, a token recognition of the growing awareness of the possibility that the Congress might not be the most productive agency for suggestions concerning executive reorganization.[6] Nonetheless, the important innovation here was the emphasis upon "methods" rather than a concentration upon data alone. The feeling that there existed business or technical procedures with which government needed to be familiar was developing in government itself, just as it was among men like Henry R. Towne and Frederick W. Taylor who were attempting to call the attention of their colleagues in engineering to many of the same elements.

The Dockery Commission, set up by Congress in 1893, was the last of the solo efforts by Congress to achieve economy and efficiency through reorganization effected by the legislative branch. Again the mountains of detail were collected; but this commission had produced a slightly better method of tabulation which did contribute more effective data for future analysts. Its own contributions as an administrative adviser, however, were no greater than those of its predecessors. Congress had proved the possibility of gathering endless reams of data on government operations, some of it even well organized, but it had not proved the efficacy of its labors. However well taken the need for more efficient executive management might be, the Congressional view, buttressed by increasingly objective, rational intention, was still too far from and too foreign to the practices and purposes of executive government.[7]

### III

Woodrow Wilson's early study of Congressional government in the United States seems in retrospect an excitingly perverse view of the problem. Its perversity lies in its surprising emphasis upon Congressional inefficiency at precisely the point in time when Congress was concentrating a good bit of its attention on executive inefficiency. By accepting the unstated Congressional preference for a weak executive, Wilson could take the position that an alternative in the form of an efficient parliamentary system was the only logical, indeed practical, answer. The exciting aspect of the thesis, however, from the vantage point of over half a century's distance, is the author's recognition of the fact that Congress stood at a crucial turning point in its own history. An executive was a necessary component of modern government, and the chances were he would have to be a strong one. Either Congress provided itself with the necessary means to accomplish the practical ends demanded by that fact, or it would have to recreate the presidency in a stronger image of its powers. Despite Wilson's advice but in keeping with its own traditions, Congress could not reconstitute itself an efficient executive body. Its recognition of the need took the form of investigations of the executive branch. What it continued to refuse to give was an explicit recognition of the independence of that branch not only from its constant control but from the specifics described in its well-intentioned advice.[8]

Theodore Roosevelt's appointment of a Committee on Executive Departments under the direction of Charles Hallam Keep was a milestone in executive organization and administration on several counts, the most important of which was its explicit recognition of the fact that executive reorganization was an executive responsibility. Equally important but considerably less central to the committee's work at the time was the fact that the continuation of the Congressional concern with economy and efficiency took new lines when approached from the executive point of view. Roosevelt was concerned as well with the competence of the administrative staff and the relation which such competence bore to salaries. In addition the dissemination of knowledge and scientific information was a key point in Roosevelt's charge to the commission and in the report it produced.[9] Economy and efficiency remained the basic emphases, to be sure, but there were clear signs that executive reorganization could become the vehicle for approaches to problems other than the purely fiscal. Executive concern with the quality of personnel and the efficacy of routes of knowledge and information in government had been added to the Congressional concern with costs.[10] Congress and the President had come to understand that something else beyond the attitudes and approaches which the legislature could see was involved in the idea of executive management. It was difficult to tell what that was; but certainly the presumption that individuals and the knowledge they might possess could share a status equal to that given to methods of doing business was an indication of possible directions.

President Taft's appointment of a Committee on Economy and Efficiency under Frederick A. Cleveland's direction was in part a direct outgrowth of possibilities opened up by the Keep Commission. Dr. Cleveland's position, described in the previous chapter, was clear. The emergence of what he called "the budget idea" as the new device for correcting inequities and inefficiencies in government gradually developed into the dominant point of contact between the executive, which now directed its own quest for improved organization, and the legislature, which would have to pass the necessary legislation to effect such reorganization. But here the difficulties which would occupy reorganization proponents for some time to come were gradually becoming clearer.

It had taken Congress almost half a century to recognize that the information relevant to reorganization of the executive and the suggestions regarding it would have to come from the executive branch itself if they were to be of any ultimate practical use. But reorganization of the executive was still, from Congress's point of view, to be accomplished only by legislative action. That the executive could be free both to propose and to dispose seemed well beyond the realm of possibility. To leave the President free to reorganize the executive branch of the government looked like a violation of some form of checks and balances, although it was difficult to say how this could actually be the case. Certainly with respect to the appointment of cabinet officers as department heads as well as in the case of other high executors of administrative policy, the "Advice and Consent" clause had, early in American history, been taken to mean that the executive was free to make his own choices within the broad limitations of Congressional review. Congress, however, chose not to apply the doctrine to other aspects of executive operation. Certainly where expenditures of funds were concerned the lines were more difficult to draw. Proponents of more effective executive authority could well have argued that increased responsibilities of the presidency brought about by the historical circumstances of an industrial society made it necessary that "advice and consent" be applied more generally to executive authority. Congress could not actively control all executive action by legislation and it had begun to admit it, even if at times it resented limitations which were both constitutional and practical. But the nature and extent of the "enabling" power necessary would become increasingly difficult to determine. Meanwhile it seemed easier to create new executive agencies to solve new problems and let their control depend upon opportunity.

Throughout the first phase of executive reorganization, 1879–1901, the emphasis had been upon Congressional legislation which could limit and possibly even rationalize the activities of the executive branch, thereby effecting economies, primarily, efficiencies, secondarily. In the second phase, 1901–1936, the emphasis was upon executive proposals which would result in legislation to produce economy and efficiency, again in that order. The results of the two phases were almost totally in the realm of "business" efficiency, a reorganization of accounting procedures to bring them in line with current business practices, and the introduction of a national budget in 1921. But here a difference was beginning clearly to emerge. Congress could feel secure, rightly or wrongly, in its capacity to supervise through adequate procedures of bookkeeping and accounting. Budgets were another matter, not only in the view of the Congress but in the minds of those who argued for them.

Woodrow Wilson had been forced to politic shrewdly to get a budget system past a Congress already quaking at its experiences with a strong, wartime President. But in March of 1921 Congress passed a budget act which made the Director of the Budget an appointee of the Congress. Wilson's veto of the bill was one of his last acts as President. In the early days of the Harding administration the act was repassed, giving the President the power to appoint the Director of the Budget. Even so, Congress continued to see executive management of economic matters as a problem requiring immediate congressional surveillance and direction at the same time that it was forced to admit that its own ends, whatever they were, could not be accomplished by the direction it wished to give. During the emergency of the first World War it had acknowledged its inability to direct efficient reorganization of governmental administration by giving to the President broad reorganizing and consolidating powers under the Overman Act of 1918; but such powers ended with the emergency. The importance of even a temporary grant lay in the recognition of the fact that when the cards were down, reorganization was fundamentally an executive responsibility. Congress could gather information and it could complain about what it found; but it could work out no way of acting which was practical, let alone constitutional.

Even in the palmy days of the twenties executive reorganization continued to play an important role. Under Presidents Harding, Coolidge, and Hoover executive proposals for more efficient and economic government were toyed with by the Congress and either rejected or ignored. The growing emergency of the depression won Hoover the power to reorganize by executive order—essentially the old Overman Act authority —but with the added feature that such orders could be vetoed by resolution of either house. All fifty-eight of the orders issued by Hoover in December of 1932 were vetoed thusly by the House on the ground that the incoming President ought to be allowed to effect his own reorganizations. At the beginning of March of 1933, just before leaving office, Mr. Hoover signed into law a renewal of this act. Earlier, the Attorney General had declared the veto provision unconstitutional on the ground that it gave a lawmaking power to one house of Congress exclusively. The authority now carried with it the condition that all orders lie before the Congress as a whole for sixty days while in session.

Such was the authority for reorganization which Franklin Roosevelt had when he took office, and he used it in the spirit in which it was intended both by President Hoover and by the Congress—as a means of cutting out overlap of functions as well as those which he considered unnecessary. It was an authority which he used initially under the advice of such men as Lewis Douglas and Raymond Moley and with recommendations from his Cabinet. But it was soon clear that the problems of reorganization would have to be postponed while piecemeal shots aimed at moneysaving would be used from time to time to maim if not to destroy some of the subsidiary functions of the existing system.[11]

As far as executive reorganization was concerned, the New Deal from 1932 to 1936 differed in no way from the major lines of a tradition of attitudes stretching back to the Civil War. The basic premises of that tradition were retained: that government was excessively large and sprawling, hence excessively expensive; that the rationalization of its structure would ultimately produce less government more economically and efficiently run. This was good business and good business was good government.

The fact that during these years reorganization continued in piecemeal fashion to pare, consolidate, and economize, presumably, without being formed along lines significant of some over-all approach was symptomatic of the greatest difficulty involved: that there seemed indeed to be no over-all approach which had emerged within the tradition itself. The federal tradition had depended upon two assumptions. First, the arguments over the division of responsibility between the President and the Congress assumed that ideally they could agree on effective organization and that the only real difference was which one could more effectively accomplish the agreed upon end. Secondly, there was the older assumption, both liberal and conservative, that the machinery of government properly structured and appropriately oiled was essentially self-regulating; that there was some one series of corrections which was "right" and which would return government to its proper place, whatever that was. Indeed, many of those who had been seeking and supporting moves toward the consolidation of executive power in state and city governments as the route to greater efficiency were opposed to any parallel in the federal executive. In many respects this seems to have been the basis for one level of agreement between Franklin Roosevelt and the Congress throughout most of the first term of the New Deal.

During 1935 and certainly by 1936 it was clear that something larger and more important than the correction of machinery and the application of oil could cope with what was happening to American government. While this may have been obvious much earlier to many of the advisers, technicians, and experts who made up the New Deal, it seems to have been an idea approached with much caution and a certain amount of inner misgiving by the President himself. The Supreme Court, however, forced the issue. In keeping with its traditional role as examiner of the constitutional principles of American government, the Court issued warnings in the form of disruptive and truculent denunciations of New Deal legislation. If one removes much of the debatable substance of the Court's decisions and concentrates only on the fact of its disagreement, the Court becomes less the nine "bad boys" of the New Deal, more the enunciator of the fact that change was taking place and that such change would have to be woven into the traditional fabric of government or dealt with as a revolution.

The traditions of over half a century were giving way to practices new to minds inured to older views. It was clear even to those who did not doubt either the necessity or the constitutionality of the practices that their disorganized, piecemeal relationship to American government as a whole, regardless of the doctrinal content which could be seen in them, constituted a serious threat to the future stability of that government. The Court said that such structures as the National Industrial Recovery Act were dangerously unconstitutional. Others, within and without the government, argued that they were dangerously disorganized. But the relationship between "organization" and "constitution" of government was no less tricky now than it had been all along.

In fact, however, the Court was not simply criticizing methods. Its declarations of the supposed unconstitutionality of New Deal legislation was a condemnation of much of the available methodology brought to bear on the crisis. Yet regardless of the questions which can be asked of the criteria which the Court used in stating its judgments, it was still raising a voice which needed to be raised. The first term of the New Deal and its emergency efforts were, in method at least, a continuation of the piecemeal practices which Congress had used since the Civil War and which had raised all of the basic issues of reorganization in the first place. But the futility of Congressional practices certainly did not justify turning the same methods over to the President. What Congress had been doing was, in part at least, relatively clear. Despite its periodic hesitancy over the strength of the Presidents of the United States, Congress had recognized the need for an executor of its will, particularly in the past half century as demands upon the federal government increased. What it had done was to use its legislative power to create an executive branch of the government which was only partly under the control of the executive designated by the people. Commissions, regulatory agencies, various agencies of administration, and ultimately heads of the departments themselves stood midway between the Congress which legislated their offices into existence and the President who appointed them. Concerned over the efficiency of this growing multiple executive, Congress had sought to maintain its independent control of the powers represented by the different groups; at the same time it testily delegated such authority, as a painfully practical experience came to demand, to the man constitutionally charged with executive power.

In the heat of the "hundred days" and in much of the legislation subsequent to the famous initial period of the New Deal, Congress relaxed its guard, as it had had to do for Wilson during the war, encouraging a direct leadership unprecedented in any peacetime period. But the difference between the physical threat of war and the large-scale social threat of a depression aroused a Court which could not see the depression as an emergency justifying such delegation of authority. More important was the implicit if confused recognition that a modern definition of the relation between Congress and the President had yet to be made. The Court may well have left itself open to the justified criticism that it was preserving as "constitutional" practices which were the traditions of little more than half a century. But in their desire to retrieve a miscalculated view of stability, they put the responsibility for justification squarely where it belonged, on the President.

While one cannot completely justify the Court's arrogantly negative and obstructionist view during a period of national emergency and the logic with which it supported its complaints, it is still possible to see in its actions the working out of a justifiably historic point of view, and, indeed, a service to a real and necessary purpose. By calling attention to the need for stabilizing government operation in a manner consistent with constitutional safeguards and national values it is possible that they were far more useful than they had intended to be. The Court and other opponents of the President insisted on seeing the chaos of experimental activity as a deliberate mask for sinister intentions; but in their own way the President and his associates had come to see it as a serious danger to the security and continuity of American government.

After fifty years of a successfully practical avoidance of the issue, the country was faced directly with a crisis in effective executive government. Theretofore the problem had been couched—indeed, concealed—in terms of the economy and efficiency of executive machinery. The emphasis upon fiscal policy as the basis of effective government rather than as simply one of its tools had been as much a basic belief of all of the Presidents of the period as it was now of Franklin Roosevelt. But the transition from that point of view to a new consideration of executive government was beginning to take place.

By the time Roosevelt appointed his Committee on Administrative Management in 1936 it was clear, if only by the personnel he chose, that the old lines of thought were being broken. Among the initial, significant decisions concerning the committee's work was the separation of the studies of departmental organization and overlap from the committee's expressed intention of concentrating on what it called "over-all top management." As significant as was the name of the committee itself, its view of its function expressed a new idea in the long history of executive reorganization. Despite Congress's insistence upon its own point of view over the years since 1901, the relation between executive management and executive reorganization had, since the Keep Commission, been moving slowly toward the foreground in discussions of the presidency. The President's Committee on Administrative Management put it squarely in the center of the stage.

IV

The change in Franklin Roosevelt's own attitude toward executive organization, occurring as it did toward the end of his first term, was another example of the peculiarly flexible processes of his own thinking. Despite his initial attitudes toward reorganization as President of the United States, he had, as Governor of New York, stood high among the proponents of the modern executive demanded by changing social problems. New York State had a history of executive reorganization going back to the Hughes administration and culminating in that of Roosevelt's immediate predecessor, Al Smith. Roosevelt himself had, as Governor, been forced to resort to the courts to defend his budget authority from legislative encroachment. He had studied the state executive reorganizations effected by Governor Lowden in Illinois—the nation's first major executive reorganization—and by Governor Byrd in Virginia. But like Byrd, who would become one of the major opponents of his proposals for reorganization of the presidency, Roosevelt's commitment to the tradition of economy and efficiency as joint, correlative terms which defined one another touched springs in his beliefs which went deeper than the political.

At some point during his first term Roosevelt came to separate the two ideas in the sense of recognizing the crucial nature of efficiency as a safeguard of democracy, regardless of cost. The process is impossible to trace beyond the obvious impact which the first years of the New Deal must have had upon him. The ceaseless activity, experimentation, responsibility, and with it all the carping voice of the Supreme Court could scarcely have been an unimpressive education. But even in his experience as Governor he had learned the weakness of arguing economy as the justification of reorganization, a lesson he transmitted to members of his presidential reorganization staff.[12] Still, during the campaign of 1932 he had castigated Hoover's presumed profligacy with the federal purse. And he had made the financially conservative Lewis Douglas his Budget Director. He had continued as President to look at reorganization through the eyes of those who saw in it a means of saving money, balancing the budget, and thereby giving security to the nation's economy. By 1936 this viewpoint had undergone drastic revision. What had happened?

Brownlow attributed the change to the effect of the experience of the New Deal itself, and from the standpoint of Roosevelt's essential pragmatism, his capacity not only to learn from experience but to insist that experience teach him, this is the clearest explanation. Through the first two years of the New Deal he was considerably more effective and even systematic in his organization of his administration than he was often given credit for being. He used an enlarged cabinet under a general secretary—Frank Walker, the first of the "assistant presidents"—until the institution got too large to work on the sort of "New England Town Meeting" plan which Roosevelt enjoyed. Like the press conference, it utilized his talents for communicating his views and intentions to an informal group at the same time that he extracted from it the information and varying opinions which he needed to test or to buttress his own. The failure of the constantly growing group to provide him with what he needed probably led to his experiment with another administrative system in 1935.[13]

The Emergency Relief Appropriation Act of that year gave to the President a lump sum which he had authority to administer. The system by which Roosevelt decided to govern this new shift in Congressional attitude toward executive expenditure came to be known to students of administration as the "five-ring circus." Under this scheme applications were to be sent to Frank Walker of the Division of Applications and Information. An Advisory Committee on Allotments under Secretary Ickes would examine them and advise the President. Harry Hopkins and the WPA were to coordinate execution of the work, while Secretary Morgenthau would set up disbursing and accounting facilities with control of funds for administrative expenses being managed by Budget Director Bell. Shocked at the fact that the circus worked, the professional administrators tended to attribute its peculiar effectiveness to the fact that Roosevelt was running it and that it involved no real delegation of his authority. Certainly given the contact into which it threw some of the touchiest and most controversial figures of the New Deal, its operation was a tribute to the individual skill and energy of the President and the devotion of those who served him.

Nonetheless, the "five-ring circus" had some interesting lessons to teach. First, it demonstrated the growing dependence of the President on official staff other than cabinet members (whose departmental duties were already sufficient to occupy them fully) working exceedingly close to the President's own sphere of daily operation. Ideally speaking they executed the President's will without possessing direct authority of their own; but it was difficult to say where the line was to be drawn. Cabinet members who felt that their own territory was being invaded resented what seemed to them to be interposition. Such a staff had existed on various levels and in many forms from the beginning of the New Deal; and Roosevelt had, even before his election to the presidency, shown a predilection for flexible, informal, semi-social groups acting as little "families" whose personnel changed with needs or even whims. It was a technique of administration which defied charting in any systematic fashion; but its personal nature does not mitigate its status as a technique. The "five-ring circus" gave more definite form to the technique than it had had before by intermixing cabinet officials with other administrators without making the group a formal committee of the Cabinet.

Secondly, the system recognized that lump sum appropriations could underline, as few other things had done, the weaknesses of the executive with respect to the management and control of expenditures. Congress had made the appropriation in this form because it seemed to be willing, at least for the moment, to recognize the fact that it could not administer and control so complex an operation as federal relief. But there was some question at first as to whether or not the executive could do so either, given the inadequate machinery in his possession. Roosevelt's system, regardless of its weaknesses, was an attempt to deal with the problem.

Finally, and in part as a result of questions raised by the recognition of the above problem, the system called the attention of the President to those who had been suggesting that the emergency agencies had to be absorbed into the existing executive framework, regardless of the length of time they were supposed to exist. Whatever offense this may have been to those who viewed emergency measures as temporary accretions to be dropped as soon as conditions permitted, some form of absorption could meet a very practical question by placing agencies within the purview of budget and accounting procedures already in existence. Despite the problems inherent in the fiscal machinery as it stood, a continued development of governments within governments could only lead to a dangerous chaos over which the President would have no control whatsoever.

By such outlines one can document some of the circumstances

which led to the President's change in point of view regarding the question of reorganization, from economy and efficiency as it had always been argued to problems of over-all top management. But it is quite likely that for Roosevelt the switch was far less dramatic than it seemed to those who had watched the administrative directions of the earlier years. Roosevelt in changing attitudes did not attach to them firm commitments to systematic ideologies concerning the functions of government, as those who now found themselves advising him would discover. For him it was primarily a practical problem. During the 1932 campaign he had written to Anne O'Hare McCormick, "The Presidency is not merely an administrative office. That's the least of it. It is more than an engineering job, efficient or inefficient. It is pre-eminently a place of moral leadership." [14] By 1936, following the November elections, he could tell the newspaper reporters quite frankly that his opponents had failed to touch upon the weakest spot in the New Deal, "administration." [15]

The transition from one definition of administration to another was accompanied by the adoption of new advisers when prophets of previous positions were dropped. But the transition was smooth, a fact facilitated by the presence within the administration itself of proponents of alternative attitudes. Here again Roosevelt's unwillingness to allow doctrinal dispute to alienate his trust in a personality worked to bring into active service within the administration opponents and proponents of many positions. In this case the important elements were working in and through the Public Works Administration whose chief, Harold Ickes, was the center if not the source, of many of the New Deal's most dedicated oppositions and devout faiths. While Ickes may not have been the originator of the new ideas, his willingness to entertain them gave them an earlier, more effective role in the New Deal than they otherwise might have been able to obtain. [16]

In 1933, prior to the passage of the NIRA of that year but during its planning stages, the President had asked General

Hugh Johnson to head the endeavor. Johnson took on the industrial aspect of the plan himself, but turned the public works end over to Colonel George R. Spalding of the Corps of Engineers, who asked the American Society of Civil Engineers for help in planning a program. Colonel Henry M. Waite, engineer and former city manager of Dayton, Ohio, was one of those who answered the call. Louis Brownlow was called in to provide contact, from his vantage point as Director of the Public Administration Clearing House, with organizations in state and local government. By the time the Act was passed, tentative organizations had been established in each of the states to bring qualified engineers into the program.

Roosevelt's decision to separate the industrial title of the Act from the public works title and place the two under separate committees of the Cabinet gave Johnson almost total control over the industrial section and turned public works over to Harold Ickes. Ickes, apparently knowing nothing of the plans already established by Waite, Brownlow, and the engineers, called Charles Merriam in Chicago for a recommendation of someone to handle public works. Merriam referred Ickes to Brownlow who recommended Waite and thus brought the group already organized to Ickes' attention.

The public works aspect of national recovery posed problems which were in some respects different from those envisioned by its original proponents. To be sure, it could stimulate the economy through government spending, as the economists thought it would. And for those concerned with the social and psychological effects of relief and "dole" it provided useful, respectable work for citizens seeking livelihoods rather than charity. But above and beyond these functions was the fact that the "works" were "things," presumably useful and purposeful whether or not the economy was spurred and people put to work. Roads had to go where people wanted to go, just as bridges had to cross rivers with some intelligible utility. Schoolhouses and post offices had to be built with a view to their functioning long after immediate emergencies were over.

As requests poured into Washington for a road here, a school-house there, a bridge somewhere else, it became clear that the complex of motives could produce chaos and waste if left un-directed. A rationality would have to be provided to give logic to the relationship of needs to one another, to balance the relief function of public works against local and general economic needs, as well as against the functions of the works themselves. There was no point sacrificing future needs for the satisfaction of immediate demands. What was required was planning, yet it would not be easy to find plans that would please economists, local governments, and Congressional politicians, let alone the engineers who would have to execute them.

Brownlow's role as consultant to or informal representative of such a large number of the groups involved in public works gave him an importantly catalytic position in the events which followed. When Ickes asked his advice, he recommended the establishment of a planning committee for public works. Asked whom he would suggest for such a committee, Brownlow by-passed the dedicated particular interests and chose three men who placed planning in a separate, over-all category, Frederick Delano, whom Ickes had known as head of the Chicago Region-al Planning Association (and an uncle, incidentally, of the President), Charles Merriam, an old and respected friend of the Secretary, and Wesley C. Mitchell, the only one with whom Ickes was not acquainted. His presence on the list reveals part of the intention behind Brownlow's recommendation. Merriam and Mitchell had just finished their work on President Hoover's Research Committee on Social Trends. That report had sug-gested the urgent necessity for more governmental planning, in line, perhaps, with its general conception of its own functions.

Ickes' concurrence in these suggestions broadened the scope of public works importantly, gave a new place to planning within an agency of the government, and provided the possi-bility for important utilizations of a kind of planning which was not specifically oriented toward either the budget or toward such specific interests as transportation, conservation and natural resources, or industry. A generalized concept of over-all planning such as that reflected in *Recent Social Trends* and represented in part by such organizations as PACH and the Social Science Research Council looked to the gathering and the interchange of specialized knowledge and specific techniques in an effort not only to produce new effects through the cross-fertilization of ideas but also to arrive at a broader understanding of needs and purposes.

Brownlow's choice of such interested and knowledgeable men for the job would not in itself have been sufficient had he not also been aware of the particular problems posed by Ickes' habits of administration. Ickes knew Merriam and Delano. Merriam, like Ickes, had been one of the early members of the Progressive party, although Ickes' Republicanism was of a steadier sort. Ickes trusted Merriam and Brownlow. For a congenitally suspicious man, this was an advantage of the highest order. Merriam and Brownlow together operated to manipulate Ickes into more useful administrative attitudes than his personality sometimes permitted; but most important of all, Ickes' respect for Merriam gave the latter an independence in the Ickes' camp which few others would have been allowed.

The original National Planning Board became a truly effective device for bringing the agencies which had developed outside the federal government into useful relationships with federal problems. The existence of rational groupings of national organizations which dealt with local governmental problems and which could unify and generalize knowledge and information about those problems provided the needed logical channels through which an intelligent examination of public works could move. Without such ready-made instruments, the New Deal effort would have been considerably slower and possibly even unsuccessful in its attempts to cope with the nation's anguished cries for help. The indications of democratic society's capacity to help itself efficiently came from the fact that the means existed prior to the urgency, that such means had been developing all along. When in 1936 the President began to look for new definitions of efficiency he had the individuals with whom and the institutions through which to discover them for himself.

v

The seeds for a new kind of study of executive organization were planted by the advisory committee of the National Planning Board in November of 1933. The idea was discussed originally under the rubric of planning, but planning of a rather new variety. The committee separated into three groups for purposes of pursuing different contributions to the idea. Delano and the Secretary of the Board, Charles W. Eliot 2nd, undertook to study physical public works planning as such. Mitchell proposed to examine economic planning, and Merriam investigated what he called a scheme for a "governmental and political plan." Merriam's project came to be known as "the plan for a plan" and in 1934 he prepared an essay entitled "A Plan for Planning," which accompanied the final report of the National Planning Board on the eve of its becoming the National Resources Committee, a change which signified, among other things, the President's increasing interest in its work.[17]

During the spring and summer of 1935 as committee meetings in the White House brought Merriam and the President into constant contact, Roosevelt began to express curiosity about Merriam's view of a broader concept of planning and its relation to the presidency. He asked Merriam to prepare a memorandum on the subject. The memorandum, written by Merriam in consultation with Brownlow, opened with the statement: "One of the greatest assets of America is that of executive skills, sometimes developed in industry, sometimes in education and engineering, sometimes in the domain of government. The city manager, the large-scale industrial executive, the national executive officer, are examples of leadership which have justly attracted attention everywhere."[18] In that memorandum the basic statement of planning as a guide to governmental and political policy, distinguished from problems of personnel and budget—indeed well above them—was set forth.

Merriam envisioned a historic study of "trends," going back in time to the Civil War. For the actual carrying out of the study he recommended the Committee on Public Administration of the Social Science Research Council. That committee had been established in 1928 with Leonard White as its chairman. White had been succeeded by Luther Gulick, and Gulick by Brownlow in 1934. In suggesting the committee as a center for a study of the executive, Merriam was aware of the interest which the committee had already shown in research problems in public administration as well as in its conduct of such investigations as its Commission of Inquiry on Public Service Personnel. The latter, which *Recent Social Trends* had recommended in 1933, included Merriam and Brownlow, with Luther Gulick as its director of research. Its report, published in 1935, revitalized standards of investigation into civil service practices, shifting focus from the reform arguments and techniques of a previous era to studies of professional status and educational needs. The committee was as logical a place outside of government for Roosevelt to look for advice as the SSRC as a whole had been for Hoover's examination of social trends.

Delano and Merriam discussed with the President the possibilities represented by Merriam's plan in November of 1935, and Merriam reported to Brownlow that the President was very much interested in the whole idea. But the President added that he also felt that a study ought to be made of the possibilities of reorganization of the several departments, commissions, and agencies of the federal government; and that such a study, too, should probably be undertaken by the Public Administration Committee of the SSRC.

Roosevelt's linking of the administrative study with the reorganization study was the first meeting of the two camps at the level of the White House itself. It is probably the first direct reference by the President—or any President—to the idea that a study of the presidency was a two-fold task, one involving over-all, top management, the other dealing with the older, indeed the traditional, notion of executive reorganization.

Members of the Merriam-Brownlow camp had not tended to entertain for any length of time the possibility of an old-fashioned reorganization study. They were essentially in agreement with Lewis Meriam of the Brookings Institution who wrote in a memorandum prepared for Merriam in October of 1935: "To some observers of public administration in the United States such a study seems infinitely more promising than any new study of the reorganization of the administrative departments because reorganization is static whereas Presidential control of the administrative departments must be dynamic." [19] Yet, despite the virtual agreement among the "observers of public administration" there were those among the older remnants of reform who tended to look upon the problem differently.

The President continued to express interest in the idea through the remainder of 1935, although without committing himself to a special date, or even the promise of when such a date might be announced. The Public Administration Committee of the SSRC continued to plan, but maintained its insistence, first voiced to the committee by Lindsay Rogers, that its work would not effectively begin until and unless it received a specific request from the President. This had been the procedure with the appointment of the Recent Social Trends group and had particular meaning in the present instance because the absence of such a request would obviously cripple the committee's efforts at inquiry. But the statement from the President was not forthcoming.

The President's decision early in 1936 to order a study made, but not to request it of the SSRC, was to some a surprise which was nonetheless based upon some interesting points. First, he felt that it would be politically inexpedient to have such a study financed by anyone connected with the name Rockefeller. He thought that Congressional and general public reaction to this might be severe. Secondly, he had serious doubts about the use of an organization outside both the executive in particular and the government as a whole. Such an organization could issue a report which would be in disagreement with his own views. By so doing the organization could raise more debate, solve no problems, and put him in a needlessly defensive position. A committee appointed by him and financed by him would be subject to his approval.

Merriam argued against both of these points. He had himself contributed greatly to the useful development of the Spelman Fund and the Rockefeller Foundation as aids to local and state governments in the solution of public problems. More important, however, was the second point. The President's response here touched upon the objectivity of social science in relation to political control, and to many minds it might have hinted at the fundamental question of academic freedom since it placed academic research completely at the disposal of political ends. Merriam's willingness finally to agree to the President's reversal of position reveals to some degree Merriam's own views about these questions. It also serves to indicate in advance some aspects of the nature of the report produced by the President's Committee on Administrative Management. More important for the moment it revealed an important difference between Hoover's approach to science and politics and that of Franklin Roosevelt. For by requesting these products of knowledge and research, Roosevelt was committing himself deliberately to a course of action, but one which he could control.

The difference in the two points of view—Hoover's and Roosevelt's and, indeed, Merriam's and Roosevelt's—indicates the major transition which the President's Committee on Administrative Management represented. Hoover had appointed the Committee on Recent Social Trends as an objective, external voice of social scientists examining the society of which they were members. He did nothing to hamper their actions or restrict their findings. At the same time, he was totally uncommitted to the use of their opinions and committed only to the extent of responsibility for their appointment but not to agreement with their conclusions. He had requested advice. They gave it. He was presumably as free to respond to it—or not to respond—as he was to the advice of any individual or group. This was a viewpoint which Merriam had shared and, to some extent, encouraged as the function of an advisory committee. It was a viewpoint characteristic of the distinction between politics and administration as well as between politics and political science held by members both of the older political science and the newer administrative professions.

By choosing to commit himself at the beginning, in effect, to the conclusions of his Committee on Administrative Management, Roosevelt both drew more sharply than ever the line between politics and political science and obscured it. For he was admitting that he could not commit himself as a politician to objective conclusions before he had had an opportunity to examine them and test his agreement with them, at the same time that he was admitting the need of the advice of the community of social scientists for purposes of running his government. The refusal to commit himself in advance to unknown conclusions marked a difference, crucial in the extreme, between the conclusions of the politician and those of the social scientist. But the recognition of and selection of the community of social science as the center of the best advice was a request to that community that, in the interests of politics, it enter the arena of government but divested, temporarily of course, of its traditional commitment to objectivity. For some, as we shall see, this proved to be a request which would have been rejected—had they understood it at the beginning.

Brownlow was asked to sketch a memorandum for the President, giving his ideas of what such a study would include. Brownlow's outline, produced on hotel stationery, formed the basic plan which eventuated in the report.

Several weeks later, Brownlow was approached by Senator Harry Byrd and asked to head a study of government reorganization for the Senate Committee of which Byrd was chairman. It was clear from Byrd's description that he had in mind an examination of duplication and overlap. Brownlow explained to him his tentative commitment to a study for the

President, but one which would not be likely to conflict with that to be undertaken by the Senate.

The official announcement on March 22, 1936, of the appointment by the President of a Committee on Administrative Management had behind it a series of attempts to smooth pathways of potential dispute. These are worth setting out because they form, in the light of the history of debates over reorganization, a particularly interesting list.

First, the President had previously written to the Senate and the House telling them of his intentions to appoint such a committee and suggesting that they appoint groups to conduct similar investigations. The letters, drafted by Brownlow, were intended to prevent the appearance that the President's reorganization hand, so to speak, had been forced by Senator Byrd's plans, or that the President and the Senate might be seeking to by-pass the House and Representative Buchanan's Committee on Appropriations. It was important to the President that executive initiative in the matter be clear.

Secondly, in an effort to achieve some unity in the work of the three groups, Presidential, Senate, and House committees, it was initially planned that Brownlow would serve as head of advisory committees for all three. Representative Buchanan saw no difficulty in it, but the Senate Committee ultimately came to find the work of the Brookings Institution more in keeping with its own interests. This was important because it succeeded in reinforcing the distinction between executive and congressional views on reorganization.

Thirdly, although the President's committee was quite literally the President's, the research staff of the committee was chosen from among the same or similar groups as would have been involved in the original study proposed by Merriam to be conducted under the auspices of the social scientists of the SSRC. The initial presumption of joint involvement by the Brookings Institution was predicated upon that group's undertaking the separate studies of the departments, originally conceived as an important and useful adjunct to the committee's report. As an SSRC venture the two were to be coordinated; but while such coordination was originally planned by the President's committee, it disappeared without anyone quite knowing why. While it is difficult to say why this happened, it was important. The closeness with which the three members of the President's committee worked with the President after the November elections and before the submission of the report; the President's objection to outside agencies and his awareness of the political nature of the report; the possible proclivities of some of the Brookings' people for the economy and efficiency tradition more in keeping with congressional concerns—all tended toward a division of responsibility, interest, and ultimately, conclusion. There was even indication, as we will see in the next chapter, of a tendency of the committee to separate itself at times from its own staff; this was as much necessitated by the committee's particular interests as by the President's original assumption that the community of social scientists would not be fully in agreement—let alone unanimous —about its suggestions and advice.

The letter which was sent to the three committee members was drafted for the President in the Comptroller General's Office. To say the very least, it failed to express Roosevelt's ideas, but despite some annoyance he sent it along anyway. Still, it illustrated a rather strong difference of opinion on the subject of reorganization and served as an additional prophecy of dispute by informing the committee that its function was "to make a study of the relation of the existing regular organizations of the Executive Branch of the Government, of the many new agencies which have been created during the emergency." It concluded: "Some of these agencies doubtless will be dropped or greatly curtailed, while others may have to be fitted into the permanent organization of the Executive Branch." [20]

Regardless of portents, the President now had his Committee on Administrative Management. It included a representative of the tradition of American academic interest in the conduct of government, Charles Merriam; a representative of the professions of public administration, Louis Brownlow; and a representative of the study of economy and efficiency modernized in budget reform, Luther Gulick; all three representatives of the ideas embodied in a long tradition of continual social reformation. But the three, despite their commitments to the fields in which they were educated, turned their attention to the larger interest which unified both the histories of their own endeavors and that of the man in whose service they found themselves, as well as—most important of all—that of the office they had been selected to review. Franklin Roosevelt, like so many of his predecessors, had determined to examine the ground on which he stood to make certain that it would bear the weight of generations of Presidents to come. That it would also, for a time, have to bear his own raised questions as old as the office itself.

OLD AND NEW

*The Battleground*

I

THE PROPOSAL for a study of executive reorganization attracted to Washington a group the like of which had not been
seen since the meetings of the Social Trends Committee. The
staff of the new group included some of the most brilliant
academic minds of the twenties and thirties as well as many
younger men who would, over the next decades, assume equal
prominence. This is not to deny the obvious impact which the
academic community had already had on the New Deal but
rather to point to a difference of some importance. Men like
Tugwell and Moley forsook the academy for administrative
responsibilities in government, to be sure, but in doing so they
had become administrators, giving up the academic community
as well as its methods and approaches to the study of governmental life. They sat at desks in offices giving commands, not
in libraries engaged in research. They were public servants who
had been academics.

Those men who were invited to Washington to study the
executive branch were invited in their capacity as academics,
as men trained in the avenues of research and methodical
analysis. Like the Social Trends group, they were asked to
apply the standards and experience of their special fields of
study to problems of government. The Social Trends Committee, however, had been planned from the beginning as a
public voice which would, at the end of its labors, speak its
opinions not only to the President who had appointed it but to

the public at large. Had the original plan for the new study to be undertaken by the Social Science Research Council gone into effect, the study of the presidency would have concluded, one assumes, with a similar public presentation.

Roosevelt's decision to support the committee's work himself cast an entirely different light on its ultimate function, although not on its personnel. The decision, however, raised questions which the committee's work could not answer. For as academics the staff members were being called upon to engage in research—as their predecessors on Social Trends had done—but also to make, certainly by implication, a commitment to the policies of the administration as their colleagues in government had done. The mid-position between academic independence and political commitment was for some no mid-position at all but a contradiction in terms. Their zeal to be of help may well have obscured their doubts at the beginning; but at the end when they wondered to what use their work had or had not been put some of them could scarcely avoid a sense of disillusion. Particularly for those who respected Merriam's views of the purity of science or who sided with Gulick on the separation of politics and administration the basically political function of the committee came as a rude shock. Even so, the shock or the disillusion could not be blamed on any lack of explanation by the men who headed the committee.

From the beginning the three members of the President's Committee on Administrative Management looked upon themselves as staff to the President. And it was clear to them that the President's wishes were the controlling factor in their assignment. Roosevelt had told Brownlow that he hoped the committee would assemble a staff who already knew enough so that they could "skim the cream off the top of their own memories." [1] Furthermore, Brownlow told the committee's staff at its first assembled meeting, the President hoped for a report on "principles," not "methodology." He was concerned lest disputes over details bury public interest in the principles. The staff was further warned not to be distracted by substantive operational or internal administrative problems in Bureaus being investigated. They were to think and to analyze "with only enough factual research to prevent . . . egregious errors." [2]

In an effort to distinguish even more clearly the work of the committee from the research project initially planned, Merriam asked that the staff be conscious of the fact that individually they were not independent students but a staff, that monographs for eventual publication were not their primary concern. "The report is to be for use by the President in the manner which he deems most effective. He may prefer to restate the proposals in his own language and publish nothing." It was thus made clear from the beginning that the committee had chosen to follow a course between research and politics which differed in considerable degree from that originally defined in the traditions of academic progressivism.

The choice of a chief of staff or director of research had been something of a problem. Brownlow and Merriam had agreed that Clarence Dykstra, then city manager of Cincinnati, would be ideal; but Dykstra's own commitments there forced him, despite his great interest, to decline.[3] Joseph P. Harris, then director of research for the Public Administration Committee of the Social Science Research Council, was given the job, at first on a temporary basis which was later made permanent.[4] Interestingly enough, Luther Gulick had expressed to Merriam his own desire for the job during the early days of discussion of a possible examination of the presidency. His preference for the position, even over and above an interest in being a member of the committee, indicates his views toward the function of research and the importance which its direction could have for such an analysis. Insofar as the director of research allocated problems to be studied and guided the final direction which the studies would take, he gave much of the life and substance to the conclusions reached in the ultimate report. Despite the continuing emulation of the laboratory sciences, subtler thought would be found to reveal the fact that problems in social science were not so clearly delineated and historically received. Nor

were the circumstances under which and the methods according to which investigation could proceed a matter of fundamental agreement. The scholars who came to Washington to
study the federal executive during the latter half of 1936
brought methods and purposes with them. The extent to which
their immersion in the data transformed their thinking could
be a matter for some debate.

The committee outlined its plan of research at its first full
meeting in New York. But the Brownlow memorandum had
already, even earlier, made the general plan clear. And Merriam's memorandum of 1935 had drawn the distinction between
"the political relations of the Executive" and "the technical
services." The latter posed, he felt, the problems in need of
"over-all" examination. He envisioned such a study, even from
the beginning, as involving the three parts: personnel, budget,
and planning. "Steps have already been taken on the personnel
side," he wrote, "in the establishment of the merit system and
the civil service commission; on the fiscal side through the
establishment of the budget director and the comptroller-
general; and in the coordination of long time planning policies
through the National Resources Committee." [5] Still, in its
earlier form, Merriam's idea was to construct a historical study
of "trends," almost as though the presentation of the roots were
itself the point of the endeavor, the revelation of principles
imbedded in the past.

Brownlow's initial draft of his own memorandum had spoken
of the three centers for investigation, to which he had added
the term "legal," which he followed by a bracketed question
mark. In a revision of the memorandum for committee purposes,
Brownlow had retained "legal" and added "statistical, etc.,"
which he designated as "staff" functions. In so doing he was
considering most of the regular departments and agencies as
"line," utilizing the older administrative distinction between
offices responsible for gathering information to be used in
formulation of policy and those which issued the commands in
fulfillment of that policy.[6] In the course of the committee's

deliberation the distinction was apparently dropped. The three "managerial arms" were left without additional accompaniments, in part for the simple reason that the committee finally chose to isolate what it considered essentially nondelegable functions. Even so, it was difficult to find the old staff-line concept in the committee's report.

The staff-line scheme, important to the early development of public administration in this country, had originally been derived from the German "General Staff" idea which Elihu Root had modified for the War Department during Theodore Roosevelt's administration.[7] This effort was part of the new attitude toward executive organization which had been developing since the Keep Commission and part of the transition from the economy-efficiency attitudes to the independent concept of executive management. Its aim involved two factors of much importance to the growing awareness throughout the western world of the need for the application of rational, systematic processes to the complex bureaucracy which all governments had tended to develop in the wake of modern industrialism.

First, there was the need for greater communication between knowledge or technical skill and the actual, day to day operations of government. Secondly, and almost as a correlate, there was the recognized need for the delimiting of arbitrary executive will in areas or under circumstances where that will could be inefficient or incorrect. It must be noted here that these concerns were neither necessarily liberal nor democratic, although they had certain affinities for problems traditional in liberal democracy, particularly the concern for limitation upon arbitrary executive authority. But from the point of view of scientific government (or later, "rational-legal bureaucracy," as Max Weber, the German sociologist would call it), it was the "arbitrary" which characterized the fault in older governments, not the "executive" or the "authority."

The movement toward revisions in the traditional view of executive authority was as important in turn-of-the-century events in American government as it was in many European countries, although the forms it took depended upon the historic base on which the problems rested. In the broadest sense, modern industrial organization had centered attention on problems raised by the application of parliamentary methods to complex mechanical and economic systems requiring technical skills and specialized forms of knowledge which were nonpolitical in the traditional sense of the word. The resulting evolutions of government had, in England, produced an increasingly effective cabinet system resting on a strong civil service and responsible to the electorate through a parliament which tended more and more to debate the results of decisions rather than the decisions themselves. Insofar as executive authority rested in the office of Prime Minister, the popular base of that authority was indistinguishable from the popular base of the parliament as a whole, since the Prime Minister and his cabinet were presumably elected as representatives first, receiving their executive authority from their position in the legislature, not as a result of popular designation. In American government, of course, the public makes a deliberate choice of executive leadership which is completely separate from its expression of its legislative will.

In Germany, by contrast, executive authority had stronger traditions and parliamentary government was itself in a perpetually embryonic stage. The application of industrial knowledge and techniques to government produced more systematic institutions through the immediate transfer of problems from strong monarchy to strong leadership in any rational, nonarbitrary form. This could avoid the presumably clumsy mediation of a strong parliamentary tradition. The absolutism of reason, knowledge, and technology produced a pyramidal, bureaucratic structure the aim of which was to achieve impersonal, scientific authority as a protection against the basic inefficiencies of personal, arbitrary rule. To idealists like Weber, Germany's history seemed almost to have provided the perfect method for coping with industrialism, perhaps

even precisely because Germany had been historically preserved from the now useless chaos of legislative self-government better suited to agrarian communities of the past. The
development of truly knowledgeable executive government
could thereby be effected more easily. The German intellectual on the eve of World War I had reason to look at the
highly developed, effective structure of the German civil
service; at the efficient, socially useful operation of the German city; at the increasing knowledge and awareness of the
uses of such administrative structures as the General Staff and
find the future a hopeful one, in which a great Germany could
guide the world through the complex problems of the industrial age. The Kaiser may have made some German intellectuals
almost as uneasy as Hitler later would make their sons; but
public heroes seemed useful devices to insure a certain amount
of public spirit and popular support.

There were Americans who looked hopefully in Germany's
direction, who studied in its schools and who felt that the
German experience could somehow be grafted in modified
form onto the democratic American one. Others felt that the
British experience, having evolved through the democratic era,
provided a more nearly indigenous pattern to be emulated
usefully by America. The important thing, however, is that
Americans were considering the various possibilities, that they
had, through their own experience with industrialism, come
face to face with the same problems being dealt with by other
countries of the western world. Industrial development and
scientific advance produced the same dilemma everywhere
they occurred. But in America, unlike either Britain or Germany, democracy had come to be so exclusively associated
with legislative control that the virtues of executive authority
could be hidden effectively in a tradition of debate. True, the
tradition of legislative control was not as old as it appeared to
be; and those who sought revisions would point this out. But
the 1830's, even more than the 1790's, had marked modern
American government with an individual stamp; and the fig-

ure of Andrew Jackson returning government to the people would loom larger than that of George Washington formulating it and preserving it for them.

The transition from the legislature to the executive as the center of reform occurred in the United States during the period with which this study has dealt. Men like Merriam attempted to balance their interest in the sciences of society and their educational experiences in Germany with an understanding of the nature of democratic leadership and the process of democratic politics. Brownlow sought some effective separation of the process of democratic politics from the necessary professionalization of the increasingly technical processes of government, but a separation which would retain for the two a real and a useful responsiveness to one another. The tradition to which Gulick belonged had searched for objective techniques which could preserve the functions of government regardless of changes in politics and purposes. In some respects all three were related closely to one another but, while many of the elements seemed the same, their uses were different.

Merriam and Gulick both looked to "science" as basic to the development of social and governmental structure, but Merriam's emphasis was on principles of science while Gulick stressed methodology. Gulick and Brownlow both were concerned essentially with the administration of government as separate from politics; for Brownlow, however, the priority of politics as the ultimate source of knowledgeable decision was crucial; for Gulick the rigorous separation of administration from politics tended to make administrative investigation and analysis the true source of a somewhat rarified political knowledge. Merriam and Brownlow agreed on the priority of politics, but Merriam's science of politics was different from Brownlow's operational, dialectical view of the nature of political debate.

In many important respects all three men clearly reflected the traditions in which they had been educated and in which they continued to work. Merriam's approach was essentially academic in that he saw social science as a group of disciplines with principles which provided direction to the processes of investigation and the examination of evidence. "Planning" and "science" came to have a peculiar identity in his thinking, peculiar in that they were identified as being fundamentally democratic and oriented to public will, hence well within the orbit of politics and its debates. For men like Gulick who belonged to a basically antipolitical tradition, the amalgam of pure science and the administrative areas of practical politics was possible only in the sense that out of the conflict between them one could abstract a kind of essence, in the form of methods and techniques which were "pure" without being useless and practical without being partisan. Brownlow, virtually alone among the three, had grown up in the tradition of the practitioners, the "hired-hands" of government who, long before the debates had been formulated very clearly, had begun to apply professional skills and codification to the activities in which they found themselves engaged. Through his aid to and interest in the greater professionalization of public service, Brownlow had come to search for generalizations which he would refer to as "principles."

All three men continually sought definitions of what they meant by "principles." It is likely that, in the final analysis, the only thing they really had in common as far as their definitions were concerned was the endeavor. Principles, for Merriam, were the old philosophic concepts of purpose, broad generalizations about fundamental existence by which actions could be guided. Principles for Brownlow were closer to being definitions themselves, in the sense of being generalized descriptions of facts, categories according to which classes of actions could be understood. Principles for Gulick were methodological analyses of kinds of action. Different as the three meanings might be, they complemented one another to a large extent; and when Franklin Roosevelt asked his Committee on Administrative Management to provide him with the "principles" of executive authority, he was perhaps thinking of yet a fourth definition. For it was clear by his injunction that he was seeking effective, forceful justifications, consistent with the values embodied in American history and its Constitution, for actions which present and historical necessity had forced upon American government. The principles he sought were justifications for accepting necessity and dealing with it in a fashion which could deserve the security of the American democratic tradition. Thus, as far as "principles" were concerned, the basic outlines of the report of the committee had been determined by the President's choice of staff and by his definition of his purpose.

Nonetheless, the range of possible purpose was considerably larger than that reflected in the three members of the committee and the President. Roosevelt had realized this when he chose to appoint his own committee, dependent upon him rather than upon any outside agency. Still, in the efforts to utilize all available talent, the members of the committee in their own choice of staff had succeeded in representing a wide range of opinions, as the collection of unpublished studies in the committee's files would testify. In a sense the extremes were represented by the view, perhaps exclusively the President's, that, whatever the presidency was as a historic institution, it was *his* job which he had won by election because he represented to a large portion of the voting public across the nation what they wanted to see in the office. Had the victory in 1936 not been as great as it was, Roosevelt still would have held the proprietary attitude toward his individual possession of this very individual political position. It is an attitude which has been characteristic of a good many presidents and comes, perhaps, from the immense isolation and individuality demanded by the role. At the other extreme are those who view the office as an objectively observable and methodologically analyzable administrative institution which is both practically and historically separate from the men who hold the office.

The two points of view, as extremes, have consequences which would be bound to affect any attempt at systematic study, even beyond the personal concerns of Franklin Roosevelt himself. Blocked by the Court in his efforts to provide public services necessitated by the depression, he was painfully aware of the practical necessity of a more effective executive. Recognizing the dangers inherent in constitutional reformation as the means, the President sought a public statement in appraisal of executive authority. Such a statement could be an intelligent, public affirmation of faith in both the flexibility and the security of the American Constitution and the executive office it defined. This would lead to definitions of executive machinery which would be commensurate with that authority. While this attitude toward the committee's function undoubtedly reflects Roosevelt's rather extraordinary faith in the ultimate rightness of his own views, it is a logical position to be taken by anyone who seeks theoretical security for a job in which he feels practically secure.

In contrast to the President's more political and pragmatic view stood those who, from the vantage point of a developing interest in a science of politics, sought a complete restructuring of executive authority in American government. Some had already suggested constitutional amendment as the basic, most effective means of building into the presidency the kinds of precise executive machinery represented by various forms of general staff, cabinet government, or even more authoritarian devices of more absolute control. Others, while not completely certain of the necessity of constitutional revision, were nonetheless adherents to programs of complete structural reorganization within the existing constitutional framework.[8]

Some of the members of the research staff of the President's committee saw the endeavor as a hopeful means of introducing scientific administration into American government, both as an instrument for practical operation of government as well as a research technique for the general examination of government. From the beginning Roosevelt's disclaimer of any commitment to wholly objective research to be publicly debated—and the committee's declared intention of preserving his wishes in the matter—hampered and at times offended members of the research staff who felt that their own commitments to objective research were being interfered with by purely political, not to say partisan, ends.

In a very important sense, the three members of the committee stood as mediators between the extremes. They distributed projects to the scholars whom they had assembled. They listened to the reports which were ultimately turned in, absorbing some, ignoring others, commenting at times rather ironically on the academic paraphernalia (Merriam likened one session to a "damned Ph.D. exam" [9]), requesting revision where it seemed to them necessary—in subject matter as well as in form—listening to all recommendations made to them from within and without the government. The basic method followed was, in effect, a combination of the "assembly of scholars" approach as represented by the Recent Social Trends group and the "gathering of direct evidence from participants" approach as reflected in the work of the Commission of Inquiry on Public Service Personnel. But in the final analysis the actual report was written in large part by the three members of the committee who, with selected members of the research staff (surprisingly few, considering the size of the staff), hammered out the fifty-three-page report. To it were appended nine "Special Studies" which Merriam, with a wry mixture of poetry and justice, called the "nonsupporting documents." [10] Some of those who had considered their mission to Washington a new step forward in the relation between government and the academic community left with the feeling that they had, in part at least, been subjected to a political trick. But it was possible also to see in the compromises, mediations, and adjustments the emergence of a new approach to the problems which all of them, including the President, were trying to solve.

II

Merriam and Brownlow spent most of the summer of 1936 in Europe and England, while Gulick's visits to Washington were limited by his own prior commitments to the state of New York and at the Institute of Public Administration.[11] J. P. Harris and his staff concentrated on interviews with representatives of the various departments, amassing data and points of view, while various individuals who had been assigned special studies continued in their preparation and revision.

In a Washington occupied with presidential nominating conventions and the forthcoming elections, the work of the committee was not likely to arouse much attention. And undoubtedly the possibility, however remote, of a change in incumbent of the office they were studying cast some shadow of influence upon those who were seeking principles which went beyond the immediacy of individuals or elections.

In addition to the domestic circumstances which could scarcely help but serve as background to the committee's work, foreign events were pressing in, particularly to Brownlow and Merriam who were attending meetings of international groups concerned with public administration. In Berlin Brownlow was received briefly by Hitler, whose shadow had already been clearly marked elsewhere in meetings with various public officials some of whom were of the older German tradition of service in local government. Others equally well-known in professional circles were absent, and one could only speculate on the reasons. In Warsaw Brownlow and Merriam helped fight off an attempt by fascist delegates to a congress there to state as the sense of the meeting that efficient executive government and democratic processes were, in effect, incompatible.[12]

On the train back from Warsaw Merriam gave Brownlow a running translation of Leon Blum's book, *Governmental Reform*, a study which impressed both men with its clear and warmly written recognition of the problems of governmental organization in a world in which the traditions of western democracy were being assailed both from the right and the left.[13]

Europe in the thirties provided a strained and tormented

testing ground for ideas of previous generations. Both communism and fascism could propose relatively programmatic support for their reformations of existing western institutions of government. Both could attack the inefficiencies of liberal systems and in doing so utilize arguments which critics loyal to the systems were using against themselves. The conversations which Merriam and Brownlow held with such respected British civil servants as Thomas Jones and Sir Henry Bunbury and students of government like Harold Laski and Herman Finer, revealed to them an awareness of common problems and a reaffirmation of the frameworks of tradition as guides in the search for solutions. But while in general terms Americans could manage to reject the rebellious propositions of the extremes, as the English tended to do, the affirmation of tradition was not either as customary or as specific in America as it seemed to be in England. Somehow the refusal to entertain the extremes in the first place had put Americans in the peculiar position of being innocent of the demands that they defend their traditions, yet subject to the same historic circumstances which were threatening those traditions. To the extent that America's depression, like the general economic collapse in the rest of the world, had been part of a complex response to problems in western society as a whole, American government had, through the Hoover administration and beyond, demonstrated precisely the kind of inefficiency which fascism and communism both were using as their major criticism of democratic government. What was interesting was that American critics of the New Deal who did not attack it on the grounds of the extraordinary powers given to the executive, attacked its "inefficiency," using the term as synonymous with waste and inextricably tied to the old question of the expense of government.

What the differences reveal are in fact two definitions of efficiency. Both were products, in a sense, of modern industrialism; one, the traditional American, used the expense of government as the external sign of efficient government, the other, the European emphasized the distribution of wealth, and class differences served as the external sign. America assumed an ultimate equality of distribution—an essential classlessness—and concentrated on the cost, while Europe assumed the cost of government and concentrated on the method and manner of the distribution of social goods. In these respects the American dream of a government which would be efficient and inexpensive is no more unrealistic than the European dream of a society which would be both efficient and classless.

By comparison with world-wide governmental crises in the twenties and thirties, the New Deal was from its inception as efficient in the European sense as were any of the traditional or revolutionary governments of Europe in that it was finding effective means for solving problems of distribution without regard for traditional barriers imposed on methods. But unlike governments in Europe, the New Deal sought no systematic or ideological justification for its methods, seemed to take little or no pride in them, and, particularly as far as the President seemed to be concerned, insisted on the temporary nature of changes most obviously opposed to past methods and the traditional nature of those now deemed permanent.

By the time Brownlow and Merriam returned to America in the late summer of 1936, they could bring back with them an experience which moved them even closer, perhaps, to an understanding of the needs which their report would have to serve. It would not be sufficient to decry dictatorship as immoral or undemocratic as long as the strains which produced it were endemic to all of western society. One would have to provide an alternative in practical efficient democracy which recognized the confusions of a new age and attempted to cope with them, but which was buttressed by the truths of an older, secure tradition. America had needed strong Presidents before and it had found them, but not in a world so replete with illustrations of the effects of obedience to brute, primal strength. If industrialism and technology had produced a need for strong leadership, it had done so in ways and in an atmosphere which made that need capable of terrifyingly destructive realization.

In his opening of the introduction to the committee's report, Merriam placed many of the problems of the surrounding political scene into the context of history.[14] Criticisms of democratic government were not new. "From time to time," he wrote, "the decay, destruction, and death of democracy has been gloomily predicted by false prophets who mocked at us, but our own American system has matched its massive strength against all the forces of destruction through parts of three centuries." The current need for reconstruction he traced to three sources: the depression, the tremendous growth of the nation, and "the vexing social problems of our times." In words which forecast the language and the tone which the President would use in his forthcoming inaugural address, Merriam sought to broaden the interest in effective government, looking back to the history of the American presidency and forward to increasing concern with "much bitter wrong" which needed to be "set right in neglected ways of human life." ". . . facing one of the most troubled periods in all the troubled history of mankind," he continued, "we wish to set our affairs in the very best possible order to make the best use of all of our national resources and to make good our democratic claims. . . . We seek modern types of management in National government best fitted for the stern situations we are bound to meet, both at home and elsewhere."

These words set the report on a course which would take it well beyond the immediate issues of the depression and into considerations of the future responsibilities of the nation, not only to itself but to the rest of the world. "If America fails, the hopes and dreams of democracy all over the world go down." [15]

Gulick found good management a universal factor present in of "The Foundations of Governmental Efficiency." Gulick pinpointed the problem of definition by resting governmental efficiency on two factors: "the consent of the governed and good management." The relation between the two had been a crucial part of the whole Frederick Cleveland, efficiency-budget tradition, the corner stone of which was, as it had been from the beginning, the "responsible executive," with responsibility defined by reference to the consent of the governed.

Gulick found good management a universal factor present in any public or private instance of effective operation, whether of business or government: "Stated in simple terms these canons of efficiency require the establishment of a responsible and effective chief executive as the center of energy, direction, and administrative management; the systematic organization of all activities in the hands of qualified personnel under the direction of the chief executive; and to aid him in this, the establishment of appropriate managerial and staff agencies. There must also be provision for planning, a complete fiscal system, and means for holding the executive accountable for his program." [16] As previous discussion has suggested, the problem of accountability and responsibility had been the major point of difference between budget reformers and those who took a broader view of management reform problems for many years. Within the research staff of the President's committee one could also find the same disagreement. Some considered the President's political position in the government a hindrance to real responsibility because of his inability to dissolve a reluctant Congress and take the issue to the people. Others saw no necessity in the constitutional change that this would entail, either as a requirement of effective responsibility or as a practical possibility in any case. There were gradations of agreement and disagreement between the extremes of quasi cabinet government, on the one hand, and absolute maintenance of the status quo on the other. To be able to increase the sensitivity of the President's control over legislation was a highly sensitive issue in itself. The tradition of argument had ranged from item veto, which would have given the executive more direct power, to the potentialities inherent in older initiative and referendum arguments which would have strengthened the executive hand indirectly; the latter would give him an effective electorate, presumably, to which to appeal over the heads of the legislature. However, neither the item veto nor initiative and referendum entitled the president to appeal to the public for a new legislature as a means of discipline.

It is important to note that the committee would seek no such extremes in its adjustment of executive-legislative relations, that its methods of adjustment were purposely and insistently within the framework of existing constitutional provisions. Gulick's section of the introduction closed with a statement which reinforced the basic view of the committee toward its function vis-à-vis the President as well as the traditions of development and debate. "What we need," he wrote, "is not a new principle, but a modernizing of our managerial equipment." [17] Not everyone could be completely sure of the difference.

In an interesting reflection of his earlier Massachusetts study, Gulick reminded his readers that the modernizing of managerial equipment was not a revolutionary suggestion. He referred them to recent historical events in state and city government, to large-scale revisions in private industry, to the reorganizations effected by Frank O. Lowden in Illinois, Alfred E. Smith in New York, Harry F. Byrd in Virginia, and William Tudor Gardiner in Maine. While the federal government admittedly presented a problem of larger magnitude, "the principles of reorganization are," he wrote, "the same." He then summed up the five major points to be undertaken in the report.

1. To deal with the greatly increased duties of executive management falling upon the President, the White House staff should be expanded.
2. The managerial agencies of the Government, particularly those dealing with the budget, efficiency research, personnel, and planning, should be greatly strengthened and developed as arms of the Chief Executive.
3. The merit system should be extended upward, outward,

and downward to cover all non-policy-determining posts, and the civil service system should be reorganized and opportunities established for a career system attractive to the best talent of the Nation.

4. The whole Executive Branch of the Government should be overhauled and the present 100 agencies reorganized under a few large departments in which every executive activity would find its place.

5. The fiscal system should be extensively revised in the light of the best governmental and private practice, particularly with reference to financial records, audit, and accountability of the executive to the Congress.[18]

Brownlow concluded the introduction with a peroration on "the Purpose of Reorganization." He took pains to point out that too close a view of "machinery" could inhibit inquiry in accordance with the "true purpose of efficient management." In a listing which summarized in effect the history of hesitant starts in reorganization of the presidency, Brownlow noted that neither economy nor elimination of duplication and contradictory policies, nor simple and symmetrical organization, nor higher salaries and better jobs, nor better business methods and fiscal controls were singly or together the ends of reorganization, although each was a useful, even necessary, factor.

"There is but one grand purpose," he wrote, "namely, to make democracy work today in our National Government; that is, to make our Government an up-to-date, efficient, and effective instrument for carrying out the will of the Nation. It is for this purpose that the Government needs thoroughly modern tools of management." [19]

In sum, while the committee acknowledged its debt to the traditions which had produced it, it seemed to have in mind elements which went beyond those traditions; but its purpose, it kept insisting, was modernization, not revolution.

The nature of the report, its fundamental emphases and the basic character of its innovations were revealed by the structure of the report as prefaced not in the introduction but in the first section which followed. While the committee based its arguments on the five points listed above, it did not organize its report according to them but rather took the lead posed by Brownlow in his chapter on the White House staff. For the committee, in keeping with its basic argument, began with the heart of the executive branch, the office of the President, rather than with the sprawling parts of the executive establishment. The committee's view was to be "over-all" and its vantage point was the top.

"The President needs help," Brownlow wrote, and for that help he suggested the appointment of no less than six assistants, men who "should be possessed of high competence, great physical vigor, and a passion for anonymity." [20] He suggested also that "the President should have at his command a contingent fund to enable him to bring in from time to time particular persons possessed of a particular competency for a particular purpose and whose services he might usefully employ for short periods of time." In addition he asked that the President be given direct control over "the great managerial functions of the Government," and he designated these as personnel management, fiscal and organizational management, and planning management. "Within these three groups," Brownlow wrote, "may be comprehended all of the essential elements of business management." The next three sections of the report, then, deal with the three "managerial arms of the Chief Executive." [21]

The first of the three sections, Personnel Management, was divided into three parts. Gulick opened with an enunciation of the importance of adequate provision for selection and training of qualified service personnel, an enunciation which held echoes of the words which had been written twenty-five years earlier by Mrs. Harriman and Cutting in their pleas for a training school for public service. In the fifty years which had passed since the institution of Civil Service reforms throughout the country needs had changed. Mere "protection" was no longer sufficient. Positive steps to advance, guide, encourage, and educate were required by the complexities of modern government. Certainly the New York Bureau of Municipal Research, as well as the Institute of Public Administration which Gulick headed, had sought originally a transition from critical faultfinding reform and corrective-punitive agencies of reform to positive and constructive reform through improved methods and techniques of governing. The Commission of Inquiry on Public Service Personnel, on which Merriam, Gulick, and Brownlow had all served, had called for such changes. The request was now written into the report of the President's committee. Its specific base was to be the extension of the merit system upward to cover all but the most clearly policy-determining positions at the top; downward to cover all of the technical positions, including both skilled workmen and laborers; and outward to take local positions out of the hands of the President and place them under the control of the relevant departments.

In what would later become one of the most controversial sections of the report, Brownlow described the administrative organization through which the revisions in personnel administration would be effected and controlled. He proposed abolition of the Civil Service Commission and its replacement by a Civil Service Administration consisting of an Administrator appointed by the President, with the advice and consent of the Senate, on the basis of an open competitive examination conducted by a special board of examiners appointed by the Civil Service Board, and a group of seven "non-salaried" (i.e., "lay") men appointed by the President with the advice and consent of the Senate. The Board members would serve seven-year, overlapping terms. The Administrator would serve "at the pleasure of the President."

The plan is interesting here for several reasons. First, it is consistent with the committee's argument throughout its report that commissions and boards holding administrative responsibility were, in effect, relics of the post-Civil War Congressional committeeism which had created the kind of chaos which

Woodrow Wilson, as well as many others, had criticized. Secondly, the new plan with its emphasis upon a single, technically competent individual to be overseen by a nonsalaried commission bore familiar marks, not only of the arguments which developed and sustained manager-council government but in every area where technical, professional competence and democratic public process were forced into effective relation to one another. Thirdly, the use of the nonsalaried, "lay" board, not only here but also in the section on planning, was a device which subjected the committee to much criticism. There were reasons, however, which underlay their choice of this method. For one, members of the committee felt that personnel and planning, especially, were areas in which the misuse of specialization could be damaging to the needs of the general public. In both cases it seemed wiser to have men who were specialists in other fields bear partial responsibility for judgment lest planning and personnel become rigid specializations in and of themselves, thereby restricting the necessary free flow of influence from other endeavors and concerns. The use of a full-time, civil servant as administrator would insure continuity and adequate technical control. The use of part-time laymen from other areas would insure that neither planning nor personnel would be treated within government as new specializations or new additions to the already fractionated agencies and departments. By now it was beginning to be clear that by "managerial arms" the committee did not mean another set of departmental functions.

Advocates of professional personnel and planning techniques or of planning as a subject matter and specialization different from the things being planned could not help but object to such a view. Some even felt that Merriam had sought by this device to insure his own continuity in government. From the standpoint of a personal device for aggrandizement this seems most unsupportable. But this defense does not deny the fact that Merriam and other members of the committee sought a continuing use by government of specialists from the academic or other technical communities who would not have to give up the values of their own professional engagement in order to serve government. For their continuing and productive involvement in their own fields of inquiry was the greatest value government could expect from them in their capacities as planners and advisers.

In addition, however, the use of laymen at the highest levels of government assured a flow of new individuals from various sectors of American society in and out of government, thereby building into bureaucratic structure a modern democratization which could help prevent administrative bureaucracy from becoming a self-generated, self-judging world separate from the responsibilities of society as a whole. This point of view was inherent in the whole structure of the committee's report and reflects its particular variety of neo-Jacksonianism which sought to place democratic involvement in self-government at the top, policy-making levels of government, separating it from the technical services which needed to be dealt with through the traditions, if not the methods, of Civil Service reform.

In a concluding section on "Compensation and Classification" Gulick raised the touchy twin questions of salary and executive latitude in determining it. His major arguments were directed toward bringing government to levels and standards competitive with business and professional life. This would be both efficient and economical because it would raise standards and lower the rate of turnover. His appeal was to good business sense.

The second of the three management chapters discussed "Fiscal Management." This posed problems rather different from those involved in either the previous chapter or the one to follow. Federal personnel practices had evolved out of reforms now fifty years or more old. Planning practices scarcely existed. Fiscal practices had been modernized as recently as 1921 in the Budget and Accounting Act. The Director of the Bureau as its chief administrator reported directly to the President; but, as we have already seen, the peculiar status of the

Comptroller General had preserved the "commission psychology" of the Congress by creating a post midway between the President and the Congress and effectively responsible to neither. The report of the Committee on Administrative Management, therefore, concentrated on two major problems: the effectiveness of the Director of the Budget as the administrator of this managerial tool of the President, and the problems involved in Congress's failure in 1921 to separate audit from control.

The first problem was taken up by Gulick with J. P. Harris and Herbert Emmerich in an opening section on Budgeting and Administrative Control. The burden of its argument rested on the need for a closer relationship between the Bureau and the rest of the executive branch through enlarged and improved staffing which would enable the Director to concentrate more upon fiscal policy and planning, at the same time that the Bureau's contacts with the other departments would be improved. It was originally intended that the Bureau should engage in "research" in organization and management, as well as serving as a center for the dissemination of information concerning common departmental organizational and fiscal problems. But in some respects the Bureau had fallen victim to the economy-efficiency aspects of the movement which had created it and had tended to be as parsimonious with its own size and development as it was with respect to the departments. Enlarging the Bureau would enable it to serve not only in the preparation but in the execution of the Budget. In short, the Bureau was treated basically as the right unit for its purpose, only insufficiently staffed and hence weak in its effects. Certainly there was an undercurrent of criticisms which were deeply involved in the history of arguments over economy and efficiency.

The problem of the Comptroller General was central to the committee's discussion of fiscal policy, just as were the boards and commissions which also represented Congressional interference with executive authority. But it was not ultimately to be dealt with easily. In a section prepared by Gulick and Harvey

C. Mansfield the report recommended separation of audit from control, turning over to the Secretary of the Treasury the power to settle accounts and allow expenditure and setting up an Auditor General who would be directly responsible to the Congress and who would function solely as an auditor. The Attorney General was to be given authority to settle jurisdictional disputes between the Secretary of the Treasury and other Departments over account settlements—in short, control was to be made a function entirely within the executive branch itself, while audit would belong exclusively to Congress. As we shall see, opponents of the plan tried to define control as a check on the money *before* it was spent, audit a check on it *after*, thereby making the watchdog of control a much sharper and wiser creature than it could in practice be. But the recommendations of the committee, consistent with its proposals on personnel, were in effect an attack upon the tradition of fear and mistrust which had blocked the modernization of government.

In some respects the chapter on Planning Management provides the most interesting insight into the authors of the report and the effects upon them of their careers and the traditions which stood behind them. The committee staff, in particular Charles McKinley, had labored long over questions of the adequate and appropriate context for a discussion of planning in American government. The final statement is undoubtedly a reflection of the many minds which had been assembled to consider the problem. In particular, the experience of Merriam and Brownlow, who finally produced the text, can be found in the fundamental philosophy of democratic planning suggested. The Social Science Research Council, the Committee on Social Trends, the Public Administration Clearing House, and, indeed, the President's Committee on Administrative Management itself provide a background in method for the institutionalization of planning:

> The first function of such an agency is to serve as a clearing house of planning interests and concerns in the effort to prevent waste and improve our national living standard. Another

is to cooperate with departmental, state, and local agencies, and in general to use the Board's good offices to see that planning decisions are not made by one group in ignorance of relevant undertakings or research going on elsewhere. Obviously much of this is a matter of diplomacy and intelligent interest rather than legal authority and high command.[22]

Here was the clearing house idea again, the antihierarchy, antiauthoritarian notion of the community of knowledge which was to be kept a community by not being crystallized by structure or routinized by chains of command. "Diplomacy and intelligent interest," "good offices," all of these were terms and characteristics which Brownlow and Merriam had learned from one another as well as from their own contacts and conflicts with others whom they had sought to help and whose interests they had encouraged. They hoped to make a place for the kinds of careers they had established for themselves and to see it institutionalized in the presidency itself.

"Another function is that of collecting and analyzing data relating to our national resources, both human and physical, and of shaping up advisory plans for the better use of those resources. The gains of civilization are essentially mass gains. They should be distributed as fairly as possible among those who created them." [23] These are the principles upon which rested the faith in the communal nature of research and its relation to the communal nature of democratic government. The economy of time and effort involved in the effective and efficient interchange of information—the clearing house—were to be represented now in the federal executive by the presence at the top of a Planning Agency to enable the President to do for the country as a whole what these men and others like them had been working to do from their own particular positions in American society since the turn of the century. As members of the President's committee they could now suggest the necessity of looking closely at the problems of change which had been concerning responsible men throughout that whole era, for it was in effect the "point of view" of the committee, so to speak, its position at the top of executive government which gave it its unique vitality and which, in the minds of its authors, pointed to the answer to the continuing problem of American government. As they went on to say: "Unless some overhead central agency takes an over-all view from time to time, analyzes facts, and suggests plans to insure the preservation of the equilibrium upon which our American democracy rests, there is danger that it will be badly upset." [24] This was "planning," but its philosophy came from the role which the President's committee had chosen for itself.

The agency was to be established as a board consisting of five nonsalaried members with indefinite terms, with a director appointed by the board and an executive officer in the classified service. It was to be a national clearing house of knowledge and research, a permanent examiner and evaluator of social trends.

With the White House staff and the three managerial arms defined, the committee proceeded then to an examination of the Administrative Reorganization of the Government of the United States (chapter v), and the Accountability of the Executive to Congress (chapter vi). The division between the chapters described thus far and the remaining two raises one of the most important questions of the report, for the committee had, at the outset, clearly disavowed any intention, presumably, of doing anything beyond reviewing questions of "over-all management," an aim which later critics of the report would see as having been accomplished in the first four chapters. What such criticism misses, however, is the meaning of "over-all" in the committee's mind, for it meant less a limitation than, again, a point of view. It distinguished, as we will see later, the approach which began with the departments and analyzed its way to the chief executive—essentially the old Congressional approach—from that which began with the executive and worked its way outward to the departments. To be sure, the committee had no intention of doing detailed studies of the departments, that being the province of the Brookings studies; but to ignore departmental organization would have been to ignore one of the most obviously important elements of management—that which is being managed. That there was room for disagreement about this raises some additional questions of theory and intention. It is certainly true that the mere presence of this discussion in the committee's report could be considered at most an overlap of functions assigned the Brookings staff, at least an attempt to indicate a direction which departmental analysis would properly take. Since no one at this stage anticipated dispute between the committee's report and that to be issued by Brookings, there was no reason to be overly protective about questions of jurisdiction.

Brownlow in his discussion of the departments recommended that they be increased in number to twelve, that all existing agencies be placed under them according to the relevance of their functions, and indicated that this included the administrative aspects of the commissions and boards as well as the various government corporations. This suggested augmentation also provided the focal point for some of the professional criticism of the report. Advocates of vastly increasing the number of the departments rather than their individual size joined E. S. Corwin in his disapproval of expanding the power of the President himself rather than the effectiveness of his administrative departments.[25] This group found the argument that the departments should be kept within the immediate range of command of the President a spurious excuse for an increase in personal power, possibly even at the expense of efficiency. Small departments seemed far more useful units than big ones. The President was not a monolithic, all-seeing god who could administer equally monolithic, all-encompassing departments. If he needed more help, and no one doubted that he did, the cabinet was the place in which to find it, once everyone recognized that the President had more responsibility than he could justly exercize. Schuyler Wallace had prepared a memorandum to this effect for the committee.

Others on the committee's staff, William Yandell Elliott in

particular, felt that the committee's role threatened to become simply that of a professional stamp for the continuation and expansion of Roosevelt's chaotic predilections as an administrator.[26] Elliott had prepared a plan which was, to some extent at least, midway between the expanded cabinet views of the Corwin school and the expanded presidency views ultimately to be taken by the committee. He had proposed to the committee what was in effect a cabinet secretariat, which would function more or less with and through a partially expanded cabinet under the general direction of an executive secretary acting as a combined assistant president and a prime minister.[27] To him one of the most objectionable characteristics of the committee's proposal for assistants whose functions would be determined only by the President and who would be equally subject to and responsible to presidential will was the lack of any clear organization, structure, or, from his point of view, purpose. Certainly the committee's views seemed to suggest interposition between the cabinet and the President of an authoritative group as extraconstitutional as the cabinet itself. Lindsay Rogers prepared for the committee a detailed study advancing a modified cabinet secretariat which is, in part at least, an interesting critique of the position finally taken by the committee. As we shall see, the committee's original recommendation suggested a compromise closer than one might have suspected to the approach suggested by Rogers and Elliott. It was vetoed by the President.

These objections all pointed to differences of opinion as old as the traditions which had combined to form the experience of the President's Committee on Administrative Management. The growth of executive responsibility since the end of the Civil War had not been accompanied by a corresponding development in the instruments of executive power. But this was true only where the President himself was concerned. Congress had created new executive departments, new executive agencies, commissions and boards, new executive corporations. But these were clearly identifiable as bureaucratic institutions and could be separated from the political personalities of the succession of men who held the various offices. The same was not true of the presidency itself. There the identification of the office with the political personality of the man caused misgivings in the minds of those who saw personal, individual power as the threat to democratic government.

The creation of the "second executive" had cast its image over the whole departmental structure of the government, creating an ever-widening gap between the executive branch and the political figure who was, by constitutional authority, its chief. This satisfied many public concerns, the very sort which had given rise to the reform movements which sought institutional or legislative bulwarks against the evil, politics. But the technician-executive and the political executive in the federal government were not as effectively separable a pair as were the city manager and the mayor in local government. Those who sought executive secretaries or prime ministers were looking for a solution to the problem of this division.

The main difficulty lay in the consequences of the common agreement—professional administrator, academic, and even congressional—that the gap between the executive and his branch of the government would have to be bridged, or filled, or in some way removed. Yet there could obviously be only three logically possible solutions, a fact which went no way at all toward finding agreement on one of them. The first, the interposition of a "fourth branch," had been the method since the 1870's and had resulted in the creation of commissions and agencies appointed by the executive, sanctioned by the Congress but often responsible in fact to neither one. A modernization of this method could have involved the creation of a highly rationalized bureaucracy located midway between the President and his cabinet and connected logically to both by some distribution of functions. The Rogers and Elliott "cabinet secretariat" was part of such a notion, as were later—and earlier—theories of multiple executive, redistributed executive power, assistant presidents, and the like.

The second solution would involve a vast increase in the

number of departments to fill the gap between President and executive branch with smaller, presumably more effective departments which would have all executive functions distributed among them, the President acting as a general overseer. This approach, advocated in part by E. S. Corwin,[28] would do away with independent agencies of various kinds and reduce the managerial demands on the President himself by dividing his functions departmentally. The gap would thus be filled not by creating new or quasi-new institutions but by bringing the departmental structure closer to the President.

The third of the logical possibilities in the situation would be to fill the gap by what would in effect be an enlargement of the President himself. But the problem of institutionalizing democratically an enlarged executive required innovations in structure of a seemingly dangerous order. Nevertheless, the basic approach of the committee was directed toward this view.

The heart of the method lay in two points: the idea of assistants to the President and the notion of three agencies as "managerial arms." The first was an almost physical extension of the President himself, the addition of eyes and ears only, with the power to command left solely to the President. These men were to act as anonymous servants, exercising no initiative independently of the President's wishes. No authority was delegated to them. Their function was to extend the President's power to listen wherever useful information could be gathered and to see whatever needed to be seen to provide the information required for decisions. In order to give them the utmost responsibility to presidential will, as well as ultimate flexibility, their functions were not to be defined except as the President saw fit to define them. As such they would not constitute either an additional institution or certainly not an independent one, but rather an extension of the presidency itself.

The second feature of the committee's method was the idea of three "managerial arms," personnel, fiscal, and planning. If the assistants were to be eyes and ears, channeling to the President such information as he felt he needed, the "arms" were to be literally that, not in the sense of independent sources of command, that being the prerogative solely of the President, nor flexible sources of information, that being the function of the assistants, nor sources of information with respect to the precise distribution of executive functions, that being the responsibility of the departments. Over and above the departments but not as either a supervisor or collator of the functions, the three managerial agencies were the devices, the tools by which the President could act as a manager, not his own Cabinet Secretary. The specifically managerial questions common to all the departments and through which the President as a chief executive exercised his particular form of control over departmental activities necessarily involved the choice of individuals for jobs, the allocation of funds, and the formulation and interrelations of policy. Insofar as the President would be required to exercise his influence in a department it would be through these three questions rather than through questions of detail in the structural organization or the operation of the department itself. The latter questions could, of course, enter his sphere of control, but only insofar as they impinged on his managerial responsibilities. As managerial arms, then, the three agencies implemented presidential responsibility for impressing on the executive establishment the President's image of the mandate from the public and his party by giving him direct means of overseeing activities common to all departments of government at the points of their interrelation. These means were to be managerial, a term which was distinguishable from the functions distributed among the departments.

Thus, the definition of twelve departments and the consolidation of all agencies, boards, and the like under them were necessary to the explanation and operation of what was essentially the expansion of the President within the executive branch of the government. With the gap filled by what was in effect now a modern presidency, it was necessary that the committee define the role of that presidency vis-à-vis the executive departments and the Congress. For here lay the efficiency of the new executive and the democratic control over it.

Brownlow's recommendation that the bureaucratic structure of the executive branch be simplified was a direct consequence of the recommendation for the expanded presidency. The President should have a more circumambient organization to oversee once the means of oversight were present. The managerial arms assured him a systematic and unified approach to all departments, while the more or less free-wheeling flexibility of the six assistants assured him freedom from structurally rigid chains of command which could prevent needed information from reaching his desk. Systematic managerial control plus fluid channels of information were essential to the committee's whole view of administrative principles and processes. In keeping with this twofold analysis, Brownlow defined the functions of the department secretaries as being to "advise" the President on problems within the department's scope, and to manage the department.[29] The dual structure of presidential aids was thus reflected in the committee's view of the department: information plus management.

The sense in which the committee's concept of management deviated from the older administrative distinction between staff and line, information and command, is important, for it is the committee's most unique contribution to the study of administration. What the committee had done, in effect, was to distinguish two forms of information relevant to administration, only one form of which could be directly and specifically defined as administrative information—that relating immediately to the three managerial functions. The other form of information came specifically from concerns in the world itself and were scientific or diplomatic or economic or sociological—anything which circumstances would, from time to time, define them as being. To take an obvious historical instance, the now famous information concerning nuclear research given to the President by Albert Einstein in 1939 was information initially relevant only to the study of nuclear physics. Its acceptance by the President as being relevant to political and military ends did not change the nature of the original information, but it did bring the information within the orbit of questions specifically oriented toward the management of government. The questions relevant to the setting up of the Manhattan project and the relation between that project and other projects being undertaken by a government at war were questions of management, not of nuclear physics. The problem, however, lay in the tendency of the two kinds of information to affect one another, of administrative policy and approach to affect questions being asked by nuclear physics and of nuclear physics to be determining administrative policy. Even if one did not, or could not, separate pure physics from pure politics, the recognition of a distinction and a systematization of the means of making it would be useful in determining the limits of human judgment. The committee's definition of the three managerial questions set not only the scope but the limits of the function of executive authority.

Finally, in the chapter on Accountability of the Executive to Congress Merriam repeated the earlier emphasis upon the necessity of an audit which would be independent of the executive branch. He recommended the setting up by Congress of committees to hear regular reports from the proposed Auditor General. Here again the separation of audit from control was consistent with the committee's effort to distinguish information from action, review from management. Equally important, it designated fiscal review as the basic democratic control over executive management, affirming in the context of the federal government the principles which, in other forms, had been part of the traditions of local and state government reform since the turn of the century. That they were also part of the whole history of western liberal democracy would account, in part at least, for some of the argument that followed.

From the November elections of 1936 until the final presentation of the report, the committee worked closely with the President. He was even more approving of and enthusiastic about their recommendations than they had initially hoped. He had one serious reservation about the original form in which the report had been presented to him. The committee had suggested a larger staff than that finally recommended, and had organized them at least to the extent of providing for an executive secretary as a general head of the group. Roosevelt had strong objections to this. He felt that information of the kind needed by the chief executive was too complex to be channeled through one official position. He also doubted that the public would tolerate anything which looked like the German General Staff, an idea which he himself had opposed as Assistant Secretary of the Navy. While he felt that one of the assistants would probably become *primus inter pares*, he insisted upon complete flexibility in his choice of that one. This was the most obvious instance of the committee's acquiescence to the President's wishes.[30]

While in some respects the President's insistence upon this point was characteristic of his own personal habits of administration—the White House "family" had been from the beginning a group of such flexibility and indeterminate status—it was still consistent with the committee's aim that information requisite for decision be channeled ultimately to the top, to the President himself. In some respects it extended the committee's intentions rather than contradicting them, solving for them a dilemma they were unable to solve among themselves. Franklin Roosevelt was always careful to preserve the powers of the presidency whole and undivided, and the committee strove to create a system whereby the power could be both undivided and efficient, as well as undelegated. Hence, the first function of each cabinet secretary was to advise the President about matters relating to the policy problems of his department, not to decide for the President. From the committee's point of view the essentially undelegable powers of the presidency were the managerial responsibilities represented by planning, budget, and personnel, since these were the ultimate control over any process of executive management. But as the committee recognized, information for purposes of management was in part and of necessity a function separate from the process of management and decision. And as the President was uniquely aware perhaps from his experience as President, the problem of information was the central problem of the presidency, given the essential isolation and singularity of its constitutional responsibility. For where the power to inform and the authority to decide rested in the same hands, one could define for that particular function a chief executive. It was therefore necessary that on the major issues of national policy where constitutional authority was placed squarely on the President that the two powers come together only in him.

The committee had provided the President precisely what he had asked for, more precisely in fact than he might have had reason to expect. For this was not simply a document in justification of the necessity of clear executive authority. It was a document in explanation of it, affirming historically the meaning of the presidency and bringing to bear on that office the fruits of a half-century's experience in improving the efficiency of a society democratically governed. But it was only a beginning, a mapping out of the image of the modern presidency. As such, its importance was immediately apparent.

Some of those who had labored on staff reports were disheartened by the results of their efforts—when they could find them in the materials finally presented by the committee. The files of the committee, ultimately sent to the Roosevelt Library, are a dramatic testimony to the masses of intellect brought to the study of the problems of executive government in the United States. Essays, study papers, replies, admonitions and rejoinders, all of the debates and disputes which could conceivably pertain to the subject are there. In some respects their totality alone provides the supporting documentation of the report, more so than the materials the committee chose to append. But those who looked through the report for solutions to their dilemmas or rebuttals of their disputes rarely found them. And those who sought evidences for their own contributions often found them only in clearly reflected ideas or perhaps a phrase or two whose authorship they alone knew they could claim.

Luther Gulick wrote the draft of the message with which the President transmitted the report to Congress. With rare and appropriate eloquence he communicated the sense of urgency which each of the members of the committee shared with the President as they looked about them at the world in which democratic processes seemed imperiled by the effects of their own successes over the previous two centuries. The President read the draft message approvingly. When he arrived at the sentence which read, "I have examined this report carefully and thoughtfully, and am convinced that it is a great state document of permanent importance," he paused, and, picking up his pen, crossed out "state." [31]

### III

The election of 1936 would be cited at the time and by later historians as a clear and undeniable affirmation of the leadership which it continued in power. In that respect unique in the history of American elections, it nonetheless shared with all other elections the difficulty of precise interpretation. The nature of the affirmation would remain obscure, not only for those who sought historical understanding of it, but for those, like the victor himself, who had the practical necessity of reading into it some kind of mandate for a future course of action.

Roosevelt's attempts to turn that approving mandate into improved leadership took three forms in a succession of efforts, each of which suffered open and public defeat. He tried to improve executive administrative efficiency by reorganizing the presidency. He attempted to free executive action from what he considered the fetters of a conservative Supreme Court. And when each of these had been rejected by the Congress, he sought to reorganize executive-Congressional relationships by instituting party discipline through direct influence in the off-year elections. Thus for two years, 1937 and 1938, the President sought a readjustment of the position of his office in the federal government on a scale which covered all three branches, executive, judicial, and legislative, creating, in effect, a crisis of constitutional proportions. Not since the eve of the Civil War had the constitution of American government been subjected to such thoroughgoing re-examination and debate. That the debate did not center itself on any clear-cut constitutional issue as subject and substance gives a makeshift appearance to the relation among the three stages. And to all of the participants, with the possible exception of the President, the relationship was indeed obscure. The members of the committee were shocked at the embroilment of their report in the subsequent Court bill battle. Members of the Court were undoubtedly unmoved by the President's reorganization proposals which went to the Congress on January 12th, three weeks before the President's attack on the Court. And the Congress was slow, very slow, to make any connection between the two. In committee hearings the opposition to the reorganization proposals was relatively mild, much more so, even, than had been expected. And despite the fact that the Supreme Court bill was defeated finally on the 22nd of July, the House on the 12th of August passed the reorganization bill by a vote of 283 to 75. The lateness of this triumph, however, meant that the bill could not go to the Senate and would have to be delayed until the next session. At this stage of affairs, any relation between the two fights seems to have been only a matter of an unfortunate proximity rather than any intrinsic connection.

Committee hearings during the summer showed the generation of an opposition more formidable than that yet encountered, with Senator Byrd at the head of it. The introduction of the bill in the Senate the following winter met heated and organized furor, with cries of "Dictator" and the fantastic charge that Roosevelt was seeking the power to abolish the Congress, a grotesque interpretation of the committee's recommendation that the President have the power to reorganize and possibly to abolish executive offices. Even so, the defeat of the bill was far from being a foregone conclusion. Senator Byrnes succeeded in getting it passed by one vote, but failed through a parliamentary maneuver to get the House bill substituted for the Senate bill and a joint conference to resolve the differences. Someone pulled his coattail to ask a question in the midst of debate and by the time his attention could be returned to the discussion, it was too late. The House then proceeded to kill the Senate measure by more than a two-thirds majority, despite the fact that it differed little from the one they had passed in the previous session. By summer the President was campaigning for revenge.

It is difficult to abstract the report of the committee from the years which saw the defeat of its first legislative form. Yet the drama of the Court bill—a drama made consequential as much by the method of Roosevelt's attack as by its substance—has obscured the defeat of the first reorganization bill, while the quiet and thoroughly unobtrusive passage in 1939 of another reorganization bill embodying many features of the first has tended to conceal the relations of executive organization to the revolution which occurred, successfully, during those years. Parenthesized by dramas its authors had seen no reason to anticipate—the Court fight and the attempt at party discipline—the first reorganization bill seems almost a forlorn actor on stage in the wrong play, a nightmarish situation which could be comic but for its consequences. Even its defeat was virtually an accident, a piece of parliamentary pie throwing which, had it not occurred, would have enabled the bill to pass.

Accidental as many of the actions would appear, and the intensity of the debate was most certainly in a heat reflected from the Court fight, the arguments themselves were more in keeping with oppositions familiar from pre-New Deal traditions and concerns. To return for a moment to the 12th of January 1937, the day on which the first message and its accompanying documents were sent to Congress, one finds a statement issued by Senator Byrd, cautious, tentative, and, read in the light of both the ensuing events as well as the previous history, a bit threatening. He could not, in the first place, quite see the savings and economies which were, in his opinion, essential to reorganization. Secondly, he did not feel comfortable about the committee's proposals with regard to the Comptroller General whose watchful eye he felt, under the immediate circumstances particularly, was an absolute necessity. He went so far as to suggest that Mr. Roosevelt and his Secretary of the Treasury were a good distance from having evidenced sufficient regard for economy, and that their most recent behavior scarcely justified placing control of expenditures in their hands, leaving the new Auditor General with nothing to do but to complain to Congress after the fact. Thirdly, he did not see that the President's committee had taken much heed of the problem of abolishing unnecessary emergency agencies and returning government to more normal practices. The committee seemed to him to have accepted too much of the "temporary" structure of government as permanent—indeed had recommended making it permanent by fitting it into the regular structure of government. In some respects the fat was in the fire from the day the report was issued.[32] It just took it a while to start sizzling.

Throughout the testimony before Congress these points were labored, albeit quietly and almost ineffectually by members of Congress in opposition to the bill, in large part conservative economy and efficiency proponents of past reforms. Other older traditions were awakened. Congress seemed notoriously misinformed on the provisions of the original Civil Service Act, believing that the members of the commission were independent of the President and "politics," even though of all the "headless" agencies and commissions, Civil Service was the one most under direct presidential control and had been from the beginning. One could even argue that the President's committee could have avoided this issue had it anticipated the objections, since its changes were really relatively small. But there the traditional reform arguments of Civil Service groups had done their work too well, for the public and Congress alike could be induced to see the single Civil Service Administrator in the White House as an out-an-out return to the spoils system, while shrewder minds could spot the recommendation for extending Civil Service as a direct threat to old-fashioned Congressional spoils.

The substance for opposition, however, came from more stable sources than public opinion or the standard percentage of Congressional innocence and ignorance. The Brookings Institution had provided Senator Byrd's committee with a report more to his liking, particularly with respect to the need for the vigilance of the Comptroller General, as well as the necessity for reducing the size and cost of government. Backed by professional, extragovernmental advice, Byrd could appeal not simply from entrenched Congressional opposition but from sources as objective and as unimpeachably academic as those employed by the President. And in any case, if the President's committee could give the President the advice he wanted, there was no reason why Senator Byrd could not have a committee to provide him with equally suitable justifications of his own opinions.

The possibility of a serious difference of opinion between the Brownlow group and the Brookings people might have occurred to those who checked back into the materials which had been prepared by the Institute for Government Research some fifteen years earlier during the discussions which preceded the Budget and Accounting Act of 1921. In March of 1921 the Institute circulated a mimeographed and unsigned study of the problem of executive reorganization, presumably the work of the Willoughbys and their staff. A massively detailed examination of the entire administrative establishment, the report proposed, among other suggestions for change, four new departments: maritime affairs or transportation, public works and public domain, education and science, and public health. It suggested also the abolition of the Departments of Commerce and the Interior. What is most significant for our purposes, however, is the fact that the report devotes a total of twenty of its four hundred and ten pages to the office of the President. It gives him a Bureau of General Administration (later acknowledged to be virtually identical to the proposed Bureau of the Budget and a replacement for the former Bureau of Efficiency). The section on the presidency, furthermore, opens with the statement: "The executive, as distinguished from the administrative, branch of the government, embraces only the single service, The Executive Office of the President. . . ." This distinction between the executive and administrative sets at once the general line of argument and suggests even an extra-constitutional elevation of the Cabinet to the status of a fourth branch of government. In addition, and in keeping with the language of business as analogous to government, the report identifies the President as a "General Manager" of the government and the Congress as his "Board of Directors."

This latter relationship—General Manager and Board of Directors—is used in the Brookings report's discussion of the proposed Office of Comptroller and Auditor General as the rationale behind the development of an independent audit. This point is, in the language of the report, rather difficult to understand. The office is always referred to by its combined title, but it seems clear that two separate individuals are intended. Their relation to one another is, however, rather obscure. For the report seems to seek the establishment of an audit which would be independent of control, but seeks as well to have both independent of the executive and responsible only to the Congress. Here the author or authors of the report seem already to have been influenced by Congressional concern and to be sounding out directions of compromise. Ultimately, of course, while Congress in the Budget and Accounting Act did set up the Office of Comptroller General as the report had suggested, contrary to the advice of the report, it did not separate audit from control. In any case, the point of view, daring with respect to the departmental structure, sees the Presidency from a position quite opposed to that to be taken by the President's Committee on Administrative Management. To the extent that that position would still be reflected in the Brookings staff, the potentiality of disagreement might have been predicted.

Nonetheless basic opposition between the Brookings Institution and the President's committee seems not at first to have been envisioned. Brownlow had initially recommended to Byrd that he employ Brookings to do technical studies and it was announced at the outset that the work of all the committees, presidential as well as Congressional, would be complementary. As we have already seen, Brownlow was originally intended as chairman of all of them. But as early as March 27, 1936, the Brookings people had sent a memorandum to Senator Byrd stating clearly that "it is the view of the Brookings Institution . . . that a satisfactory plan of organization can be arrived at only by proceeding from the particular to the general, from the parts to the whole. What is needed is a series of special studies of the various service fields with a view to ascertaining what changes might be most likely to effect efficiency and economy." [33]

For the President's committee the direction had been exactly the opposite: "over-all, top management" as a point of view sought to move from the whole to the parts, from general principles to the particulars. The assumption at the beginning, perhaps, was that the two working in opposite directions would meet at some common, intellectually congenial point. But Brookings had said "only."

In some respects the Comptroller General was the point at which they met, in head-on opposition, with Brookings' belief that audit and control could and should both be independent of executive authority. During subsequent hearings the Brookings' report was partially discredited, at the very least, by the revelation that Brookings' advice to numerous states with regard to fiscal management had been exactly the opposite of their advice now to the federal government. To the states they had consistently recommended the separation of control from audit, recognizing control as an executive responsibility to be checked by an independent audit. No real attempt was made to explain why a measure so appropriate at the level of local government was now to be considered inappropriate when applied to the federal government.

The intensity of the disagreement between the President's committee and the Brookings Institution was sharpened later, in November of 1937, when, for reasons no one could quite understand, the Brookings Institution issued an apparently unsolicited pamphlet attacking the single Civil Service Administrator proposed by the President's committee.[34] It did not take much research to reveal that here again Brookings was attacking at the federal level recommendations which it itself had been making to the several states. Nor were they alone in their strange about-face. Harry Byrd as Governor of Virginia had recommended changes which, as Senator, he now denied the President.

To say that personalities lay at the root of it—Roosevelt versus Byrd, Brownlow and Merriam versus H. G. Moulton of Brookings—is to touch upon a truism of political history which can become meaningless. Gulick, who had advised Byrd on the Virginia reorganization, tried to mend the dispute between Byrd and the President by arranging a luncheon meeting. Gulick knew that where reorganization was concerned their sympathies were too close to justify the current bickering. But the President chose to confine his attention to subjects where he knew real disagreement lay, and by pricking his adversary insistently managed to draw blood. Byrd left even angrier.[35] Even so, the disagreement was older than both of them, and if their personalities lent fuel to the fire, it was still a fire which other generations had tended.

The real question lay in the meaning of "whole to the parts versus parts to the whole." It sounded interestingly objective, yet beneath the distinction in direction lay a difference of approach more fundamental than method. The President's committee had sat at the desk of the President and looked down at the government for whose operation he was constitutionally responsible. What they saw was a sprawling chaos which the President, any President, would be unable to manage because he lacked the one necessary power for bringing the government within his grasp—the power to organize it. Brookings, on the other hand, had absorbed itself into what had been the congressional viewpoint of the presidency, looking outward to the agencies of executive government with which it dealt and upward, way upward, to the President himself. It had never been a comfortable position from which to view American executive government.

In short, the President's committee began with the office of the President and ended with his accountability to the legislature, an accountability which they rested on the oldest protection in the history of democratic government, the power of the purse. Brookings and the legislature began with that responsibility and, like all of the proposals for executive reorganization which had originated in Congress, their proposal never quite got to the President. Equally important, like the reformers for generations prior to it, the Brookings report and the Congressmen committed to it sought "parts," piecemeal correctives and cures to specific abuses, the only effective generalization for which was their expense. The denial of the executive implicit in their approach was consistent with an older view which saw politics as the major evil and individuals as the center of corruption. "Perfect the machinery and you lessen the need for honest men" was an implied slogan which carried with it two important assumptions: (1) that the honesty of most men was suspect anyway, and (2) that the liberal community ran itself and had no need for executive authority. That there might be some conflict between the two assumptions could be lost in the course of any debate; but most of the institutions for reform since the 1870's had been built on this creed.

The Brookings Institution report and Senator Byrd's enthusiasm for it were in some respects the last major statement of the legislative approach to executive reform, the approach which had, since the Civil War produced the major changes and developments in American federal government. But extension of this approach into the New Deal added the final straw to the weight of increasing concern which had grown up almost parallel to the institutions themselves. The President's committee sought to apply new standards to old concerns, to state in principle an approach which could include the best of the past with an awareness of new demands. The objections were old and dying echoes of John Randolph of Roanoke, made by those whose chronic fear of the American presidency would always remain an inevitable leg of every congressional seat. In 1937 it would have been likely that, except for the expected brief flare-up, the recognition of the experience of the previous half century would override more traditional concerns.

The bill should have passed. As the Brookings report so amply illustrates, with assistance from the early objections of Senator Byrd, the opposition had scarcely much voice to raise beyond the concern over economy and efficiency, the perennial well-worn pair. Arguments over the fear of executive authority were not raised at first, even by Byrd, beyond his reflections on Roosevelt's light hand with the purse. Conservatives grumbled but not with much effect or the expectation of effect. Such opposition scarcely played much of a role in the first House debate, and the provisions of the bill giving the President the power to reorganize by executive order were of little importance to the investigating committee. It was a method they had found necessary to approve before, during World War I, and there seemed no good reason to object to it now. The opposition seemed not to see the potentiality of public furor until the President pointed it out to them when he attacked the Supreme Court. The two arguments seemed to have no necessary relation to one another, yet in tandem they revealed inherent fears which, like images in a hall of mirrors, reflected endlessly the historic shape of the fear itself. Those who had been lamenting, without effect they thought, Roosevelt's increasing power were suddenly and unexpectedly given evidences of wider public appeal than they had ever dreamed possible.

The relation between executive authority and economical government was, in one of those rare historic moments, revealed by the speed with which opponents of the bill, aroused to indignation by the attack on the Court, switched their arguments from fear of expensive inefficiency to fear of a dictator.

In Byrd's case it seems even more instinctive than the political convenience it could well have been. For years later, during the reorganization discussions of 1945 when he recanted his position of 1937–1939 vis-à-vis the President's power to reorganize his own administration, he did so with the open candor of a genuinely repentant heretic, confessing his new belief that the President and only the President could reorganize the executive branch.[36] He seemed not to remember the relatively late emergence of his concerns with that aspect of the first reorganization bill. Be it noted, too, that all recantations to the contrary notwithstanding, the Comptroller General remains today the watchdog who carries his own leash.

Even so, the defeat of the bill was more in the nature of a delay than a clear defeat. By 1939 many of its provisions were quickly and quietly absorbed into American government. The President was given the power to reorganize, not by executive orders, but through the submission to Congress of reorganizations plans, acting in effect as an agent of the legislature. This device was a brilliant stroke which allayed many fears. The Executive Office of the President was created; the Bureau of the Budget as well as the National Resources Committee (renamed National Resources Planning Board) were transferred to the Executive Office. Forbidden to set up two new departments, the President created the Federal Security Agency and the Public Works Agency as repositories of the welfare and works functions recommended by the committee. He was given his administrative assistants, and, since he was refused permission by Congress to have a single Civil Service Administrator in place of the Commission, he named one assistant to be in charge of personnel and to act as liaison man with the Civil Service Commission. These powers to reorganize expired in 1941 but were continued in the War Powers Acts, and thence provided again by the Reorganization Act of 1945. They have continued, with brief periods of expiration, to be powers of the President. Subsequent reorganizations have followed the lines laid down by the first. The report of the committee initiated a process because it effectively outlined principles by which such a process could evolve. In that respect, the most enduring effect of the work of the committee would never be found solely in any one reorganization, or in any element of any reorganization, but in the historical evolution of the institution of the American presidency. More important, perhaps, it can be found in the report itself, the document which called attention to the need for such an institution and offered recommendations on the course it might take. The basic concern with "over-all, top management" was the innovation which provided the pattern for the future. The President's Committee on Administrative Management handed the President a mirror in which he could see himself, not the President which Congress saw, or the Departments, or the professionals of politics as practice or as science. From their report emerged an image of the President as President, and if it looked much like Franklin Roosevelt, it was an understandable consequence of the image which he impressed on the presidency. In revealing what it saw, the committee could scarcely have obscured the most basic fact of the Roosevelt era—Roosevelt himself.

IV

The report of the President's Committee on Administrative Management is better known as a beginning than as a conclusion. Even then, it is to the student of public administration or of political science that it is best known, not to the historian. It is to its now familiar offspring, the Hoover Commission appointed by President Truman, that those who study executive reorganization are most apt to turn in their analysis of the recent history of the presidency. Buried in the last hectic days of the New Deal's efforts to sustain its revolution, the report of the President's committee was in some respects the Thermidor, the institutionalization in American government of one of Roosevelt's greatest contributions to American politics: the presidency as the movable weight in the balance of democratic government, providing that rapidly adjustable point which might seek to maintain equilibrium in a rapidly changing world.

The Reorganization Act of 1939 was passed quietly. The still settling dust of the skirmishes of the previous two years prevented any fanfare of victory, if victory it was; and the gathering clouds of war in Europe made clearer the necessity of change and the meaninglessness of flourishes in domestic successes. There would be other victories and other defeats. When the war came, Roosevelt would have the power he needed to organize the nation's defenses under his immediate control and to guide the campaigns. In the years to come Congress would legislate and delegate, giving to the President the powers he needed to conduct the war; but the power to act efficiently and to control effectively the authority given him did not come from those years. It came from the earlier battles of 1937 and 1938. In this sense, the report was a beginning.

That it was also a conclusion has been a subject of this study. The problems which the New Deal sought to solve were not new problems, despite the drama with which they had affected the nation as a whole. The desire to effect efficiency and economy, to bring honesty to government, to refurbish the city halls and state capitols across the nation was not the fetish of petty minds given to the saving of string and pencil stubs, although there would always be a good number in any group who could translate the larger issues into smaller terms. When the depression as a national affliction brought forth the innumerable peddlers of remedies and cures there was the possibility of separating quackery from experimental treatment because the institutions of the latter had been in operation throughout the country for years. Social science, for better or for worse, had grown out of the moral philosophy taught to and by a previous generation. Public administration had sought to rebuild reform on more stable, objective, and practical lines.

This essay has sought to bring public administration into the perspective of the history of which it is a part, not because it is, or ever was, so drastically new a way of looking at the world, but because so many of the older ways have been and will continue to be channeled through it. Equally important has been the attempt to redress a balance deliberately and necessarily disturbed in the early days of the new century. It was with good reason that men of this vintage looked with suspicion and distaste upon reform, moral do-goodism, and the "politics" of bossism and graft, seeking as curb and corrective the objectivity of scientific method, professional training, and principles of practical government. The President's Research Committee on Social Trends had brought the new academic of social science to a position of prominence which, quite possibly, more than satisfied his demands for recognition. He was secure in his objectivity, in the freedom of his endeavor from the taints of politics; but was he secure in his power, in the sense of responsibility which a certain acquiescence to the needs of temporal rule gives to the ideals and the abstractions of those who feel they really know? The difference between the Committee on Social Trends and the Committee on Administrative Management marks the line between the old academic and the new.

Yet all of their roots were in reform. Their zeal for improvement, for accepting moral responsibility for the conduct of lives other than their own, and their inner compulsion for doing good were not lessened by their rebellion against the methods of a previous generation any more than by their desertion of their own. They shrank disdainfully from some of the words and invented new ones of their own, but the song was one which Whitman had heard and Emerson before him, and all of the others who sought toleration, or suffrage, or abolition of whatever hampered the development of the dignity of man.

Translation into the new tongue took its toll as the excesses it corrected found their way into history and their improvements began to breed new excesses. A new generation often listened to the words but found the music either obscure or, for the moment, irrelevant. Merriam's students sometimes seemed to him to seek the rigors of science where he himself had not sought them—or had found that, in his opinion, they ought not to be. All three men, Merriam, Brownlow, and Gulick seemed to some to act more like politicians than scientists, to use scientific methodology loosely, conveniently, even irresponsibly. For to the new generation science could be the faith, while to their teacher it was only the tool. The faith came from elsewhere, from the history they revered; from the soul-searching, conscience-searing doctrines of the American Protestantism which they had endeavored to modify in their own lives; from the heroes, the "Leaders of Men" who marched out of the Civil War tales their parents told, into their boyhood novels and on to the great stage of American presidential politics where they found that faith in men like Theodore Roosevelt, Woodrow Wilson, and Franklin Roosevelt. This was objective because it was real, not because it was scientific. To them these were facts because, in the most ageless sense of the word, they had witnessed them.

It was difficult to explain this faith in the kind of reform which had created first a colony, then a nation. Merriam tried to make a new philosophy out of it; Gulick concentrated his attention on methods; Brownlow touched older springs in his parables and tales. But if one rejected the basic element of reform, its spiritual zeal, however valid the reason for doing so, it would be difficult to transmit conscience from one generation to the next. Even so, one could find the spirit beneath the words. The report of the committee contains it, in a basic, quiet way, in the philosophy of government it reflects, in the alternatives it rejects.

First, and in some ways the central point of the whole analysis, the report presumed that there would be "great" Presidents of the United States. There had been some in the past—they might have disagreed among themselves which they were. They believed that the future would provide the nation with more. Most important, they assumed that nothing they or anyone else could do to the presidency, no organizational machinery and no science of government, could produce that greatness or substitute for it if by popular election the public had not willed it. The experience of the presidency might make a man great. The organization of it could not. The organization of the presidency was not to be a hedge against mediocrity or a guard against misuse, but an adjunct to the people's choice.

Secondly, since their purpose was neither to curtail the President's power nor to increase it, but to give it modern efficiency, they defined the "managerial arms" accordingly, placing ultimate decision squarely in the hands of the President, not in the hands of experts or professionals in the various possible fields. This decision could not help but run counter to those who saw modern society as requiring specialized, skilled guidance unhampered by ignorant public or political interference. But here again the position of the three men as mediators between past and future is important.

In a world coming more and more to ally the process of planning with the purposes of planning, men like Merriam and Brownlow could still insist upon a rigorous distinction between the two. For them planning was a fact gathering, knowledge producing enterprise conducted without regard for any single social design. For them any single or fundamental design hampered the process of planning by limiting it to a predetermined channel. The control over planning was fundamentally political, to be determined in this case by the complex relation between the President as public leader and guide and the President as the servant of public will. This kept ultimate responsibility in the people, to whom the President would in turn be responsible. It rejected the idea of placing responsibility in the expert-technician-scientist, lest the paternalism to which that would lead dissipate and destroy the necessary functioning of democracy. Thus, the basic faith in the future of American society could be its continued reliance on democratic process, not on scientific method.

This definition of planning moves logically to the problems of constructing a democratic view of personnel in a society increasingly concerned with specialization and professionalism. Brownlow and Gulick, who prepared these sections of the report, had been particularly concerned with the relationship between professionalism and training for public service. Brownlow in particular had long been in opposition to attempts within the various professional groups he had helped to develop to model themselves along what he called "guild" lines. Like doctors, druggists, and lawyers, administrators had sought to establish the definition of professional status by setting standards to be tested and certified by professional associations. Brownlow's election as president of the City Manager's Association had, some years before, broken the efforts of professional engineers to imply that their professional training constituted a standard for city management.

That the problem was an old one in American history can be found in the efforts of men like Washington, Jefferson, and John Adams to find a means of educating a governing group which would not at the same time create an unwanted aristocracy. The basic question of personnel in government in modern terms rested on the relation between professional civil service and democratic processes. Here again, more effectively direct control by the elected President could assure flexibility within the system—that, plus more universal recruitment and the increase in the attractiveness and security of the profession. The key to the democratic nature of specialization lay in keeping the fundamental standard of judgment separate from the group being judged.

This last point, finally, was symbolized practically by the committee's objections to the presence of both control and audit in the hands of an "unresponsible" appointed official. The elected executive of the people should be judged democratically by elected representatives in Congress, not by a nonelective official. Control was executive in nature, audit the legislative check. The constitutional separation of executive from legislative seemed to imply and to necessitate the separation of audit from control.

In each instance democratic process was brought to bear at its most effective modern point, a point identical with its most effective classical point in American history, the constitutional provision for the election of a chief executive and a Congress. The committee sought to restore the old balance by restating it in modern terms, utilizing in that restatement all of the techniques and tools which had been developed through the years of their work in a field which they were now proud to call public administration.

The work of the President's Committee on Administrative Management was more a summary of the years which had preceded it than many of its observers were quite able to admit. The arguments which surrounded it and the criticisms which grew out of it in fact illustrate its midway position between the extremes whose battles had contributed much to the study of administration as a separate field. For public administration had grown out of reform and, in the process of its growth, had reached toward the rapidly developing awareness of methodology in the social sciences. Yet while a position between the zealous chaos of old reform and the relentless rigors of young science was not an easy one to maintain, it was nonetheless a dynamic one, producing a continuity which drew upon opposing views of the process of government as old and as rich as the debate between Alexander Hamilton and Thomas Jefferson. That it could also be as bitter was a tribute to the vitality of its endeavor.

To the extent that rigorous methodology produced aristocracies of knowledge and specialized elites, that side of administration which looked toward political science and systematic professionalization would, whether led by academics or practicing technicians, find itself in league with those whose fear or mistrust of the potential excesses of democratic government were as old as the idea of democracy itself. Those who had looked back to reform and sought individual action of a democratic citizenry through increasingly systematic forms of representation as the only basis for lasting administrative efficiency, fearing private decisions and interest group control, were one historically with those who had followed Jackson's economics against Biddle's politics, fearing men and institutions which separated themselves from control by public will.

Between them, in a continuity which stretched back to the very beginning of American history wherever one sought to mark it, were men who found the debate an exciting dialectic whose poles changed with needs, the inclinations and demands of history, and a practical wisdom which could be systematically described only to the extent that it was consistent with the dictates of a fundamental faith in the process of democratic government.

Chapter 1. Reformers Old and New: the Meeting Ground

1. *Survey Graphic*, XX, no. 1 (October 1931).

2. Lincoln Steffens, "As Steffens Sees It," *ibid.*, p. 12.

3. Louis Brownlow, "A New Deal at City Hall," *ibid.*, p. 22.

4. Jurgen F. H. Herbst, "Nineteenth Century German Scholarship in America," unpubl. diss. (Harvard, 1958), gives an account of five Americans, H. B. Adams, J. W. Burgess, F. G. Peabody, R. T. Ely, and A. W. Small, representing the fields of history, political science, theology, economics, and sociology. These men were among the last of the 8,000 or so Americans who studied in Germany during the century from 1820 to 1920. 1895–1896 was the peak year of American enrollment in German universities with some 514 students matriculating in the fall semester.

5. Herbert Croly, *The Promise of American Life* (New York, 1909), chap. ii, "Federalism and Republicanism," pp. 27–51. Compare the criticism there of Jefferson and the praise of Hamilton with such statements later as, "German nationality as an efficient political and economic force has been wrought by skillful and patriotic management. . . ," p. 246, and ". . . the modern German nation has been at bottom the work of admirable leadership on the part of official responsible leaders. . ." p. 247.

6. Miss Addams delivered one of the speeches seconding the nomination of Theodore Roosevelt by the Progressive party. He telegraphed her in August of 1912, "I prized your action not only because of what you are and stand for but because of what it symbolized for the new movement." *Letters of Theodore Roosevelt*, ed. Elting E. Morison (Cambridge, 1954), vol. 7, item 5753, p. 594.

7. *Ibid.*, vol. 6, p. 942.

8. Theodore Roosevelt to the Progressive Party Convention, August 6, 1912.

9. "Germany with shallow soil, no mines, only a window on the seas and a population more than ten times as dense as ours, yet has

a sounder business, a steadier prosperity, a more contented because better cared for people." August 5, 1912, to the Progressive Party Convention.

10. *The Political Battle of 1912*, ed. Thomas H. Russell of the American Academy of Political Science, p. 286 (no publisher, no date).

11. Frederick C. Howe, "The German and the American City," *Scribner's*, 49:485–492 (January–June 1911). "The German city is a part of the traditions . . . the universal efficiency, the far-sighted outlook, the paternalism vitalized by the patriotism of the German people. The American city, on the other hand, has no traditions. There is no sense of responsibility. It is efficient only in spots. . . And measured by the services rendered, or the sense of the paramountcy of the State, it is far less democratic than the German." p. 285.

12. Woodrow Wilson, "The Study of Administration," *The Political Science Quarterly*, 2:197–222 (1887).

13. *Survey Graphic, ibid.*, p. 6. It is in fact a painting entitled "Stump Speaking," by George Caleb Bingham, 1854.

14. Walter Lippmann, *Public Opinion* (New York, 1922). World War I had given men like Lippmann and David Lawrence a particular concern with the uses of propaganda, accurate or inaccurate, for persuading public opinion. In the publication which was later to become *U. S. News and World Reports* Lawrence sought to continue that strand of progressive reform which relied on the presentation of facts and documentation as the bases of informed public response. Lippmann turned in a more psychological direction, seeking unconscious influences. *Public Opinion* draws some interesting distinctions between "images" of politics and "realities" of politics; but its conclusions were still not far from those more dramatically urged by H. L. Mencken when he said, "Public Opinion? Walter Lippmann, searching for it, could not find it. . . Public opinion, in its raw state, gushes out in the immemorial form of the mob's fears. It is piped to central factories, and there it is flavoured and coloured, and put into cans." *Notes on Democracy* (New York, 1926), p. 192. Lippmann, on the other hand, had said, "You cannot take more political wisdom out of human beings than there is in them. And no reform, however sensational, is truly radical, which does not consciously provide a way of overcoming the subjectivism of human opinion based on the limitation of individual experience . . . when they ignore [the principle of intelligence] . . . they elaborate their prejudice instead of increasing their knowledge." Lippmann, *Public Opinion*, p. 397. The way around

the barn was longer for Lippmann than for Mencken, but it was the same barn.

15. Efficiency and economy platform planks as recorded in *The Political Battle of 1912* (see n. 10 above) are as follows: Progressive: "We pledge our part to a readjustment of the business methods of the national government and a proper coordination of the federal bureaus, which will increase the economy and efficiency of the government service, prevent duplications and secure better results to the taxpayers for every dollar expended." p. 352. Republican: "We commend the earnest effort of the Republican administration to secure greater economy and increased efficiency in the conduct of government business. Extravagant appropriations and the creation of unnecessary offices are an injustice to the taxpayer and a bad example to the citizen." p. 221. Democratic: "We call attention of the patriotic citizens of our country to its [the 62nd Congress] record of efficiency, economy, and constructive legislation. . . We demand a return to that simplicity and economy which befits a Democratic government and a reduction in the number of useless offices, the salaries of which drain the substance of the people." p. 264. They called also for a reorganization of the administration of civil and criminal law. The Prohibition party stated simply and succinctly: "Efficiency and economy in governmental administration."

16. Speaking before the House Special Committee to Investigate the Taylor and Other Systems of Shop Management on January 25, 1912, Taylor said, "Now, in its essence, scientific management involves a complete mental revolution on the part of the working-man . . . as to their duties toward their work, toward their fellow-men, and toward their employers. And it involves the equally complete mental revolution on the management side. . . The great revolution . . . is that both sides take their eyes off of the division of surplus as the all-important matter, and together turn their attention toward increasing the size of that surplus until this surplus becomes so great that it is unnecessary to quarrel over how it shall be divided . . . the substitution of peace for war; the substitution of hearty brotherly cooperation for contention and strife; . . . of becoming friends instead of enemies; it is along this line, I say, that scientific management must be developed." Testimony reprinted in F. W. Taylor, *Scientific Management* (New York, 1947), pp. 27–30.

17. *Proceedings of the American Society of Mechanical Engineers*, May, 1886, quoted by Towne in his introduction to Taylor, *Scientific Management*, p. 6.

18. *The Public Papers and Addresses of Franklin D. Roosevelt*,

ed. Samuel I. Rosenman (New York, 1938), vol. V, items 43 and 43A, pp. 144-146.

19. This memorandum is quoted at length by Louis Brownlow in his *Autobiography*, pt. 2, *A Passion for Anonymity* (Chicago, 1958), pp. 378-382. Much of the quoted passage, however, was omitted from the printed text and can be found only in the manuscript now in the Harvard Library.

20. *Ibid.* Brownlow also quotes from a press conference following the election of 1936 in which the President said that his opponents had not really attacked the chief weakness of the New Deal. Asked what it was, Roosevelt replied, "Administration." Brownlow, p. 392.

### Chapter 2. *Charles Edward Merriam: Politics, Planning, and the Academy.*

1. This was the official title chosen by the committee. The title of the published report was "Recent Social Trends in the United States," and the committee later became generally known by that title.

2. The committee as officially appointed included, in addition to Merriam, Mitchell, and Ogburn, Shelby M. Harrison, Secretary-Treasurer, Alice Hamilton, and Howard W. Odum. The executive staff, with Odum as Assistant Director of Research, had Edward Eyre Hunt as Executive Secretary. The working committee was in fact considerably larger, of course, and drew heavily on the faculties of the various universities with which individual members were associated. Thirteen individual monographs actually appeared in print. For a listing see *Recent Social Trends in the United States* (New York, 1933), p. ii.

3. *Ibid.*, p. v.

4. *Ibid.*, p. 1540.

5. The SSRC, founded in 1924 with Rockefeller funds, gave its support in not too indirect a fashion through the aid given individual staff members, travel funds, secretarial and accounting services, etc. Throughout this period, 1929-1934, the Spelman Fund of New York (originally the Laura Spelman Rockefeller Memorial) was one of the central factors in the sponsorship of research into social and governmental problems. But the newspaper and general public antipathy to the name "Rockefeller" made it imperative that the connection be kept as anonymous as possible. Thus, it is not quite correct, from a legal standpoint, to speak of the Laura Spelman Fund of the Rockefeller Foundation. But this is the connection in fact.

6. President's Papers, University of Chicago Archives, William R. Harper section. On several occasions in 1910–1911, Harper expressed himself to Merriam as interested in the idea which Merriam had proposed for an institute for governmental research; but in transmitting Merriam's communication to other administrative officers of the university, he indicated that the idea had exceedingly low priority. On one occasion a University trustee had to intercede with Harper on Merriam's behalf. Harper was not sure that faculty members ought to engage in local politics. Merriam's papers contain ample evidence of continuing suspicion on the part of University officials of his constant and active interest in local politics.

7. President Judson to Merriam, March 27, 1920, Merriam papers.

8. A quite complete history of these negotiations can be found in the Merriam papers, 1921–1924.

9. Haskins to Merriam, December 5, 1922. Merriam papers.

10. Jameson to Merriam, May 11, 1923. Merriam papers.

11. Haskins to Merriam, December 5, 1922. Merriam papers.

12. Haskins to Merriam, May 10, 1923. Merriam papers.

13. Merriam to Jameson, May 24, 1923. "I do not know just what is going to happen but it seems to me, with a reasonable amount of patience and forbearance, we can make material progress without neglecting the Humanities on the one hand, or falling short of our scientific possibilities, on the other." Merriam papers.

14. The Laura Spelman Rockefeller Memorial had as its purpose the dispensing of aid to "women, children, and Baptists." The Spelman Fund stated as its purpose in its charter of December 27, 1928, the following: "It is formed for exclusively charitable, scientific and educational purposes, including the advancement and diffusion of knowledge concerning child life, the improvement of interracial relations and cooperation with public agencies." It was not long before all these could be subsumed in effect under the single title, "public administration." Beardsley Ruml, then the active young genius which he remained for the next two decades, was the guiding administrator of the fund. His acquaintance with Merriam was a happy one and led, among other things, to Ruml's becoming Dean of the Division of the Social Sciences at the University of Chicago.

15. John Gaus in his important monograph, *A Study of Research in Public Administration* (New York, 1930), (mimeo.), placed much importance on this book, as did later "theorists" in public administration like Dwight Waldo.

16. The New York Bureau of Municipal Research, founded by Robert Fulton Cutting in 1904 with the help of Frederick A. Cleveland, William Allen, and money from John D. Rockefeller, was the first. Boston, Chicago, and many other cities soon followed.

17. Charles E. Merriam, *Chicago, A More Intimate View of Urban Politics* (New York, 1929), chap. viii. Also fragments of Merriam's autobiography, Merriam papers, and unpubl. lectures (Chicago, 1950), mimeo., Merriam papers.

18. Cleveland to Merriam, April 5, 1911. Merriam papers.

19. Biographical detail comes from numerous sources including the manuscript autobiography (through 1911 only), notes for the autobiography which Merriam kept, and family correspondence. Merriam papers.

20. This was one of the Seth Low campaigns. Of professors interested in current city politics and willing to say so in class, Merriam mentions only James Harvey Robinson.

21. Despite his doctrinal disagreements with Preuss's rather traditional constitutionalism, Merriam looked to him as the greatest influence on his own career, particularly the example he set of active political participation.

22. *Systematic Politics* (Chicago, 1945), p. 328.

23. "Present State of the Study of Politics," *American Political Science Review*, XV, no. 2, May 1921.

24. To my knowledge, no one has been able to find the source of the Kelvin quote.

25. *Ibid.*

26. *Systematic Politics*, p. 17.

27. *Political Theories, Recent Times*, p. 12 (New York, 1924).

28. *Ibid.*

29. *Political Power* (Glencoe, Ill., 1950), p. 279.

30. *Ibid.*, p. 329.

31. *Ibid.*, p. 320.

32. *Columbia University Studies in History, Economics, and Public Law* (New York, 1900), vol. 12, no. 4.

33. See particularly, Morton White, *Social Thought in America, The Revolt Against Formalism* (Boston, 1957).

34. See above, Chap. 1, n. 12.

35. Columbia notes, 1896–1897. Merriam papers.

36. There exists among Merriam's papers a number of poems, many of which were written in his later years. In them he refers constantly to "the Master's hand," and to unseen influences which move him and which he serves.

37. Charles E. Merriam, *Prologue to Politics* (Chicago, 1939), p. 75.

38. Merriam, *American Political Theories* (New York, 1903), p. 348.

39. Merriam, "The Present State of the Study of Politics," *American Political Science Review*, 15:183 (1921).

40. *Ibid.*, p. 176. See also *Political Power* for a later restatement of this position. "The logician may readily discover flaws in the inconsistency of a political system, but this may only show that he does not understand the logic of politics, if such it may be called, in which consistency may be inconsistent with reality." And, "There are many curious fish in the great sea, and the proof of piscine quality is not a special uniformity of shape or scaliness, but ability to swim, or crawl, or both perhaps, and survive, indifferent to the measurements made by the juristic icthyologists." pp. 54–55.

41. Among his early manuscripts is a book review of Roe's *A Knight of the XIXth Century*, and a short story in obvious imitation of it. He seems to have been in high school at the time. Merriam papers.

42. "The National Resources Planning Board, A Chapter in American Planning Experience," *American Political Science Review*, 8:1086–1087 (1944).

43. *Ibid.*

44. See R. G. Tugwell, "The Utility of the Future in the Present," *Public Administration Review*, 8:49–59.

45. Quoted from manuscript draft of the report. Merriam papers.

46. *Ibid.*

47. *Recent Social Trends*, p. lxxiii.

48. Quoted in Louis Brownlow, *A Passion for Anonymity* (Chicago, 1958).

49. "The National Resources Planning Board," p. 1086.

50. *The Spelman Fund of New York, Final Report* (New York, 1949).

*Chapter 3. Louis Brownlow: The Professionalism of Service and the Practice of Administration.*

1. The biographical detail on Brownlow is from his two-volume Autobiography, the more extensive manuscript of the first volume of which is in Harvard Library, and innumerable conversations with him and his wife over the past ten years.

2. See Lincoln Steffens, *The Autobiography of Lincoln Steffens* (New York, 1931), chaps. i and ii. "And what makes grown-ups promise things to children and fail them? Charlie Prodger was the only man, except my father and Colonel Carter, who kept his word with me. He was something of a politician, and I was made to feel that there was something bad about a politician." p. 15.

3. *Ibid.*, p. 865. "In Russia the ultimate purpose of this conscious process of merging politics and business is to abolish the political state as soon as its sole uses are served. . ." And on p. 870, "The

good people whom I have found to be 'no good' who carry through no reforms, who oppose all change as soon as they understand it—these, the great obstacle to all progress, whose incomes are a wasteful graft on business, in which they are a useless hindrance, whose 'moral' influence in art, literature, education, culture, and business is 'bad' as it is in politics, these people are doomed outside as they are in—Russia." This is a rather magnificent fusion of the terms of the Marxist and the old American reformer.

4. Quoted in Leonard D. White, *The City Manager* (Chicago, 1927), p. 286.

5. Charles E. Ashburner is generally recognized as the first manager—of Staunton, Virginia in 1908; but since the Virginia Constitution made the adoption of the commission plan impossible, and there was, at that time, no manager plan specifically, Ashburner was entitled "general manager." The form of city government was not therefore changed, and there were those, later, who refused to acknowledge him as the first manager, particularly those who closely identified manager reform with a whole system rather than with an individual who governed.

6. The Lockport (New York) plan, formulated by Childs at the request of the Lockport Board of Trade, was rejected by the state legislature in 1911. Childs's activities on behalf of the city manager plan could be one of the earlier attempts in this country to apply bona fide public relations techniques to the support of a political end, although Childs would undoubtedly have not used the word "political."

7. Similar ideas were discussed by the National Conference on Good Government in 1894.

8. A history of the movement is available in H. A. Stone, D. K. Price, and K. H. Stone, *City Manager Government in the United States* (Chicago, 1940).

9. A representative collection of such discussion appears in *Commission Government and the Manager Plan*, American Academy of Political and Social Science (Philadelphia, 1914).

10. "The British city elects perhaps twenty men who sit in a single-chambered council with no other elective city officials to interfere with them, and the British city gets results." R. S. Childs, *Short Ballot Principles* (Boston, 1911), p. 121.

11. "So there are no ward politicians in England, no profession of politics, and misgovernment is abnormal." Childs, *The Short Ballot* (New York, 1915), p. 24.

12. Leonard D. White, *The City Manager* (Chicago, 1927).

13. C. E. Merriam, *Four American Party Leaders* (New York,

1926). White's method and plan is virtually identical to Merriam's.

14. White's listing of the city manager's general characteristics can be found on page 144. He is attempting to evolve a personality type, although in a manner which now appears somewhat clumsy.

15. *Ibid.*, p. 304.

16. *Ibid.*, pp. 305–306.

17. Childs served as the conscience of the City Manager's Association during its "professional-engineer" decade, the first. He sought to set up standards and ethics for the new profession and was greeted by resounding opposition from engineer-managers like Henry Waite who objected strenuously to "theorists" and their unasked advice. See White, pp. 280–281.

18. Henry A. Toulmin, Jr., *The City Manager: A New Profession* (New York, 1915). Published for the National Municipal League.

19. Louis Brownlow, *The City and the Citizen* (undated) a series of 204 articles, mimeo. and bound in four volumes. Brownlow papers, Harvard College Library.

20. There exist two histories of PACH and "1313," both unpublished. The first, an extremely valuable source of information, is by Professor C. Herman Pritchett. It was written in 1945 at the request of Louis Brownlow and remained unpublished at his request. Brownlow felt that its contents, however reliable, might awaken old feuds among the organizations. The second is by Ruth Grodzins and was completed in 1958. It is the possession of Herbert Emmerich, the second and last director of PACH, and was written at his request. *The New Yorker* magazine made numerous references to PACH in an article on Beardsley Ruml, written by Alva Johnston and published on February 24, 1945 ("The National Idea Man"). Brownlow's memoirs, of course, furnish an important description of his own view of the organization.

21. The origins of the many associations in existence were as diverse as the subject matters in which they specialized. The Bureau of the Census had established the Municipal Finance Officers' Association in 1906 as a device for providing more uniform statistical reports. The Civil Service Commission had founded in the same year the Civil Service Assembly of the United States and Canada, despite the prior existence of the Civil Service Reform League. The City Managers had, like many others, organized themselves as a group which simply chose to meet at intervals to exchange ideas and experiences. The American Legislators Association had been organized by Colorado State Senator Henry W. Toll, who had long been campaigning for some uniform understanding of

state laws. This was in some respects the most fantastic of the organizations, given the traditions of federalism and the state jealousies that entailed. All in all there were throughout the country in 1932 some 1844 organizations which could qualify as part of the field of public administration. Until PACH did its survey in order to compile its directory, no one had the vaguest notion how many there might in fact be.

22. "Communities organize themselves for the purpose of securing to the individuals who compose them certain commonly desired objectives . . . government, public utility corporations, voluntary associations of citizens (which in this country includes the church) all have a varying share in the effort to advance the community toward the attainment of its . . . objectives. And we see also that the functional divisions of the municipal governmental machinery are divided according to functions, administrative or traditional, not according to objects, aims, or purposes." From a speech by Brownlow written in 1928, quoted in *A Passion for Anonymity*, pp. 239–247.

23. It was on this ground that Brownlow objected to the amendment limiting the terms of presidential tenure. *The President and the Presidency* (Chicago, 1949), p. 136.

### Chapter 4. Luther Halsey Gulick: Administration and the Mission of Economy.

1. I am indebted to Mr. Gulick for the interview in which he recalled many of these details.

2. A history of the American Board up to 1910 is given by William E. Strong in *The Story of the American Board, An Account of the First Hundred Years of the American Board of Commissioners for Foreign Missions* (Boston, 1910).

3. My information concerning the background of the Gulick family comes from documents in the library files of the American Board of Commissioners for Foreign Missions, 14 Beacon St., Boston, Mass.

4. See Gulick, O. H. (Mr. and Mrs.), *The Pilgrims of Hawaii* (Boston, 1918).

5. See Gulick, John Thomas, *Evolution, Racial and Habitudinal*, a collection of essays published by the Carnegie Institution (Washington, 1905).

6. And in 1858, *Notes on the Grammar of the Ponape Dialect*. The Luther Halsey Gulick who became famous in America as the promoter of physical fitness and summer camping was the son of the first Luther Halsey Gulick, uncle of the present one.

7. Although suffering at the time from an inoperable cancer, he lived until 1945, maintaining during most of the thirty-odd years a very active career.

8. Gulick, S. L., *The White Peril in the Far East* (New York, 1905), and *Mixing the Races in Hawaii* (New York, 1937).

9. Gulick, S. L., *A Comprehensive Immigration Policy and Program* (New York, 1916).

10. Among them Eugene William Lyman, Edward Increase Bosworth, and William James Hutchins (father of Robert Maynard Hutchins). It is perhaps a bit inaccurate to use the term "Social Gospel" to cover men so late in the movement. None of them finds a place in Charles Howard Hopkins, *The Rise of the Social Gospel in American Protestantism 1865-1915* (New Haven, 1940). However, Gulick thought of them as such and their writings tend to identify them clearly with the thinking of the movement.

11. See *A Handbook of Congregationalism*, by Henry Martyn Dexter (Boston, 1880). In his chapter on doctrine he takes the Oberlin Council of 1865 to task for having dealt "in so vague a manner" with "so great, and grand, and vital a subject." He favored a more orthodox Calvinism.

12. See Rev. Albert E. Dunning, D. D., *Congregationalists in America* (New York, 1894). Dunning gives proud histories of the educational operations of Congregationalism. The Council of 1885 had again "equivocated" on the question of doctrine, a fact which this history finds pleasing.

13. See H. D. Seager, "Relations of the Teaching of Economic History to the Teaching of Political Economy." Paper presented on December 30, 1897, before the American Economic Association in joint session with the American Historical Association. Full text published in *Labor and Other Economic Essays by Henry D. Seager*, ed. Charles A. Gulick Jr., with an introduction by Wesley C. Mitchell.

14. "Inefficiency may be cured only by training a class of men to higher administrative standards. We need men whose training will enable them to organize and administer municipal departments in harmony with new requirements and new standards." Mrs. E. H. Harriman, *Training School for Public Service: Announcements*, Bureau of Municipal Research, 261 Broadway (New York, 1911).

15. Identification of the people involved comes, in part, from the monograph by John M. Gaus, *A Study of Research in Public Administration* (New York, 1930). See also, Luther Gulick, *The National Institute of Public Administration, An Adventure in Democracy*, chap. ii (New York, 1928).

16. *A Proposed Institute for Municipal Research: A Plan approved by Hon. Seth Low, Mr. Carroll D. Wright, Mr. Richard Watson Gilder* (New York, 1906). The authorship of this pamphlet is a bit obscure, although presumably by the already named staff of the proposed Bureau and R. Fulton Cutting.

17. *Ibid.*

18. *Ibid.*

19. See Frederick A. Cleveland, *Funds and their Uses* (New York, 1902). This text remained, for the next twenty years and through a variety of editions and revisions, the standard textbook on private and public finance in business schools throughout the country. While not really the model for Cleveland's governmental writing, it presents much in the way of the practical background of his basic thought.

20. "An Appeal by the Citizen's Association of New York," February 1, 1866. Pamphlet.

21. "Supreme Court, People of the State of New York against William M. Tweed and Other, Points for Plaintiffs" (New York, 1872). Pamphlet. See also "Report of the New York City Council of Political Reform" (1875).

22. Leonard D. White, "The Rule of Parsimony," *The Federalists*, chap. 23.

23. See Gulick, *The National Institute of Public Administration.*

24. These went out usually in the form of a double postcard sent through the mails to subscribers and interested citizenry.

25. My analysis of Beard's intentions is based in large part upon his book *The Economic Basis of Politics* (New York, 1945 ed.). I find the views expressed there quite consistent with those suggested in his writings on local government, particularly his *American City Government, A Survey of Newer Tendencies* (New York, 1912), and his lecture, "Politics," from the 1908 Columbia series on Science, Philosophy, and Art. I choose these latter two as central because they precede his writings on the Constitution, which do not give so clear a picture of Beard as a reformer.

26. Gulick has an excellent picture of Beard and the Bureau in an essay "Beard and Municipal Reform" in *Charles A. Beard*, ed. H. K. Beale et al. (Lexington, Ky., 1954).

27. See above, Chap. 1, n. 17.

28. Luther H. Gulick, *Evolution of the Budget in Massachusetts* (New York, 1920).

29. *Ibid.*, p. v.

30. *Ibid.*, p. vii.

31. *Ibid.*

32. *Ibid.*, p. viii.

33. *National Budget System*, Hearings before the Select Committee on the Budget of the House of Representatives on the Establishment of a National Budget System. 65th Congress, First Session. (Washington, D. C. Government Printing Office, 1919), p. 309.

34. Of all of Beard's attacks upon Franklin Roosevelt's administration, perhaps his opposition to lend-lease gives the clearest statement of the roots of that concern.

35. Luther H. Gulick, "Beard and Municipal Reform," in *Charles A. Beard*, ed. H. K. Beale (Lexington, Ky., 1954).

36. In *Public Budgets, The Annals of the Academy of Political and Social Science*, vol. LXII, November 1915. Included also were essays by Beard, Merriam, and Gulick's old teacher, Karl Geiser.

37. "Taken as a whole it may be said that until within the last few years the 'budget idea,' as the term is here used, has had no evolution whatever in the United States. Our citizenship, our legislators, and our constitution makers have until recently been as innocent of such an idea as an unborn babe." *Ibid.*, p. 21.

38. *Ibid.*, p. 15.

39. Among them, *The Movement for Budgetary Reform in the States* (New York, 1918), by W. F. Willoughby, and *The Problem of a National Budget* (New York, 1916).

40. Gulick, *Evolution of the Budget in Massachusetts*, p. 133.

41. *Ibid.*, p. 134.

42. *Ibid.*, p. 135.

43. See *Ibid.*, p. 144–145.

44. Gulick, *Administrative Reflections from World War II* (University, Alabama, 1948), p. 77.

45. W. F. Willoughby, W. W. Willoughby, and Samuel McCune Lindsay, *The System of Financial Administration of Great Britain* (New York, 1917). A. Lawrence Lowell wrote an Introduction in which he suggests that "To attempt to engraft any foreign institution in a new land by direct imitation is usually disappointing, and sometimes mischievous; but to study it with a view to getting suggestions for improvement of one's own methods is wholly wise." p. xi. The Series editor was F. A. Cleveland. For his view of the national budget see F. A. Cleveland and A. E. Buck, *The Budget and Responsible Government* (New York, 1920).

46. See Lucius Wilmerding Jr., *The Spending Power* (New Haven, 1943), pp. 281–282.

*Chapter 5. The Presidency: Reorganization and the Habits of Reform.*

1. This three-part distinction is stated clearly in the preliminary

materials prepared by Brownlow and Merriam for the President's committee (see Brownlow, *A Passion for Anonymity*), chap. xxviii. It is first described by Merriam in a memorandum written in 1934. By the time the committee and its members finished, it could be generalized into a recognition of the fact that an executive had to know (1) what he was going to do; (2) who was going to help him do it; and (3) where he was going to get the money to do it.

2. In 1818, 1822, and 1828 Congressional committees were appointed to investigate the possibility of financial retrenchment. In 1830 a Select Congressional Committee was appointed to report on recommendations made by the President on departmental reorganization, while 1841 saw the appointment of a House Committee to examine executive departments and expenditures. (See Brownlow papers for a chronology of executive reorganization, unpub. ms, presumably by J. P. Harris, dated January 1939).

3. Senate Report 47, 41st Congress, 2nd sess. (February 21, 1870); Senate Report 380, 41st Congress, 3rd sess. (March 3, 1871). See also Gustavus A. Weber, *Organized Efforts for the Improvement of Methods of Administration in the United States* (New York, 1919) and Leonard D. White, *The Republican Era* (New York, 1958).

4. Senate Report 289, 44th Cong., 1st sess. (April 27, 1876).

5. Senate Ex. Doc. 1, 40th Cong., 3rd sess. (December 1, 1880).

6. Senate Report 3, 51st Cong., special sess. (March 28, 1889).

7. House Report 49, 53rd Cong., 1st sess. (September 30, 1893).

8. Woodrow Wilson, *Congressional Government* (New York, 1885).

9. This was clear in T. R.'s letter of appointment to Charles Hallam Keep, June 2, 1905 (Theodore Roosevelt *Letters*, ed. E. E. Morison, vol. v). The problems of the use of technical knowledge is point number one in the President's charge to the committee.

10. See the report of an assistant committee consisting of Worthington C. Ford, Charles E. Adams, Charles M. Andrews, William A. Dunning, Albert B. Hart, Andrew C. McLaughlin, Alfred T. Moban, Frederick Jackson Turner, and J. Franklin Jameson. They were proposing a permanent Commission on National Historical Publications. (Senate Doc. 714, 60th Cong., 2nd sess., February 11, 1909).

11. Scarcely a press conference during the first two years of the first administration fails to bring up the subject of reorganization. In practically each instance the names of either Douglas or Moley or both are mentioned as the presumed architects of any plan, with economy as the major purpose. The idea is dropped as emer-

gency demands make it clear that this is not the time for retrenchment.

12. See Brownlow, vol. ii, p. 382.

13. See Brownlow, vol. ii, chap. xxviii.

14. Anne O'Hare McCormick, "Roosevelt's View of the Big
Job," *New York Times Magazine*, September 11, 1932.

15. See Brownlow, p. 392.

16. This account is based upon two lectures given by Brownlow
at the University of Chicago in 1946 (ms in Brownlow papers), a
memorandum written by Brownlow at about the same time, and
materials in the Merriam papers.

17. Typewritten ms carbon in Merriam papers.

18. Brownlow, vol. ii, p. 327.

19. Merriam papers.

20. Brownlow, vol. ii, p. 344.

### Chapter 6. Old and New: The Battleground.

1. Brownlow papers. "Minutes of Meeting of Members and Staff
of President's Committee on Administrative Management. May 9
and 10, 1936, 230 Park Avenue, New York." The address, it should
be noted, is that of the Social Science Research Council.

2. *Ibid.*

3. Brownlow papers. "Minutes of the Meeting of the Committee
on Administrative Management," Hay-Adams House, Washington, D. C., April 11, 1936.

4. Discussions of this, as well as other matters relating to the
setting up of the staff work can be found in Brownlow diaries. See
his papers. The author is also deeply indebted to Herbert Emmerich
for the loan of his diaries which give a detailed accounting of many
of the steps taken at this stage.

5. Quoted in Brownlow, vol. ii, p. 327.

6. See Brownlow papers. "Preliminary Outlines of an Inquiry
Into Administrative Management of the Federal Government."

7. See Leonard White, *An Introduction to the Principles of
Public Administration* (New York, 1939), as well as A. N. Hol-
combe, "The Administrative Principles Exemplified by the War
Department General Staff and their Applicability to the Civil
Departments and Establishments of the Federal Government," a
study prepared for the Committee but, like the many others, not
published with its report. Ms in Brownlow papers.

8. William Y. Elliott, for example, had published a book entitled
*The Need for Constitutional Reform—A Program for National*

*Security* (New York, 1935). This called for constitutional amendment along lines once suggested by F. A. Cleveland (see *supra* Chap. IV). The British parliamentary system was the basic model. Elliott was on the committee's staff from the beginning.

9. Quoted here from a conversation with Herbert Emmerich, June 1959.

10. This was one of Merriam's favorite jibes. He repeated it often and in numerous contexts. See ms of Merriam autobiography, Merriam papers.

11. He had accepted responsibility for a study for the New York Board of Regents during the delays preceding Roosevelt's final decision to appoint the committee.

12. See Brownlow, vol. ii, chap. xxix.

13. *Ibid.*

14. All quotations from the report are from Louis Brownlow's printed copy *President's Committee on Administrative Management: Report with Special Studies.* U. S. Government Printing Office (Washington, 1937). This copy bears notations of individual authorship penciled in the margins by Brownlow during the summer of 1953.

15. *Ibid.,* 1–2.

16. *Ibid.,* 3.

17. Committee Report.

18. *Ibid.,* 4.

19. *Ibid.*

20. There are many disagreements concerning the origins of this phrase, some of which are traceable to Brownlow himself. In his autobiography (vol. ii, p. 357) he attributes it solely to Thomas Jones, an attribution acknowledged in Jones's memoirs. See Thomas Jones, *A Diary with Letters, 1931–1950* (Oxford, 1954), pp. 307–308. In a lecture at the University of Chicago in 1945 (ms transcript in Brownlow papers) Brownlow related that Jones told him that he had picked up the phrase from an anonymous article on administration published in the nineteenth century. The article, according to the tale, turned out to be part of the Blum book which Merriam read to Brownlow in the train from Warsaw.

21. Committee Report, 6.

22. *Ibid.,* 27.

23. *Ibid.*

24. *Ibid.*

25. See E. S. Corwin, *The Presidency, Office and Powers* (New York, 1948 ed.), pp. 114–121. Corwin's criticism of the committee report is more detailed than one is apt to find elsewhere. He sums

it up by calling their attitude "Jacksonian." See also Edward H. Hobbs, *Behind the President* (Washington, 1954), for a more recent account and support of this general point of view. This view was also supported in a Conference on the Organization of the Executive Branch of the Government, held at the University of Michigan in 1947.

26. Conversation with W. Y. Elliott, May 1960.

27. W. Y. Elliott, "The President's Role in Administrative Management," memorandum prepared for the President's Committee on Administrative Management. Ms in Prof. Elliott's possession, kindly loaned to the author.

28. Corwin, *The Presidency*.

29. Committee Report, 34-35.

30. Brownlow, Lecture of January 8, 1946, p. 18. Ms transcript in Brownlow papers. The ms is dated 1945, but this is obviously a misdating.

31. Noted in margin of Brownlow copy of report.

32. Copy of news release in Brownlow papers.

33. Quoted in Brownlow, Lecture.

34. Brownlow papers, with reply prepared by the committee staff citing all of the Brookings' previous recommendations to the contrary.

35. This incident was described to the author by Mr. Gulick. Byrd had consistently tried to undercut the President on the subject of reorganization, an area in which he felt a particular and specialized competence, as well as a certain amount of ambition. On January 2, 1937, eight days before the President's issuance of the committee's report, the *Saturday Evening Post* published an interview with Byrd on the subject of reorganization. ("Pruning and Spraying" by Raymond G. Carroll.) In addition to harping on what Byrd insisted was the most fundamental principle of any reorganization, economy, the article implied with little subtlety that the present effort was almost entirely Byrd's idea.

36. Quoted by Brownlow, Lecture. The statements were made by Byrd with respect to reorganization proposals of 1945. (Senate, November 9, 1945.) Roosevelt, of course, was dead.

# INDEX

# INDEX

Moulton, H. G., 254
Muckrakers, 2, 5, 9
Municipal Finance Officer's Association, 114
Mussolini, Benito, 28

National Committee for Constructive Immigration Legislation, 131
National Conference on Good Government, 93
National Industrial Recovery Act, 192, 199–200
National Municipal League, 93, 95
National Planning Board, 76, 202–203; advisory committee on executive organization, 203
National Research Council, 44–46, 114
National Resources Board, 77
National Resources Committee, 79, 203, 214, 257
National Resources Planning Board, vii, 78, 79, 257
Nazism, 28
New York Bureau of Municipal Research, 136, 144, 231; transition from reform to research, 139, 150
New York City Council for Political Reform, 142
Nietzsche, F., 16
Norris, Frank, 31

Oberlin College, 128
Odum, Howard W., 270
Ogburn, William F., 37, 56
Opper, F., 3
Overman Act of 1918, 190

Party platforms in 1912, 10; economy and efficiency planks in, 16
Patterson, James W., 184
Personnel, 230–233. See also Brownlow, Louis; Planning, personnel, and budget; Policy, personnel
Phillips, Wendell, 5
Pierce, Edward, 49
Planning: Merriam theories of, 72–

75, 169; and public works, 200–201; and *Recent Social Trends*, 202–204
Planning, personnel, and budget: as categories of reorganization, 170–174; as "managerial arms" of president, 241; as organization of Report of Committee on Administrative Management, 214, 230
Plato, 55, 57
Policy: economic, 171; personnel, 172; planning, Alaska purchase, 171; planning, Louisiana Purchase, 171; in spoils system and Civil Service reform, 173
Populism, 19; and Brownlow, 124
Pragmatism, 60
Presidency: administrative assistants to, vii, 230, 241; in the Constitutional Convention, 176; differing images of, 180; Executive Office of, 78–79, 257; Washington and the Jefferson-Hamilton dispute, 175. *See also* Executive branch; Executive reorganization; President's Committee on Administrative Management, Report of
President's Committee on Administrative Management: Report of, xiii, 226–247; members as representative of post-Civil War America, 29–30; objectives, 32; and New Deal, 35; and Merriam, 78–79, 81; government and technical services, 81; Comptroller General, 164–165; compared with Research Committee on Social Trends, 206–207; and "over-all top management," 253
President's Committee on Economy and Efficiency, 52, 188. *See also* Cleveland, Frederick A.
President's Research Committee on Social Trends, 37, 201; supported by SSRC, 39, 49; social science and government, 42, 81, 260; self-examination drive of progressiv-

# INDEX